ישוע

The Disciple

The Writing of the First Gospel

The Disciple

The Writing of the First Gospel

Ronald Way

WIPF & STOCK · Eugene, Oregon

Wipf and Stock Publishers
199 W 8th Ave, Suite 3
Eugene, OR 97401

The Disciple
The Writing of the First Gospel
By Way, Ronald

ISBN 13: 978-1-4982-9369-3
Publication date 5/20/2016
Previously published by MasterMark Publishing, 2009

For my wife, Trudy, who believed, and brought me love.
For my children
Marnee, Katrine, Heidi, Lisa, and Nick,
who persevered through their dad's vision.

The symbol used on the title page is one of the oldest known Hebrew renditions of the name of Jesus. It was found carved on an ancient ossuary, a container holding the remains of the dead.

Except for two instances, all bible quotations at the beginning of each chapter are from The Living bible, Paraphrased, Wheaton, Illinois, Tyndale House Publishers, 1971, Distributed to the general book trade by Doubleday & Company, Inc. One quote was taken from The Revised Standard Version of The Holy Bible, New York, Thomas Nelson and Sons, 1957

The Question

Jesus felt genuine love for this man as he looked at him. "You lack only one thing," he told him; "go and sell all you have and give the money to the poor—and you shall have treasure in heaven—and come, follow me."

Then the man's face fell, and he went sadly away, for he was very rich.

Mark 10:21-22

For two millennia people have read the quote from Mark's gospel about the wealthy young man and wondered what they would have done on that ancient day in Judea had they been facing the man of Galilee.

If it had happened to you, and you were unable to avoid his piercing eyes, what would you have said or done? Would you have rushed home to sell everything you owned, or would you have hesitated and lost the opportunity?

Alternatively, what would you do today if you met an itinerant preacher (as Jesus was) on a street corner in your own town who asked you to do likewise? I dare say, you would walk away shaking your head in disbelief. After all, how could one be expected to give up everything to follow a wandering religious teacher? It just isn't done, right?

Still trying to get a handle on this very unusual man, let's shift the scene to perhaps ten years after Jesus' death, to Paul's vision on the road to Damascus, when he was struck by a blinding light. It was here that he saw an apparition of Jesus that turned him from a prosecutor of Christians ("followers of the Way" as they were called at the time) to a believer himself.

What would you do if, like Paul, you were granted a vision and told to give up your livelihood and follow a teacher you had never met?

Paul gave up everything—his ardor for the law as a Pharisee, his tent-making business in Tarsus, and whatever family and religious ties he had—to begin to travel the world telling the story of the Jesus he knew only from his vision.

Tell me, if Jesus touched you right now, today, in a blinding flash and asked you to give up everything you believe in and know to follow him, what would you do? Would you leave your family and friends, your job, your home, your security?

It's easy to say, "Yes, of course, I would follow him anywhere." People say that in churches every Sunday, and Christians have probably said those very words over and over again for the past two thousand years. Yet when it comes down to the reality of telling your spouse, your children, your friends and coworkers that you are going to give up your life as you know it and follow a "vision," how many would be able to do that?

More importantly for me, would I be able to do that?

I was about to find out.

Let me tell you what happened to me on a warm summer day in 1981

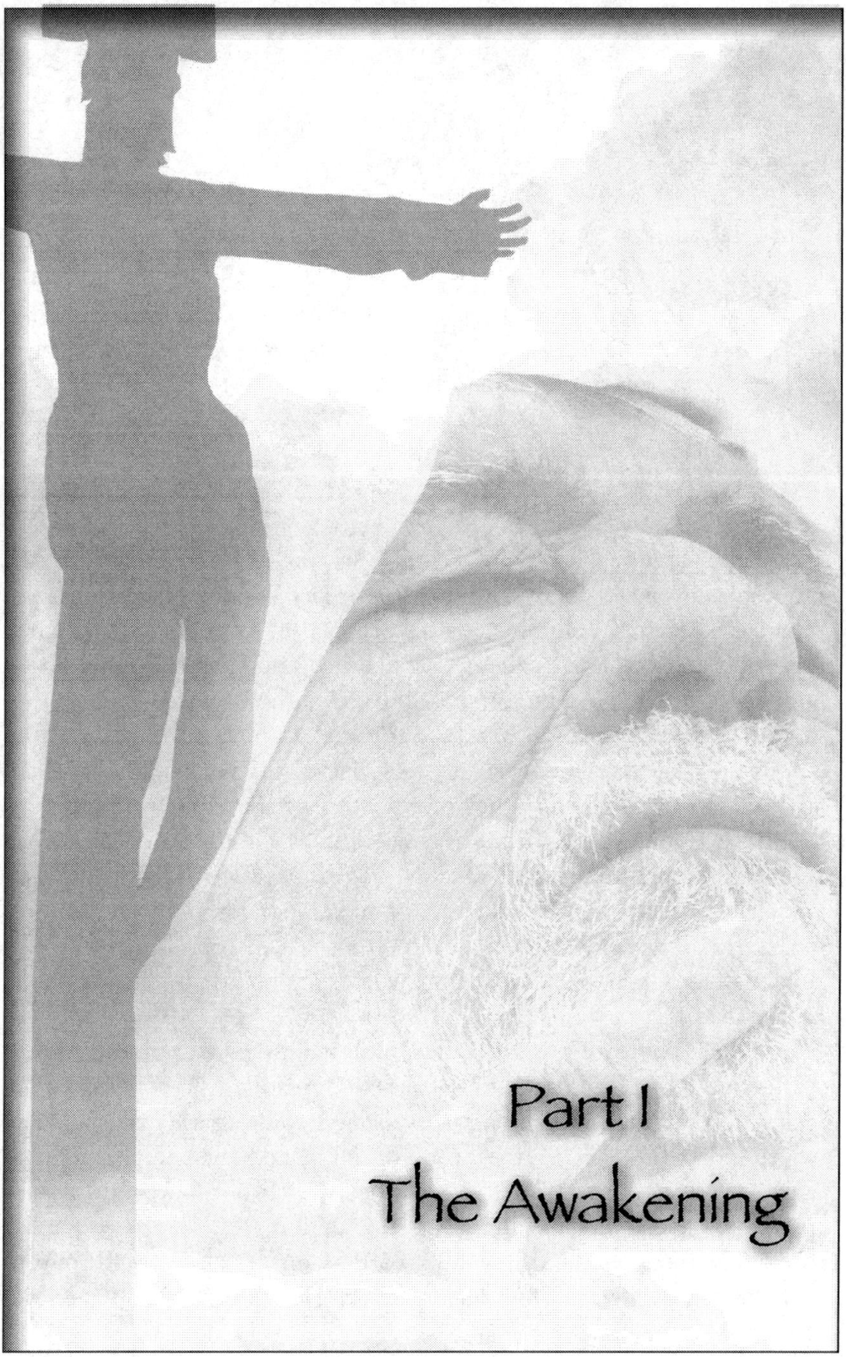
Part I
The Awakening

The Awakening

As he was nearing Damascus on this mission, suddenly a brilliant light from heaven spotted down upon him! He fell to the ground and heard a voice…

Acts 9:3–4

Bright, billowy clouds arched their way above the ocean while the sun splayed shafts of light across the sky. As we walked along San Clemente beach, the shimmering heat reflecting from the sand warmed our faces and bodies. A pair of dogs barked and snapped at the foaming waves crashing on the sand. Children laughed, danced, and sang in the surf on this beautiful July day. I glanced with warm affection at my family and friends who had come to visit for the weekend. Little did I know that this was the last day of my life—the Disciple was coming.

I was a young architect in my mid-thirties and totally engrossed in running my practice. My wife and I owned a 32-foot vacation trailer, which we parked for part of the summer at the San Clemente public campground midway between Los Angeles and San Diego. On this July 4th weekend several of our friends had come to spend the holiday weekend with us.

We left the trailer high on the bluff about 10 o'clock on Sunday morning and walked down to the beach. Spreading our towels, we decided to take a long walk along the sand. We walked perhaps a half-mile south along the base of the brooding cliffs, and then returned again along the surf. As we talked and laughed we left our footprints among the others in the moist sand on the edge of forever.

I remember thinking how all record of our passing would soon be wiped from existence when once again the earth turned and the tides cleansed the planet.

The beauty of the Southern California day was complete, or so we all thought. Little did I know that the peacefulness of the moment was soon to be shattered.

Suddenly, far down the beach I saw a fast-moving, brilliant point of light. It was blinding, like the sun flashing off of a windshield. It was accelerating; growing larger and larger, boring down on me like a comet. I was directly in its path. There was no getting away!

The light hit me with such force that I staggered unsteadily on my feet. Unconscious of my surroundings, my mind reeled from the stunning blow as the light engulfed me in its radiance. Everything turned white, and my world fell silent—*absolutely silent*—as out of the shimmering, white glow, a figure formed. It was a man not tall, nor handsome, in a coarsely woven white robe with dark hair, olive skin and eyes that penetrated my soul.

There could be no mistake. I knew him. The figure who appeared in my path was my Master of old, the one I had sought with such earnestness throughout my life, since my earliest memory as a child. Before me was Yeshua ben Joseph—Jesus of Galilee. He had finally come. On this very public beach my heart leapt in spellbound, breathless wonder.

I followed his gaze as he slowly looked down without saying a word. Between us stood a low wooden table. My architect's eye caught the subtlety of its construction. It was made of three hand-hewn planks pegged one to another. On the table there was a dull silver goblet, the hammer marks of the craftsman visible on its sides. He motioned with his arm for me to take a seat, the long sleeve of his robe glowing in the remnants of the now diminished radiance. He sat down cross-legged with an easy, youthful grace. I lowered myself on bended knees. My attention fixed on this man whom I knew I had known from the past.

Wordlessly, he reached out, took the goblet, and swirled the contents lightly, staring into the wine for a long time. Then, as if finishing a silent prayer, he lifted the chalice, extended it to me, and asked me to share the Mystery with him as I had done before, long, long ago.

I took the chalice and drank.

At that moment, the memories of another time lay just below the surface of my consciousness, struggling to burst full-born into my being. It was as if some long-past experiences were there for me to

The author, Ron Way, in ecstasy with Jesus after being struck by the "light." A friend who witnessed the event in 1982 took the picture as it was occurring.

grasp, so near that I could almost touch them, but I did not hold the key to them as yet and thus the images remained just out of my reach, a whisper of thought in the corner of my mind; calling me, urging me forward to a future I did not know.

I sipped the wine again and handed back the cup. In a wonderfully deep, resonant voice that exploded in my mind, Jesus told me that I had the ability to share with all his people a part of him that was locked within me—if I was ready to give up much. He told me I could give his people the new life he had breathed into the world, a life that had slowly dimmed over the past two thousand years.

Continuing, he said, "To do this, you must follow my words and write the story about your past with me."

In my mind, I answered fervently, "Yes, yes, my Lord," even though at that time I knew not what he meant.

There, at a simple wooden table, somewhere between the surf and eternity and totally oblivious to anything beyond what I was experiencing, Jesus began to impart to me what I had to do before I could commit to this awesome task.

"If you will share the memories I promise to awaken within you," he said, "you must be willing to let go of everything you know—everything—and trust in me."

"Everything?" I wondered, was this true? And, as inane as it sounds, the first thing that came to my mind was, "Even my Porsche?" Would I truly have to give up all the things I held close and dear to follow this man who now sat silently before me, watching and waiting for my answer? Even in a state of ecstasy the mind tends to thrash about unfocused, afraid to dwell too long on what it doesn't know or understand.

I sensed somewhere deep inside me that my life was about to change dramatically I didn't know how or when, but I knew with nothing further said between us, save that same penetrating look in his eyes, that in order for me to tell this story as he wished, I would be required to live totally on faith. I would have to give up everything in pursuit of this goal. But I tell you the truth: I didn't have the faintest idea how long it would take, or how desperate I would become in trying to fulfill his command.

All I can tell you is that at that moment my commitment was complete. In that split second of total acceptance my world began its inexorable shift. My life would never be the same again.

Without warning, my senses yanked me back into the real world. It wasn't as if Jesus faded into the mist as he had come; rather, I felt myself being jolted back and forth from vision to "reality." One instant I was sitting at the wooden table, then the next, the ocean waves were coming at me. Suddenly a terrible burning sensation filled my mouth and nose. I felt my body tumbling about and I became aware that the tide had surged in.

Conscious now of my surroundings, coughing and sputtering from the saltwater in my nose and throat, not knowing what had happened to me, I staggered toward dry sand.

There in front of me was my wife, my youngest daughter, and the friends who had come to visit, all of them staring at me, as were a number of other onlookers. I knew I was the only one there on the edge of eternity; and like Saul of Tarsus before me, the only one who had seen the blinding light.

Realizing that whatever had happened was now at an end, and observing that I could not stand on my own, my friends grabbed me and helped me to where we had spread our towels on the sand. I collapsed in a daze.

I lay there quietly for some time, and then began to sob. No one spoke or asked me anything, but I could feel their unspoken questions bombarding me. I knew I couldn't handle them yet.

With the bitter saltwater still stinging my nose and the sound of the surf pounding unbearably in my ears, I lay on the towel and buried my head in my arms. I wanted to be alone to cry. I had been so deeply touched by this man of my vision that I couldn't speak of it to anyone—not yet.

I got up, not saying a word to anyone, and hurried back along the path that led up the cliff and back to the safety of the trailer. There, away from the people and noise, I cried wondering what had happened to me. Trudy (one of our weekend guests) and my wife followed me a short time later back to the trailer, but my wife soon left, having no patience or understanding of what I had just gone through, leaving Trudy silently waiting until I could control myself; and it was to her that I explained what had happened.

"It was the goblet! I refused it last night. He had to ask again." I gasped. In an instant the memory of the evening before flooded me.

It was near midnight. I had been asleep in the family trailer parked high on the bluff above the beach when suddenly I heard someone speaking my name, "Ronald." It had been clear as a bell. I bolted straight up, wide awake, and stared into a darkened and silent interior.

My ears strained to hear who had called my name. Then in the darkness I heard the scratching of a pen on paper from where Trudy, had been sleeping.

"Trudy, did you call my name?" I whispered softly so as not to wake the rest of the inhabitants.

"No," she whispered back.

I slipped out of bed and moved back to the dining area. There, still with the lights out, I felt an overwhelming urge to meditate. Without saying another word, I sank to the floor of the kitchen, leaning up against the refrigerator, closed my eyes.

Instantly I was being hurled across an ocean of rainbow colored lights. On and on I went, faster and faster. Fear came up in waves, and each time as it rose, I forced myself to relax into the experience, surfing the glorious colors.

When I stopped my flight across this rainbow sea, Trudy was there ahead of me. She was standing in front of a man.

The man wore a robe. As I approached, he turned to me and extended his hands, which held a hammered silver goblet. He was asking me to do something that terrified me at that moment, but I didn't know consciously what it was. All I knew was that I was terrified of some task that he had asked of me.

Trudy was looking at me expectantly, as if waiting for me to drink, or answer, or both, but I couldn't. I panicked. Fear rose in me like bile, and I was immediately jerked back over the waves of color and back into my body so fast that it took my breath away.

My eyes flew open, and in the darkness of the trailer I whispered in a stunned voice, "It was Jesus, Trudy. It was Jesus!"

She simply said, "I know."

Not wanting to awaken the rest of the people sleeping in the trailer, we crept outside and sat in the lawn chairs under the stars. Trudy looked at me in a strange way as I sat down, as if she didn't know me.

Later she told me that as I sat she suddenly saw me as a short, old man with a white beard, dressed in a robe with a wrapping around my head. It startled her, then faded, and once again I looked as myself.

Softly crying she told me that just before I had come back to talk to her in the darkened trailer, she had awakened from a dream of Jesus, so real that she immediately grabbed a pen and her journal to write in the dark what she remembered.

In her dream Jesus was handing her a chalice, asking her to do something. I was at her side. She was afraid, but thought that with me beside her she could accept Jesus' challenge, and thus she drank—but I had fled in fear.

We talked and talked about our unusual experiences, wondering at their meanings (which we couldn't fathom), and wondering too at my fear. We talked until we could see the first faint streaks of gray dawn on the eastern horizon.

Exhausted from the night's experience, I slipped back into the trailer and went back to bed, falling instantly into a deep sleep. Trudy headed off to the beach to be alone, to meditate, and to ponder the night's events. Little did we know that night that it would begin all over again on the following day in a much more forceful way.

Over and over I pondered the strange experiences. During the vision I was told that I had one year to end everything and give up all my worldly belongings. Once I had done that, I was to write the story about my past with him. How? That too, I did not know. I had no memory to draw upon. I assumed the memory would come in time.

To carry out my part I had to place my faith totally in him, like Noah, who was told to build a boat on dry land; or Abraham, who was asked to kill his own son; and of course, Paul, who had seen his vision of Jesus on his way to Damascus and turned from a prosecutor of Christians to a follower of the man in his vision, Jesus. Could I, like Noah, Abraham and Paul, let go of everything and lay myself open to ridicule, possibly shaming my family before our friends and neighbors, all for something so nebulous as a vision?

In my heart of hearts I already knew the answer; I had answered Jesus by saying simply, "I will."

The vision settled into me over the next few days at the beach. It became a part of me, so that I could embrace with excitement the thought of what my life would soon become. I returned home eager to tell the world of my miraculous vision, only to be greeted with sarcastic, condescending words.

"Really, a vision from God, you say? I'm sure you thought it was real," spoke my best friend, Andy.

Then came disturbed reactions.

"What do you mean you are going to leave California? What about your businesses? How are you going to live? How are you going to support your family?" A natural question from Tom, my architectural partner, concerned with the future of the company if I left.

And finally, raw anger; "You're a liar! Christ doesn't speak to people like you. You're from Satan!" snarled the president-elect of the local Rotary club.

Most of my friends and business associates could no longer tolerate my company. They didn't know what to say to me. How do you talk to a man who has had a vision? They could not understand a man who would give up everything to follow a call he had heard from within. Nor could they fathom anyone who would give up their future to chase a mystical vision of some long lost past. As for becoming one with Jesus and believing that he had asked me to leave everything to follow him—nonsense. In fact, it was considered blasphemous!

Strange and angry sessions ensued with my neighbors, friends, and business partners, most of whom refused to accept that I merely wanted to follow the path laid out for me wherever it might lead. I never understood the anger of these well-meaning people. As for me, however, I had no choice. I had given my word. I would either write the story as he led me to find it and prove (to myself at least) that the vision was true or, if no memories came to me from within, then I'd know that these people were right in the end—I was quite mad.

I began my separation from my old life to make way for the new. My marriage of almost eighteen years ended in divorce. Shortly thereafter I married Trudy, who had become my best friend, as the world I knew dissolved around me. Some days I felt as if I was desperately clinging to a rocky shore, torn by winds and tides that I no longer controlled, but as the days passed, more often than not, I was becoming more excited about what lay ahead.

During the down days, like when my partners told me that I didn't need to come back to work following the Christmas break (after almost

10 years of effort building our companies), I wanted to scream to the heavens, "Okay, God, I don't know what you have in mind, but everything's gone wrong. What I didn't 'give up' you took away: my businesses, my position in the community, my home, even my Porsche. The only thing left is the vision." Had I been wrong?

Then it began to dawn on me. I had tried to sell my interest in my businesses, but he had asked, "Are you willing to give up everything if I awaken a memory within you?" Maybe he didn't mean sell my business, or any of those things I held so dear. Maybe he meant exactly what he had said—give them up. Well, whether I wanted to or not, it was done. At that moment, I simply let go and trusted the voice that was within me, for everything else was gone. And my world began to slowly change.

Little did I know how long a road it would be before I could put these words down on paper. Almost three decades have passed and, as it turned out, my lessons continued far longer than I ever dreamed at that time.

The most wonderful thing that happened to me in that year was my deep relationship with Trudy. She stood by me in front of my Master the night before the vision, when I pulled back in fear. She was present that day of the vision, never doubting the reality of the experience for one moment. She was my strength during the days of the dismantling of my world and has remained so to this day. We became best friends and constant companions after the episode on the beach during that Fourth of July weekend. Ten months later, Trudy and I were married, and one year after Jesus had appeared before me on the sand—almost to the day—our two families joined and headed east for a new beginning.

We set up housekeeping in a tiny summer cabin in northern Michigan. We passed the time pleasantly enough, for it was a beautiful land. Trudy, the children, and I played in the lake, walked through the woods, and acquainted ourselves with the town's people. Each night we returned to the cabin—and waited.

There we stayed throughout the long summer and into early fall without a single word put on paper in fulfillment of the vision that was now almost a year and a half old. Time after time I sat down to write, but nothing came. Slowly the thought of failure insidiously edged its way into the hidden recesses of my mind.

Several times I forced myself to start writing something—anything—in hopes that my Master would speak to me once again. But it was useless. The story he promised was not going to come from my mind. I would just have to wait, and trust, and pray that before our savings were completely depleted, my faith, and in turn my family's faith in me, was not woefully ill placed.

As each day passed, the doubts and fears began to eat away at the fortress of my being, for the vision that was once so clear was now, with the coming of autumn's chill, growing cold.

The colors painted their way across the wooded land while I chopped trees and split firewood, stacking twenty-two cords of wood upon the porch. Winter was coming, and with it... what?

Finally, I could wait no longer. I remember the day as clearly as if it were yesterday. I was in town looking in the store windows. I was depressed and forlorn. As I peered through the glass at a mannequin in a winter coat, I wondered if the store also had one of those coats made out of canvas. You know, the white ones with long sleeves and leather straps on the ends that attendants wrap around crazies before taking them away.

I came home and told Trudy that I had failed her and the children. I was insane with guilt. She would hear none of it. After all, she had been the one to first accept the chalice that night before my vision, that night that I had fled in fear.

"Remember your meditation where you were told that we should go to the Holy Land and Egypt?"

"Yes, but it's expensive and I don't have a job now."

"Ron, we've come this far, we have to go for broke."

It was late September when we laid our plans. We had to do everything we'd been asked.

****

From the moment we arrived at Ben Gurion airport at sunset on Sabbath eve, Trudy and I felt at home. The unfolding began the moment we stepped outside of the giant 747. The pilot, caught my eye as we started down the portable stairs that had been rolled up against the plane and said, "Look, I want to show you something." We followed his gaze as he pointed toward the mountains in the east.

While the rest of the unnoticing passengers hurriedly passed by, the three of us stood transfixed. A majestic shaft of light had split the backdrop of the rain-darkened storm clouds over the Mediterranean Sea. There, illuminated on top of the mountain, gleaming in its golden glory like a jewel against the rapidly darkening sky was my city, the City of David, the Holy City of Jerusalem.

I didn't know why I called it my city at the time. All I knew was that I felt as if I were coming home.

Trudy and I were blessed with a sensitive and knowledgeable guide who led us to the spots throughout Israel that every tourist visits: Bethlehem, the Jordan River, Galilee, Nazareth and more. He also took us to places that escape most tours of the ancient city. With each new vista, each historical site we visited, I felt I was filling in some missing gap in my mindscape. I felt as if these were places I had seen and ground I had trodden in the past, but as yet I could not quite draw them forward into my conscious mind. Ancient memories were growing, but they were mercurial. As hard as I tried, I couldn't quite grasp them. I felt as if they were always just beyond the reach of my consciousness, like a word that is on the tip of the tongue but can't be uttered. It was quite frustrating. I would see a sight, watch a person move, hear a sound that would almost trigger a memory, but then it faded again just before I could grab hold and examine it for what it was.

One Sabbath eve, Trudy and I had gone to the Wailing Wall (which is actually the last remaining section of the original western wall of the old Temple Mount built by Herod the Great). I had purchased a prayer shawl earlier in the week and had it draped over my head and shoulders as I approached the men now gathering. Being a woman, Trudy joined the women at the south end of the wall, and I followed the men to their appointed section. Just one amongst hundreds, I was suddenly grabbed by my elbow by an old man. He separated me from the crowd, and led me through an opening in an adjacent stone wall. Once past the portal I stumbled down an ancient stairway, trying to keep up with the old man who knew this dark passage by rote. At the bottom, I entered a huge, cavernous room that was as close as the Jews can come to where the Holy of Holies, the Temple, the Altar, and the Ark of the Covenant once stood millennia ago. In the semi-darkness, the men assembled there began to chant. Their deep, resonant voices rose and fell, echoing off and around the massive, ancient stone ceilings, walls and high arches. I was carried away with ecstasy. I was home. I was back amongst my people. The memories began to stir.

I can close my eyes today and feel it all over again. It was one of the most moving and powerful religious experiences of my life, but even though my memories were jarred, they didn't complete their surfacing that night. And thus later as I lay awake staring at the ceiling in our hotel room, I could hear the chanting echoing over and over again in my head. I wondered why the old man had picked me, what it all meant, and, most importantly, why even after this amazing night I didn't know why I was there or where any of this was going to lead.

On our last day in Israel, while Trudy waited in our room for the bellman to pick up our bags, I went down to the hotel lobby to pay our bill. I also wanted to check on the final arrangements for our flight to Egypt and subsequent trip to the southern end of the country where we would board a boat and float down the Nile.

With my mind occupied by these details, I sat down at a lobby desk to write a thank you note to our guide.

After writing a bit, I stopped. Oddly, I hadn't been paying any attention to the message, as I mindlessly wrote on the paper. It was like reading a book late at night. Reaching the bottom of the page you realize that your mind has been elsewhere and you have to start all over again from the top.

I reread the thoughts I had just scribed. It appeared that I had quoted from some passage in the Bible (Torah?), but I couldn't remember any familiar source. In fact, I doubted that the scriptures were the source at all. For although I was not (nor am I now) well versed in the Old Testament, I felt that nothing I had written this day had come from either New or Old Testament sources as they have come down to us today. Something strange had happened, and then it was gone. The hair on my neck was standing on end. Just then, Trudy showed up with the bellman and our bags. I stuffed the missive in an envelope with some money for a tip and let the strange incident pass for the time being.

After three days in Cairo and its surrounds, we made our way south to a point just north of the Aswan Dam, where we boarded a boat to float down the timeless Nile. For a week we saw nothing more modern than camels burdened with commerce on the riverbanks heading north toward the capital, as they had for thousands of years.

Just before dawn on the second day on board, I climbed the ladder to the topmost deck, to be alone and to have it out with God. I was upset—very upset! I sat down and told God that I thought that I had done everything asked of me. I had given up my livelihood, my friends, moved my family, and traveled halfway around the globe in search of a "memory." I had searched the length and breadth of Israel, and now I was in Egypt, all because of the vision—but there was no memory to be had.

"What have you done to me, God? What have you done?" I screamed to the heavens.

It was then that I recognized Jesus' voice in my head once again, saying, "You have done all that I have asked. Now it is all to begin."

Suddenly, the world as I knew it fell out from under me and I felt the shock of falling down a tunnel of light, cascading down, down, totally out of control, like an elevator in free fall. All of a sudden I landed with a jolt. It was such a powerful shock to my system that my eyes flew open in horror, thinking that the boat had run onto a hidden shoal and was about to sink.

There, as the first rays of light danced upon the river Nile, the sights and sounds of the ancient past surrounded me. I was no longer in the present. I was in another body, another time, and another place altogether. I was in Jerusalem surrounded by people, my people, and animals, and sights and sounds that no one has seen or heard for two thousand years. That feeling in the vast rock-hewn chamber, Sabbath past, began to awaken within me once again.

I was remembering my past—another past. I could see the stone buildings, the streets paved by Herod and maintained by Rome. I could smell the wood and camel-dung smoke that hung lazily between the buildings in the early morning calm. I listened to the children's voices squealing as they began another day of play. A dog here and there registered its presence, and the scuffling, clanking, banging, indeterminate sounds of a city coming to life for another day seemed peacefully serene to me.

I breathed in the rich air that I loved as the shofar sounded from high atop the Temple wall, and my body and mind were at ease.

I was looking out of the eyes of an old man, just on the other side of sixty, and I knew it was me. My body was short and stocky of build.

I had a white beard that felt strange on my face. I knew my name, Asher ben Ammi, and I knew and remembered everything about this life so long ago. I thought, "My God! This isn't someone I am watching; these are my memories. I am Asher ben Ammi!"

"Dear Father, you have fulfilled your promise," I cried. "You have taken me home. You have awakened my memories just as you promised!"

The powerful, strange experience lasted only ten or fifteen minutes at most, and then, exhausted, I felt myself being pulled back to the present. I took a gulp of still cool, Egyptian desert air. I was totally exhausted but exhilarated beyond what I can describe. I began to write. The story had begun. The memory was being awakened!

Each day for the next week, I got up before dawn to find a quiet space on the boat, meditate, feel myself falling, and then join a different world and a different time. I wrote what I saw, what I heard, what I smelled, what I felt, what I thought, and what I experienced. I wrote it all. I started by writing in a journal and later, returning home, I switched to my computer to record what was happening as the experiences continued unabated, every day for the next seven months.

I would rise well before dawn in our cabin home in Michigan, build a roaring fire in the giant stone fireplace, settle into a comfortable chair to meditate, and fall back two thousand years.

In the beginning I could hold onto the sights, sounds, and feelings for only a few minutes, ending totally exhausted, but as my body and mind became used to the journey back in time, I was able to stretch my concentration to hours at a time. I simply opened myself to the memory and wrote as fast as I could, describing what was happening to me. Thus started the story of my past life as an old man who had walked the path with one greater than he. His name was Yeshua ben Joseph. To me, however, he was, and will always remain, simply, Yeshu.

What follows is the story of a devoted disciple who stored within his soul the memory of things his Lord had said and done during those wondrous years so long ago. It is truly one of the first gospels ever written, beginning on the rooftop of old Asher's home in Jerusalem during Jesus' life, and more than likely buried there still, hidden by Asher's wife, Miriamme, beneath the rubble left after the Romans sacked Jerusalem in 70 CE.

It is the story of Jesus and his disciple, the old man, Asher ben Ammi. It is the story of my life that I now want to share with you with love and care.

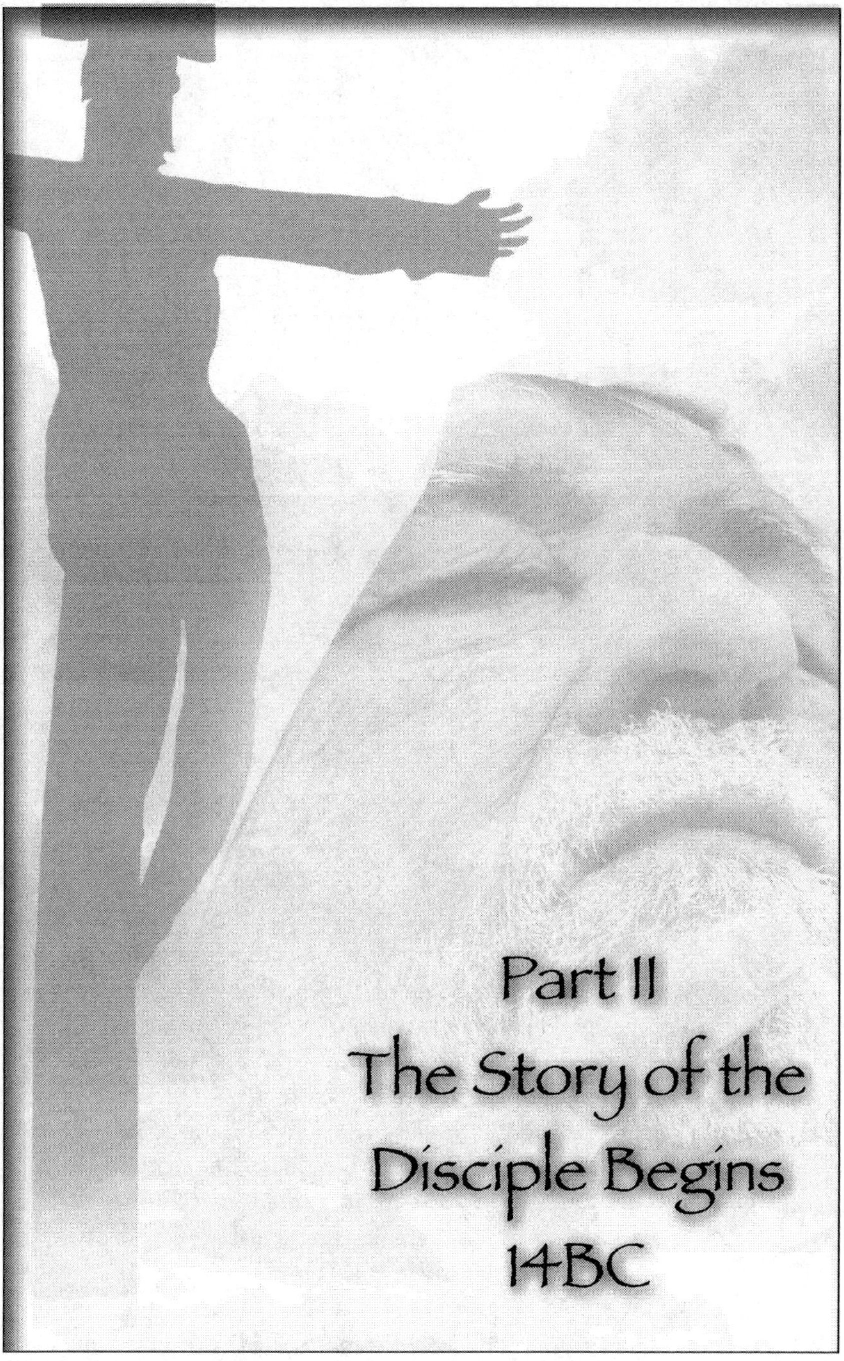

Part II
The Story of the Disciple Begins
14BC

Chapter 1

The Story Begins

Tyre: O mighty seaport city, merchant center of the world, the Lord God speaks. You say, "I am the most beautiful city in all the world." You have extended your boundaries out into the sea; your architects have made you glorious.

Ezekiel 27:3-4

Of the tribe of Asher:
"Asher is a favorite son,
Esteemed above his brothers;
He bathes his feet in soothing olive oil.
May you be protected with strong bolts
Of iron and bronze,
And may your strength match the length of your days!"

Deuteronomy 33:24–25

Asher rose early to the yellow glow of the sun just topping the hills to the east of his seaside home in Tyre, which lay along the coast in the north of Israel. He was but nineteen, yet already heady in adulthood. He was steeped in his family's business: buying, selling, and trading cloth, spices, merchandise, and objects of art with merchants from all over the world, as well as in Jerusalem, which for Asher was the center of the universe. The business fit him like a fine leather glove.

You know the kind of glove I mean. An expensive one, that fits tight, with leather cut so thin, so supple and soft, that you hardly know it is on your hand. And, as the glove is soft and warm, so could young Asher be when it suited his needs. Even at this young age his business wrapped him and became him as an outer skin. It protected him and gave him status and great strength. Just as a glove could strike hard yet protect the wearer, so too could young Asher strike boldly when it meant profits for this young businessman who was named by his father after his tribe.

Asher ben Ammi, son of the tribe of Asher; his name was given by a father to his first-born son with such pride. It said to everyone, "Look here at my son. I bring forth an emissary from our tribe, one of the twelve tribes of Israel, the tribe of Asher, one that will be our best, our brightest. He is not only my son, but our son."

Donning his robe—thin, fine, and light as air—Asher looked at himself in the mirror and straightened his cap. Then, without a backward glance toward his family's large home, he strode down to the wharf that lay along a narrow strip of land joining the old city with the more densely packed island. He couldn't wait to see what new opportunities presented themselves with the morning tide.

The early morning was still cool, but yielded a hint of the stifling heat to come. The salt air smelled of far-off lands, and he was happy in the anticipation of another day. At his age everything was an adventure, an opportunity to hone his skills against the wise old traders who outweighed him in power, money, and influence, but lacked his intelligence and drive to succeed.

What was awaiting him this day, however, would change his life forever in this small coastal city during the twenty-seventh year of King Herod's reign.

Over the years Asher's father, Malchiah, had financed his share of Herod's rise to power, and young Asher had been in his court on several occasions as his father received the return on his investment many times over from the king. But the king, a bright, ruthless, half-Jewish Idumean, was not on Asher's mind this morning; business was. His trained eyes scanned the incoming cargoes being unloaded onto the docks, looking for the unusual odd item that would catch his eye.

The morning din of voices was starting to grow as the ship captains began to shout orders to their crews. The workers on shore, freemen and slaves alike, Romans, Jews, Greeks, Egyptians, and Africans, all mixed to create a boisterous brew of languages and peoples that was the stew enticing this young man to ply his trade with such vigor and aplomb.

Suddenly, amongst the bobbing and straining ships hard at their hawsers, there was one, then two spots of brilliant moving color, vibrant against the drab, dark brown of the ships and men. The colors moved with an elegance that bespoke of royalty, or at least richness and power.

Asher drifted away from the conversation he was having with the merchant near the end of the wharf. He ducked out from under the canvas awning and pushed his way through the growing crowd to get a better view of who was departing the ship that had, by its looks, come from the north of Africa.

Walking down the gangplank onto the landing was a tall man with dusky skin and a young woman half his age and two shades lighter. The man had short black, cropped hair that shone like the sparkle of light dancing on water. Tall, ramrod straight, and fine of feature, this couple presented a regal and striking picture as the hushed crowd parted to let them pass.

They passed perhaps twenty paces in front of Asher, then turned left down the wharf and headed toward the heart of city along the causeway. The man was Asher's father's age, and the woman at his side, his own. Asher was mesmerized. The robes they wore splayed out behind them as they walked, and in such bright colors that no one could help but stop and stare.

The man was wearing a free-flowing liquid red and yellow robe of the finest material (silk, by the looks of its sheen). The young woman striding proudly by his side, head up with fire in her eyes, was likewise wearing a beautiful brilliant red robe with bright green and golden yellow swaths of color splashed across the wearer.

As the man and woman passed, the crowds parted, stopped and stared, then reformed to continue working. From Asher's distance it was like a ripple of paused humanity flowing down the long bridge jutting out from the land. Then the teaming workers swallowed up the couple again.

It wasn't until they had come abreast of where he was standing that he saw her face. Fine featured like the man she accompanied, her dark black, glistening hair reached down her tall straight back, setting off the color of her robe and making it even more brilliant in the early morning sun.

It wasn't her clothes that attracted him to her, however, it was her face! He had never seen such beauty. Asher's breath caught in his throat, then was expelled with such force that he had to lean against a nearby support for fear that his lightheadedness would cause him to black out.

This was the first time that Asher's bright mind had gone absolutely blank. He slumped against a wooden support pole in a daze for what to him seemed like an eternity. Bending at the waist, he lowered his head to get the blood rushing back into his brain.

Moments later when he felt his senses return, he raised his head and looked about to find the girl. Left, right, she was nowhere to be found. She had disappeared. Quickly he gathered himself together and rushed off down the wharf toward the old city in the direction they had gone. He strained to get a glimpse of the red, green, and yellow robes.

His friend, the master of the wharves, stared at the young man as he hurriedly dogged between slave and master, trader and dockhand, running as if chased by God. With a grin, the older man turned back to his shipping records, shaking his head, thinking that youth was far too fast for him and, more importantly, that the cool of the morning was drifting away far too quickly. The day's first drop of sweat dripped from the short pug nose plugged into his fat but friendly face and landed splat on top of the papyrus scroll before him, smearing the ink before it could evaporate into the still, dry air.

"How could I have lost them?" Asher wondered as he raced first one way, then another, in his mad dash toward the low seaside buildings that made up the majority of this side of the city.

Finally, no closer to his goal of finding the girl or the man, he slowed to a walk, feeling the first trickle of sweat run down his armpit toward his waist. Now, sobered by the loss, his mind finally caught up with his body. He turned and began to question people close by until he found several who had also taken note of the unusual pair and had seen them depart. All they knew, however, was that someone had met the couple and escorted them off along the street that paralleled the sea wall. Asher backtracked further, all the way to the ship from whence the couple had come. There he questioned the ship's captain who had brought them ashore.

He found out that the man and woman he sought owned the ship and had told the master of the vessel that they were expecting to meet the city governor's servant at the head of the wharf. A few minutes later Asher found two merchants who had seen the couple whisked away on two waiting horses, presumably to the governor's home on a high place not far from there.

"Think, Asher, think," he muttered to himself. "How can you get yourself into the governor's quarters, on what pretext?"

It struck him like a bolt. Of course! The governor was always on the lookout for something that would ingratiate himself to King Herod; or maybe this time, to a fancy and important guest. Asher had just the bait to get himself invited to the governor's home this very afternoon if all worked as expected.

Asher hurried home. The streets were now busy, bustling with people coming and going on their daily chores. Once in the house, he brushed past the servants in the kitchen area and out to the locked storeroom behind. There he lifted the key from his belt and unlocked the heavy wooden door.

In a side room, reserved for only the finest of the family's treasures, Asher lifted a cloth covering that hid an ivory elephant that he had purchased two months before from a ship captain from Egypt. The man had needed a considerable amount of funds to repair the storm-damaged rigging and sails on his ship. He had lost most of his cargo in the storm, an all too frequent occurrence in this unusually stormy year, but he had saved the elephant, which was almost as long as Asher's arm and half that in height. A bull, ears flared in full charge. In appearance, a single slab of ivory. In truth, dozens of pieces so delicately and deftly put together that they appeared as one. The captain had kept this treasure in his own quarters, locked in a chest built into the side of the ship itself for safekeeping.

Asher bought the priceless figure for a pittance really, but to Asher a deal was made based on the advantages and disadvantages of the players, and a deal would never be passed up because of emotion or pity. Somewhere deep inside he thought that one-day it might be he that another trader would be taking advantage of, which eased his conscience, thinking it only a game. Truthfully, though, his youthful mind never really thought that there would be any circumstance that he couldn't figure out, nor a path he couldn't take to win back whatever he might momentarily lose. Now the elephant was his key to the young woman who had instantly captured his total attention.

Gently he rewrapped the figure and then called for two servants to help him box the precious item in the shipping crate that had been built just for that purpose. It was loaded onto an ass-drawn cart, and with Asher astride his beautiful black stallion, his man walking beside the cart, they set out along the street that led to his destination.

Once at the gate, Asher had his servant announce his presence, telling the gateman that his master would definitely want to see what lay hidden in the crate.

Already wise in the ways of man's greed, Asher was shown into the governor's private quarters, where he was soon met by the governor himself (who knew Asher and his father and trusted the keen eye they shared for things of great value).

Asher was invited to sip a cooled goblet of wine mixed with spices and fruit. Savoring the silence and mystery of his mission, he conversed with the governor about weather and politics... and visiting dignitaries. It was now that he found out that the two guests that he sought had arrived from Africa. Jews like himself, they had come to visit the Temple in Jerusalem for the holy days that were but a fortnight away.

This man from Africa, who was widowed, was the young woman's father. They were rich beyond belief in their own land, the governor confided to Asher, all the while eyeing what had now been uncrated yet remained covered by the beautiful linen drape. Asher, already a master of patience, waited for the silence to grow to the dimension that he felt the work of art demanded, then he finally relented and, with a great show, had the drape dramatically lifted from the beautifully carved piece of ivory.

The governor gasped as he saw the detail of the workmanship, and the size! He noted that the eyes were precious black stones inset within giant, white, opalescent pearls. The tusks stood out beneath an upraised trunk, trumpeting the great creature's defiance to all that would challenge his sovereignty. This truly was a gift fit for a king, and the governor had to have it—and Asher already knew the price.

The governor immediately wanted to know how much Asher wanted for the elephant, but time was on Asher's side now; he could sense it, so he stalled. He could read the man as if he were a cat maliciously toying with a mouse, not yet ready to end his sport.

"Why don't we talk about it over dinner, my lord?" Asher smoothly suggested.

The governor reluctantly agreed. He wanted to show off the new acquisition to his guests that very evening. Why not include Asher? He could arrange to intercept Asher just before dinner started and negotiate a suitable price with the young man. He wouldn't mind at all having Asher at the dinner party; after all, Asher was an amusing, entertaining, and a well-bred guest.

Asher left with a smile on his face. He knew that once the governor had claimed ownership of the elephant in front of his noble guests, he would have to pay his price; pride would prevent him from backing away. Asher would have the money he deserved for his shrewd purchase, and as a bonus he would meet the young woman who had so attracted him that morning.

Asher arrived precisely on time that evening, in one of his finest robes. It was ivory white, with a band of pure gold thread three fingers wide sewn at the sleeves, down its front, and along the bottom hem. His hair was cut short, Roman style, and he had used some of his most expensive oil to perfume his body. This was going to be a night to remember. He could feel it. He could sense it.

After arriving, Asher was shown into the large greeting hall, brilliantly lit with a hundred lamps that flickered magically each time a gust of air stirred in the room. Given a gold-and-silver goblet of wine, he busied himself by observing the fine collectibles that ringed the room on shelves and stands built for the purpose of display.

"A bit gaudy," Asher thought to himself, "and a bit too much with the busy, Roman-style wall murals that enclosed the room on all sides—but impressive all the same."

Asher passively noted that the elephant was nowhere to be seen.

Suddenly there was a flurry of activity outside. Then, bursting through a door at the far end of the room, the governor suddenly appeared. Out of breath, scrubbed clean, pink from the exertion of dressing his portly body, his bald head glistened with little beads of sweat in the lamplight as he hurriedly crossed the room.

"Asher, Asher, so glad you arrived a bit ahead of our guests, let's not waste any time, shall we? Let's arrive at a price that makes some sense. What do you want for your prize bull?"

Asher turned away, feigning lack of interest, and instead asked the governor where the three beautiful matching jade bowls had come from. Asher had never seen such huge pieces of jade in his entire life!

"They are unimportant, young man, we have little time, and I need your answer. What price do you put on your small ivory piece?"

Amateur, Asher thought, you mistake me for my age.

"One hundred talents of gold, my lord," he hesitated to allow the shock to sink in, "...or, if you prefer, these three matching bowls."

One hundred talents was an outrageous sum! It amounted to the entire annual income later granted by the emperor Augustus to Herod the Great's son, Philip, to rule the areas north and east of Galilee (including Capernaum) upon his father's death. It was as if Asher had told the old man, "Forget it, you can't afford the piece at any price."

"Never!" the governor cried, suddenly wheezing. "I have already presented the carving to my guests, but I swear by your head, I will just as easily take it back as pay your contemptible price!"

Just as the governor spit out the last words, his face crimson with anger and sweat beginning to pour from his brow, the door that Asher had come through some minutes before swung open. Through the portal came one of the governor's house slaves announcing the entrance of the Lord Awasa of Ethiopia and his daughter, Awena.

They swept into the room with the grace that their long-practiced position in court afforded them. Asher was dazed. Once again his mind froze. No words came forth from his mouth, no thought coursed through his mind, save the picture of this beautiful creature's face.

The big man, lean, with massive upper body strength and a voice as deep and strong and clear as any Asher had ever heard, clasped the governor and kissed him on both cheeks, thanking him for the beautiful gift. "It will hold a prized place in my home for all to see."

Somewhere the meaning of the conversation registered, even though Asher stood mesmerized with the vision of the young woman in front of him.

"Asher, what is the matter with you?" the governor asked with annoyance. "Where are your manners?"

Dimly Asher realized that time had passed, and he was supposed to respond to something that the governor had said. What was it, he wondered? His mind raced without gaining a grip. He shook his head to clear it and suddenly saw, with horror, that both the girl and her father were staring at him with smiles on their faces, barely hiding what was obvious to everyone there.

Asher mumbled an apology for staring and tried manfully to recover. He was totally out of his realm here, and he knew it. Get to solid ground, Asher, he thought to himself, get to solid ground!

"I am more than honored to meet you, sir," Asher finally responded, bowing low, exercising his best Greek to match the obvious high learning of the man opposite him. Then turning to the man's daughter, he attempted a greeting, but seeing her dancing, ebony eyes, he became lost in their endless depth and forgot everything he had prepared to say.

He finally mumbled something about the weather. Realizing immediately his stupidity, he turned a far deeper shade of red than their host had earlier, thinking to himself… weather? Why on earth did I say weather? Weather indeed! What an idiot you are, Asher ben Ammi.

He was saved any further awkward silence, with the governor staring at him as if he were insane, by the dinner announcement. The governor turned with a sweep and proceeded to lead the small party through the door from which the servant had come, down a short corridor, and through a large opening into the dinning room.

Asher noted that they were to sit on Roman reclining couches that had been arranged around a low table stacked with food of every type.

Servers ringed the room waiting their appointed time and their appointed tasks. When the governor pointed out their respective couches, Asher gasped. Could it be? The governor had arranged himself at one end of the table with Awena's father next to him, and then came Awena, and finally Asher. He was to sit next to the most beautiful and exotic woman he had ever seen. God had smiled on him this night, indeed.

As they reclined with the girl's head but a short distance from his, he noticed that her long, raven-black, shining hair was braided in hundreds of small strands all over her head. He had never seen anything like it before in all his life. The finest carved features that could be imagined complemented her tall, muscular body, which she held straight and proud. Her face was one of exquisite beauty. Her eyebrows were fine and arched, joining her aquiline nose, which was straight and perfectly placed. Her eyes, like clear, dark pools, danced in the torchlight. Their blackness made them seem endlessly deep, hiding secrets that Asher could only guess about later over and over that night. Her mouth was fine and perfectly full, upturned slightly at each end. He had the immediate impression that there was devilishness hiding just behind her easy smile and mysterious eyes. He also saw determination in her intelligent face, a confidence born of her royal raising.

"Tell me about yourself, Asher," she said, as the dark black slave behind her adjusted her colorful dress to flow easily behind the couch. At the same time, she reached for the wine that had now been poured into the golden goblet on the table before her.

"There is nothing to tell, princess," Asher stammered, "I am but a humble trader of goods, a person of no count."

"I doubt that," she said with a slight grin. "Tell me about yourself."

"Truly, there is little to tell. I was born Asher ben Ammi, son of the tribe of Asher, to which I belong. My father's pride in naming me as a representative of the whole tribe, instead of choosing a proper name, was a source of great derision from others of my age as I grew. Yet I have worked hard, and I will prove to everyone someday that Asher ben Ammi is a name to be looked up to."

"Oh, is that right, Asher ben Ammi? So what have you done to date to prove your name to be worthy of respect?"

There was mocking in her voice, and that mysterious smile which Asher took as a challenge to his manhood.

"Take the elephant the old man gave your father earlier this day," he started, lowering his voice and casting an eye to the two men at the other end of the table deep in their own conversation. "That is my elephant. I wanted you to have it, so I have offered it to him, and he has given it to your father as I planned—without arriving at a price with me. Now I will embarrass him into paying whatever I want so that he doesn't have to take back the gift that was not yet his to give."

Asher could tell by her new widening smile that she had quickly grasped the situation that the governor was in, and she started to look at Asher differently. Not with outright approval as yet, but it was a start, he thought. Then, with equal delight, and without missing a beat, she turned to her father, interrupting the men in mid-conversation, saying sweetly, "Father, where is that elephant that our fine host gave us?"

"I have given instructions to have it re-crated for the trip back, my love. Why?"

"I want it, father. I want it for my own."

"And so it shall be, my love. It will be yours."

Her father turned to the governor, and lifting his goblet, toasted the older man, saying, "It appears that your fine gift has found an appreciative home. You will have to visit us and see it on display in a place of honor of my daughter's own choosing."

The governor smiled his most courtier-like smile and bowed his head before his guest, but neither Asher nor Awena missed the nervous glance in Asher's direction.

Asher pictured the jade bowls as he watched the mischievous dancing eyes of the one woman he thought might be a match for him. Now he knew that he must have her and no other. There were no other women like her in this city; no village girl or merchant's daughter in any other Jewish city within Herod's realm could match her, of that he was sure.

She was born of a different culture, one that put women equal to their men, firm of mind and equally firm of will. This was to be his greatest challenge, and his own mind was already laying the trap.

It appeared that the conversation had stopped between the two men. Awena's father sat up and began to eat from the platters laid out in front of them. Asher took the cue and leaned away from the young woman still lounging to his right. Facing the governor he said, "What activities have you planned for our guests while they are here?"

The governor began to outline some of the business that had to be accomplished before his guest left for Jerusalem.

"But what about this fine lady here?" Asher interjected. "Have you made plans for her to see our city or our countryside while you busy her father?"

Asher had a knack for making the governor turn red. It was instantly obvious that he hadn't given the girl a thought. Even tonight's arrangement, with his inclusion, was a spur-of-the-moment affair necessitated by the ill begotten elephant. Asher, instantly sensing the vacuum, began to speak as politely as he could, addressing both of the older men.

"It would be an honor for me to show your guest's daughter the sights of our poor town and beyond, sir. Would tomorrow morning suit your pleasure?" he asked, turning to his table companion with obvious anticipation.

The governor had no intention of letting Asher into his home one more time. It seemed that every time he was there, he wound up at the bad end of a deal. He could already see the empty spot that the missing jade bowls would create, and from that day forward he formed a very definite dislike for this shrewd young upstart of a man.

But before the governor could regain his composure and think of something that should have been thought out long before this, Awena's father answered for him. "That sounds like a fine idea. What do you say, Awena, would you like to take a tour with this young man instead of sitting around here waiting for me?"

"I would enjoy that very much, father," she said. Then, addressing the governor, she asked, "Kind sir, do you have a horse that I could borrow to ride tomorrow?"

The arrangements were finalized, and Asher told her that he would pick her up midmorning of the next day.

On the way out later that evening, Asher leaned close to the governor's ear and softly said, "I'll send my servant to fetch the bowls tomorrow afternoon. If you could be so kind as to have them packed for shipment, I would be most grateful."

Without a moment's pause to see the governor's reaction, Asher bid everyone a fair night. He elaborately thanked his host first, then Awena's father for his and his daughter's fine company. Lastly he bowed low before the young woman with the light ebony skin without saying a word, then turned and left the room with a flourish.

The governor went to bed that night planning his revenge. Asher fell asleep dreaming of the beautiful woman he had met and the wonder that the morrow would bring.

The following morning Asher mounted his horse and headed for the governor's house to meet the woman with whom he was so infatuated.

He entered the governor's forecourt just as Awena was tucking her skirt up and through her legs. She draped the excess under her wide belt at the small of her back, then let the fabric fall behind the saddle as she mounted her own red mare with an ease that meant that she was probably a far more practiced rider than Asher himself.

He bowed from the saddle of his stallion, one of his prized possessions, a beautiful gift for his eighteenth birthday from his father and mother. The horse was an ebony beauty, brushed and curried until his coat shone. His tail had been braided with bright ribbon and tied at the end. His mane had been clipped, and the fine horse was as proud as his rider.

Asher himself was wearing a short Roman toga as white as the full-length robe he wore the night before. It had identical gold trim around the neck and bottom of the skirt.

Asher greeted Awena with a smile that was as wide and genuine as a schoolboy's. Happiness filled his heart as they both turned the corner of the perimeter wall and headed east at an easy gallop. Once out of the town, they headed south, following one of the many country roads that led to the farms in the outskirts of the city.

Earlier that morning, Asher had dispensed one of his servants to ride about an hour south down the coast and up onto a highland bluff where a friend of the family owned a farm and a beautiful villa overlooking the sea. They lived in Jerusalem during the months when it was cool, but the older man and his family always returned to their farm during the growing season. Asher and his parents were an exception to the rule, however, for although they had a large home in Jerusalem, they lived most of the year in Tyre to be close to the ships as they arrived at the busy port of trade.

This year everyone would have stayed longer near the coast if they could have, for the summer seemed as if it would never end. Here it was the beginning of Tishrei; one week away from Yom Kippur, and less than two weeks away from Sukkoth, the festival of Tabernacles, and still there was no end to this year's unusual heat.

Upon arrival, Asher's servant asked the family if Asher and a very special lady guest might come to share their noontime meal. Simon ben Joseph and his wife, Miriam, were delighted to see one of their own son's best friends—and with a woman no less!

They had often worried during the last couple of years about Asher, so totally absorbed in trade at such a young age. They had watched as he covered his shyness with the opposite sex by immersing himself in his father's business. Within two years, he was far better at trading than his own father was. All the time spent buried in his work left people thinking Asher had no apparent interest in getting married, even though his parents and their friends had often tried to set him up with eligible young women in both Tyre and Jerusalem. Now, out of nowhere, without any warning, he was coming with a woman! They hadn't heard any news of his interest in any of the local girls, and secretly Miriam wondered why Emma, Asher's mother, hadn't mentioned this special person to her before.

Their first look at Asher told them that something was different. Usually he was too busy to care much about dressing up for anyone or anything unless it served him in his trading business. Now, as he came up the road toward their house they saw that he was attired in a toga the likes of which they had rarely seen, except at very special occasions with urbane or moneyed guests whom Asher wished to impress.

Then they saw the person who accompanied him.

She was young, proud, straight in the saddle, and an expert rider, of that no one could argue. But she was a woman of color! She wasn't a local woman at all. Immediately, without even noticing, their noses rose just a little, and they became just a touch distant and stiff. Not a conscious thing, but if you knew them, you would feel the difference, no matter the formal courtesies effortlessly extended.

As Awena brought the horse to a halt in front of the waiting couple, she swung her leg over the horse and bounced to the ground with a practiced grace.

At the same time she yanked on the front of her skirt, which instantly dropped, flowing full length around her ankles. She really was a thing of beauty.

With an easy smile, she waited for Asher to hand the reins of the horses to the waiting servant, and then as Asher breathlessly introduced her, she held out her hand and in impeccable, formal Greek told them that she was honored to meet them.

During the noontime meal on the portico looking west toward the sea far below, she kept the three of them entranced with stories of her homeland, her family, and her experiences hunting, riding, camping, and stalking game. Her people traveled far throughout a continent of which Asher and his friends had only a vague understanding, and they hunted animals seen in the circuses of Rome by only a few; and Asher wasn't counted among their number.

She told of her own proud family, which had one home near the sea and another in the cooler highlands in the interior of the country. She pictured for them the mountains and the deep gorge that split her land, within which flowed the beginnings of the mighty Nile that created Egypt's wealth.

Her father was the second son of the ruler of this Axumite kingdom. Their people had much in common with the Jews of Israel, not only by religion, but also by their subjugation by Rome. For in their land too, the Romans exerted power (more near the coast and less in the hard-to-reach heartland). Like everyone else, the indigenous people were allowed to keep to themselves as long as they did Rome's bidding and filled the coffers of the empire. Having less power than their own King Herod, her grandfather acknowledged that Caesar Divi Filius Augustus was the only true king of their land. But, because it served Rome's needs, her family had position and great wealth. Her father, however, was a younger son, thus he was not in succession to rule. As a result he had plenty of time to pursue more interesting pastimes than affairs of state.

He raised his only child, Awena, as his own heir-apparent. She went everywhere with him, and she was as shrewd in business as any man (perhaps more), for she learned early to take advantage of her unique grace and beauty to gain her way with those who were unsuspecting. She got what she wanted. Somehow, someway, she used her brains, her raw nerve, her sex, and yes, even a little guile to achieve or conquer what she desired or deserved. On the ride this fine fall morning, it was Asher that she set her sights on, and the outcome was foreordained. It was easy, really. He was shy (not in business, but with women), shorter than she would like and not that good looking, but lean and hard, and his quick mind, sharp wit, and good humor attracted her immediately.

The afternoon passed quickly. Before the sun crossed half the sky, Awena had won the overwhelming favor and approval of her hosts, yet after she left, they commented that Asher was in for a very rough time.

"That young woman is far too headstrong," Miriam said to her husband, shaking her head as the young couple galloped off and the afternoon sun began its slow fall into the sea. "Asher will suffer with her I fear," she added, shaking her head.

"And love every minute of it," her husband chuckled as they turned back toward the entry of their home.

The following few days in Tyre passed quickly with Awena's father hurriedly trying to complete his business in the seaport town before leaving to celebrate the holidays in Jerusalem that Asher's family was, of course, going to attend as well. Asher and Awena spent every available moment with one another and laid plans for their two families to travel together up into the hills of Judea to arrive in Jerusalem before the holy Feast of Tabernacles.

At Asher's urging, his father had offered to host the two visitors at their home in the city; only a short walk to the temple, baths, and gymnasium should Awena's father wish to avail himself of the facilities. Asher's family home was in the upper part of Jerusalem, near King Herod's own compound and away from the noisiest part of the city, now swelling to overflowing with the coming of the fall celebration.

The booths of the merchants and celebrants and the tents of the visitors were set up everywhere. The rich gathering that blended the Jews from all lands was in full swing when they arrived.

In their sheer joy of life Awena and Asher sampled everything to excess, wishing to stop the sun's inexorable journey so that the days would stretch into weeks, and the weeks into years.

The two fathers got on famously, and much to Asher's mother's despair, the two men were already arranging a marriage. All the while this was going on, their children sampled their youth. Unbeknownst to either of them their innocence was all too soon to be ripped from them both.

It was a perfect match, the two fathers thought. Two trading families joining hands across the sea to control markets far beyond what either of them could imagine alone. Tied by marriage, both families would prosper. It was a good thing. For Asher's father, he gained a powerful buyer in the African trade with wealth beyond his own. For Awena's father, his daughter would be sealing their offspring's legitimacy in the Jewish world by joining this old Jewish family that traced itself back to the Patriarchs; to say nothing of his family's new found access to the inner circle that controlled all trade in and around the capital city of Jerusalem. Malchiah and Awasa's grandchildren would be worldly and wealthy beyond what most could imagine—a comfortable feeling of accomplishment for both of them in their declining years.

It was arranged that Awena and her father would return to Africa, then come back six months hence, in the spring, with their immediate family for Passover. At this time of new beginnings, they would seal their two families in Jerusalem. Sometime thereafter, when the children had settled in their new home and life in Tyre, they would pack up Asher's family to visit Awena's home. There the two families could work out the details of how to put together the trading partnership that both were looking forward to.

Awena and Asher were delighted with the arrangements, and after

Asher saw Awena off on their ship back home, he counted the days and weeks until they would be able to see each other again.

Asher could think of nothing else but his bride-to-be, and he fell prey to the governor's revenge for the jade bowls in one of the dumbest trades he would ever make. But even that couldn't faze this love-struck young man. He just didn't care. His father could only count the losses, shake his head, and hope that his son would return to normal once the marriage had been consummated.

Soon after Awena left, Asher's father, in a vain attempt to re-interest his son in the everyday business at hand, sent him to the port of Caesarea, where there were whispers that an owner of a large granary was in financial difficulty. A casual investigation of the facts by Asher found that the granary was filled to capacity, and the owner was indeed telling his friends that he needed money, as he had apparently risked his reserves on a ship that floundered off the island of Rhodes on its way to Ephesus, Adramyttium, and beyond. Apparently, the entire shipment was lost, and his fortune was now balanced on the edge of a sword, poised to fall unless he could sell something of great value to pay the debts he owed.

Normally Asher would have taken weeks to quietly ferret out and verify every detail of the rumor before approaching the intended party—always through intermediaries. He would have normally heeded his father's shrewd advice: "Make three offers, each time using another trader in your employ. Offer less than half of what it is worth, making sure that each offer is lower than the one before. Then, with the owner morose, with no good offer in sight, and each offer sinking below the first, swoop in and steal the trade with what appears to be the best offer he is going to get."

It was a good plan that would work time and again for Asher during his life—but not this time. Love-sick, and wanting to return to see if any messages had been delivered by return ship, he found the price of the grain to be good, offered a little less than asked to assuage his father, then closed and sealed the contract and hurried back to his home.

If he had taken the time, he would have found out that there was no shipwreck, at least none that carried any property of the man who offered the granary for sale. This was Asher's first attempt at playing in the grain market. And, although his understanding of the market swings in grain prices was adequate, he didn't bother to find out that the governor and his close associates had already locked up all the seasonal contracts with the Temple and the Romans. That left only the small and volatile daily market, with a huge overhead, and insignificant small purchases by local merchants that would eat up any profits. It was sweet revenge for the governor, and a story that would reverberate at parties for weeks and months to come. The governor had indeed wreaked vengeance for the trick Asher had played on him by stealing his jade bowls.

Asher's return with the news that he had bought the granary without having negotiated a single advance purchase contract took the wind from his father. And, as if that weren't enough, when word spread among the small trading community in which they lived that the governor had set him up, it sent Malchiah to bed for days.

How was he to deal with this empty-headed son until the woman returned?

If Malchiah could have only known what the future would bring, however, he would have gladly given this trade and a hundred others like it in exchange for what was to come. For Asher would return to business with a vengeance less than a year and a half later, but the reason for the return and the way it was to happen, no one would have wanted.

The wedding took place as planned the following spring. After days and nights of celebration, Asher and Awena settled into their new home in Tyre, a gift of Asher's father and mother, a gift befitting this new joint venture between the two families. A right and proper place for the princess, Malchiah's son, and hopefully grandchildren if everything went according to plan.

Life was bliss for Asher. Awena and he did everything together. Asher taught her every nuance of the trading business here in his land, and she taught him as well. They were a natural team.

Most of all he learned to tread lightly with her, as she was as headstrong as her father had warned him the night before the wedding. Several times she would give him a tongue lashing in the privacy of their home that would cause him to wonder aloud to his father at their daily meetings each morning.

His father only laughed his deep belly-rolling laugh that was so infectious and gave Asher the magic words that his own father had given him many years before, words every man must learn: "I'm so very sorry, my dear. It won't happen any more. I assure you I will be more careful and attentive next time."

Malchiah would sagely admonish him; "Marriage is a dance, my son, a dance that continues from the moment you marry until the day you die. Learn it quickly and you will be happy like I am with your mother; learn it slowly, and you will twist on the spit like a heathen pig in hell." Thus said, Asher's father doubled up with laughter, as tears squeezed out of his merry eyes, now mere slits, and down the stubble of his cheeks to be lost in his thinning beard.

Asher tried the words he had learned, but Awena was far too attuned to him and rarely let him get away that easily; but his love for his young bride was total, and nothing else seemed to matter all that much after all. Despite his shrewdness in business, Asher was by nature gentle and loving in family affairs, and totally devoted to his young bride, deeply wanting to do what she wished with a glad and open heart.

Whatever else caused friction between them, however, disappeared totally a few months later when Awena presented him with the news that she was with child. Asher's parents were ecstatic. Awena immediately sent word to her father by trading ship, asking for her nanny from her homeland to make the journey to her as soon as possible to begin her preparations for the son she knew that she would bear her husband and the royal family of her homeland.

The months passed quickly as Asher split his attention between business and his young wife, whose belly grew rounder and firmer each day. She seemed to glow and mellow as the day of birth drew near. For the first time in her life, she felt vulnerable, and she pulled Asher closer with each passing day. It was a time of wonder for Asher, knowing that there was a living child within her. It would be his firstborn; the inheritor of everything that Asher hoped to build. He couldn't have honored Awena more as he wrapped himself around her each night and felt his son grow within her womb.

The day broke cold and clear. A hint of a storm was played far off over the sea, but the wind wasn't right to bring it easterly toward Tyre. As Asher strode down to the docks he gazed out over the sea and guessed that the storm would blow well north. Although he didn't know it yet, this day would change his life forever.

As he approached the end of the wharf, he turned at the sound of an urgent cry carried above the babble of the crowd. He could see among the workers already sweating under their labors even on this chilly, clear morn, the familiar head of his manservant who was waving wildly, trying to attract his attention.

Wheezing, he came to a halt in front of Asher, bending over, putting his hands to his knees to gain his breath. Then, as Asher bent over himself to impatiently look in the man's eye, he heard the news he was waiting for. Awena was about to give birth.

Joyously, Asher sprinted home just as the midwife entered his home. He immediately grabbed her by the arm and half lifted her, half dragged her into the bedroom where he could hear his wife softly moaning.

"Will she be all right?" he asked no one in particular as he adjusted the pillows under his wife's head. She was sweating profusely, and her breath was already coming in gasps.

The midwife lifted Awena's robe to see how close the baby was to crowning. What she saw turned her face immediately ashen as she gasped, putting her hands to her mouth, trying to stifle the cry rising in her throat.

Asher turned to the foot of the bed, saw the horror in her eyes, and froze. Awena's nanny began to rock back and forth, tearing at her hair and clothes in anguish. The old woman's head arched back; her tongue began to keen the warbling sound of death that sent a freezing shiver throughout all in the room.

Asher threw back the covers. There for everyone to see was more blood than he had ever seen. Awena, his beloved Awena, was hemorrhaging. The baby's head was almost out, but the blood. My God, it was flowing out of her body into a huge pool soaking into the bedding. Something was terribly wrong.

Asher stood frozen for what seemed like an eternity. He wanted to scream, he wanted to save her, but he was frozen in terror of what he saw. Then without warning he was pushed out of the way by his small mother. She had arrived without anyone's notice. She saw what was happening immediately and pushed her helpless son aside. She slapped the midwife and yelled at her to get to work and deliver the baby, before both were lost.

The midwife shook violently, as if coming back into her body from a long distance away. Then she dropped into another space, a space reserved for professionals of every ilk when called upon to act with efficiency as they were trained to do. She reached her hands inside Awena's thighs and, grabbing the baby's tiny shoulders, gently pulled the wet, slippery child to safety.

Asher's mother immediately stuffed clean bedding into the gaping wound, but nothing could stop the hemorrhaging. As Asher held his precious love close to him, wetting her face with his tears, she silently slipped away from him.

It happened that fast.

Then came his voice—if you could call it that—a long, mournful, animal sound that came from deep within his being and left the hair standing up on the necks of those who heard. His Awena had left him, and life would never be the same.

He held her there in his arms well into the night, long after she had grown cold and still. Finally, his father, Malchiah, and the rabbi gently but firmly pried him from his love. "She must be prepared for the Father," the rabbi said in a soft, soothing voice. "Let the women take care of her, my son," Malchiah advised. As Asher left the room, all the grief of the day engulfed him, and the sobs came in massive, wracking quakes.

"Why, God?" he screamed, as millions before and after him would as well, "Why didn't you take me instead?"

There was no answer for Asher that night, or the next, or the next. There was no answer the following week as his son was circumcised on the eighth day in the Temple. The day thereafter he packed up his tiny baby, the nanny from Awena's homeland, and the wet nurse. Together they set sail for Africa with the coffin that held Awena's body. He would take her home.

There was also no answer possible to the questioning eyes of Awena's father as Asher entered the greeting room of Awasa's home, placing his small new grandson in his arms.

The women there understood first; and as before, Asher heard the keening wail of more broken hearts—the sounds that would not leave him for the rest of his life. He left his wife's body there and a part of himself as well.

It was obvious to everyone that Awena's father wanted little to do with this boy-child who had caused his daughter's death. Each day

Awena's father grew more morose and distant from the child and Asher as well, until Asher decided that it was time to leave.

It was an empty man, barely 21 years of age, who returned to his homeland a month later with his son. Awena's father had named the boy, John (a Greek name, neutral, favoring neither family over the other).

Letters were exchanged for several months thereafter with news of the growing child, but it became obvious that there would be no partnership beyond the sea.

Then one day the letters stopped altogether. Asher would raise his son by himself. He would take no other woman to him for over forty years, so deeply did he love his young bride, Awena.

It would take that long, long past Asher's prime, for his longing for companionship and love to return. It would take a very special woman, and a very special time. It was a time of great changes for Asher, and soon thereafter for the world.

Forty-Two Years Later In Jerusalem

Asher and his son, John, along with John's wife, lived exclusively in their large family home in Jerusalem. Asher had long ago sold the family's holdings in Tyre. The memories there surrounding the loss of Awena were just too painful for Asher. Thus, five years after Awena's death, after both his mother and father had died as well, he sold everything he owned that tied him to the city, took his small son, and moved away, never to return.

Over the intervening years his son had grown and married. John and his wife had two daughters. The eldest daughter, John had named Awena, after the mother he never knew. They too had married in turn and left to be with their husbands in other parts of the land. It left an emptiness in the home that Asher longed to fill. John still had the companionship of his wife. Asher had no one. Loneliness was dragging at him in his old age. He wanted someone to bring happiness and joy once more into his home. He wanted a wife, and God provided.

The woman who changed Asher's life was named Miriamme. He took her as his wife a few months before turning sixty. He had seen her on a hillside in a nearby village and had fallen in love with her on sight. She was but a girl really, compared to Asher, but a woman in her late teens without a husband was considered old by most, and far beyond the ideal age to attract a suitable husband by many. Asher didn't care. She had long, silky, black hair and a face that Asher thought was far more beautiful than anything he had seen since Awena died.

After seeing her the first time, he could think of little else. Thus over the next few days he traveled outside the city over and over again until he finally caught sight of her once more. This time he would not let her slip away.

He knew that all he had to do to obtain her as his bride was to gain her father's permission. But that was not Asher's way. Before he sought out her father, he wanted the girl to approve of him; thus, he attempted something quite audacious. He approached her directly and told her that he wished to take her as his wife.

She immediately covered her face and tried to turn away, for she could have been punished severely for speaking to a strange man. He pleaded with her to hear him out before turning and hurrying away to the protection of her family.

He told her that he had seen her and thought that she was the most beautiful woman in the world. As she hid her face from him and turned away, he explained to her that he would make no demands on her of an intimate nature, for the age difference between them was indeed great and he recognized it as such. He told her that he would honor her and bring great wealth to her family if she would accept his offer and speak on his behalf to her father.

She didn't utter a word, but instead motioned him to follow her, then turned on her heels and hurried away.

A short distance away she approached a small, simple farmhouse on the outskirts of the nearby village and slipped inside the home while Asher waited outside.

Not too many minutes passed until a man appeared at the door. He paused under the lintel. Squinting through failing eyes and a sharp glaring sun, he scrutinized the old man who stood before him in robes that bespoke his wealth and position. Then, making up his mind, he motioned Asher inside.

A long conversation ensued in which Asher outlined the offer he had in mind. Even though the man was thrilled to have an offer for his unmarried daughter, especially one from a man of such apparent means, he prolonged the negotiations to see how much he could obtain from this wealthy old man for a daughter so fair.

Asher explained that he had lost his wife many years before and needed a wife to share in the running of his household and to help host his many guests. With Miriamme listening quietly in the corner of the room, Miriamme's parents told Asher that their daughter was well prepared to be a wife and well schooled in being a perfect hostess. Noting the girl's simple surroundings, Asher doubted the assertion, but he didn't care. She could learn, and he loved her no less because of her lack of learning.

The actual bargaining didn't last long. Asher was very generous, and Miriamme's father gladly accepted his offer of largess before the old man could change his mind.

Two months later Miriamme became Asher's wife amid one of the most lavish weddings that the small village had ever seen (all paid for by Asher on the parent's behalf).

Asher's life changed almost immediately. Miriamme was bright and cheery and delighted Asher in every way. John's wife, twice Miriamme's age, was a kindly woman and helped Miriamme adjust to her new household duties, training her in running the staff and her social graces. She could have resented the intrusion of this young girl, now married to her father-in-law, but she didn't. Perhaps the young woman, close to her own daughters' ages, took the place of the now-married girls.

Miriamme was a hard worker and rapid learner, grateful for any position in the home of this rich and powerful family, and the two women became fast friends.

Thus the months passed with John's wife taking Miriamme under her care. She and her husband John were happy to see Asher joyous for the first time in many years. And as for Asher, he couldn't have loved his new bride more. Although he made no demands of her in a personal way, she soon began to love him as he loved her, offering herself to him as his wife in every way, for she couldn't have found a more kindly man to wed.

Now with love in his bed as well as in his home, Asher was to find that his life was about to transformed in an even more dramatic way. This change came in another meeting, a meeting with a man who altered Asher's life forever.

What follows is Asher's own story, told in his own words, of this meeting with a man called Jesus. It is the "good news" of his meeting, his gospel if you will.

Asher began the account during his lifetime. On the rooftop of his Jerusalem home he wrote many things that he saw and heard. It is the first account of Jesus to be written—a precursor to any of the four canonical gospels by perhaps forty years. And, like other accounts written of famous people in his day, it not only combines the old man's firsthand knowledge and witness, but also captures the stories and tales of others and melds them into one, as if they were his own.

Join with Asher in a world that no longer exists, yet is as real as if it were happening today.

Welcome to my memories of Asher ben Ammi, and the man he believed to be the Messiah.

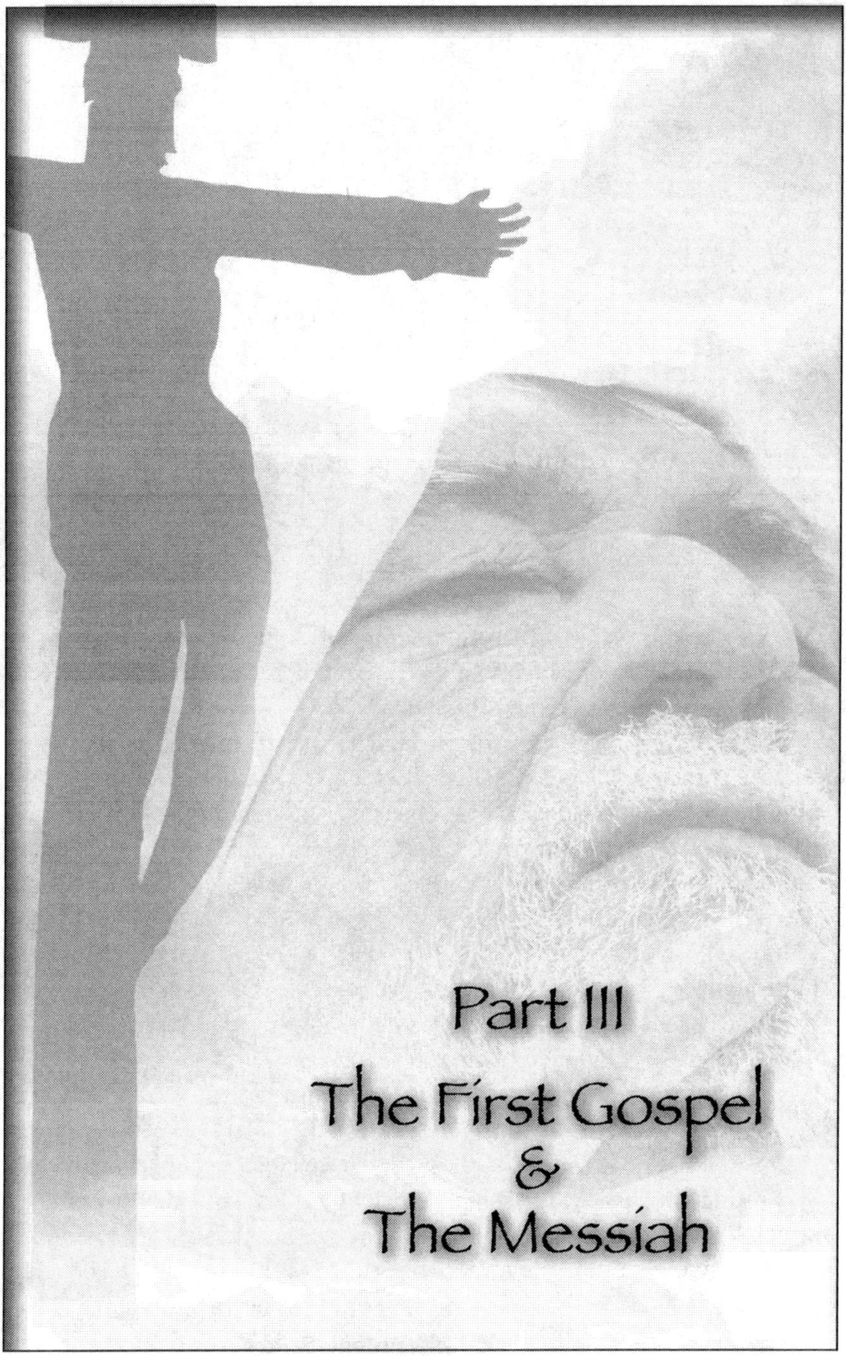
Part III
The First Gospel
&
The Messiah

Chapter 2

The Gospel Commences

But you shall receive power when the Holy Spirit has come upon you; and you shall be my witnesses in Jerusalem and in all Judea and Samar'ia and to the end of the earth.

Acts 1:8

My name is Asher ben Ammi, father of John, whom you all know. This is the story of my life—the part of it that counts, anyway—and our Teacher, Jesus, the Messiah.

My family's home is situated in what is referred to as the upper part of the Holy City, Jerusalem. It is a city that lies in the high hills of Judea, built and added to over the centuries and divided into several parts separated by protective walls, each more ancient than the next. Since the earliest times the Temple grounds have occupied and dominated the ridge to the east, surrounded as it is on one side by the Kidron Valley and on the other by the Tyropoean. The Temple pervades the high point of the ridge, where it broods over the rock where Abraham once prepared to sacrifice his son during his own test of faith and where King David gained his fame.

During the time of the Maccabees the walls were extended to enclose several other hills and valleys. Finally, in my own time, Herod completed the division by building his palace close to our home, further separating the large homes and wealthy families from the "lower city," which house the tradesmen and the poor.

Our home sits on the street that runs south between Herod's and Caiaphas' palace, and although it is not on the scale of a Roman country villa, it is yet not small. The home, built of local stone from the nearby quarries, is cool even during the warmest months. The walls enclose the living quarters for my family and the families of my servants; a beautiful garden from which our vegetables, flowers, and greens come; our warehouse; and the stables where my horses are kept. It is a most comfortable home for an old man like myself. On the roof above the family quarters, high above the resting city spread out before me to the east, I sit at my writing table in the quiet of the early dawn to begin my story.

This is the story as I know it, of the teacher from Galilee, Jesus, by name.

To begin, I wish to take you back before his birth. I have assembled this tale so that you will know us as we are. For unless you know of our land and our people and our rulers, how can you understand our Master, the man I have come to believe is the Messiah, for whom we have all waited these many generations?

When Jesus was born, Herod was the undisputed king, ruling from Idumea in the south through Galilee in the north, with no authority save Rome to tell him right from wrong. Herod was once a strong, proficient builder and ruler, able to boldly travel to Africa, win Caesar's favor, and save his own small kingdom (strategically placed between Syria to the north and Egypt to the south) even after siding wrongly with Mark Anthony and Cleopatra in their disastrous little war. Yet Herod had few friends among the people, even though he, and as a consequence our land, were allowed a certain amount of autonomy and freedom by virtue of his position in the court of Augustus.

Herod improved our city and built the Temple into one of the true wonders of the world, but he was never considered a Jew by most, even though he claimed our faith by practice. In this he was really no different than any other ruler, but toward the end, he was far crueler than any before.

He could kill and torture without a second thought and did so with impunity even unto his own family, but for these deeds God repaid him with an illness that ate him from the inside. He rotted day and night.

As he lay on his deathbed, his gasps for breath were so putrid with rot that his mercenary guards had to be changed twice each hour if they were to remain in the same room with him without becoming overwhelmed with his stench. Yet even up to his death he plotted murder and mayhem on a massive scale, and we, his subjects minded our ways so as not to come to his attention.

With this said, so that you can understand the land unto which our Master came, let me continue my tale by taking you back to my first meeting with my Master. From there, I will continue on to those days of the Messiah's birth and early life. These stories I came to learn directly from his mother and two of his brothers whom I have met, leaving me to fill in the empty places from stories told by others that circulated wherever he went.

I first knew of Jesus early in his teaching, at the time of his first trip to Jerusalem during the holy Feast of Tabernacles in the autumn. It was always a time of remembrance and reflection for me because it was during this holiday so many years ago I first tasted joy in my life with my then soon-to-be wife, Awena. It was a bittersweet memory to be sure, for in less than a blink of an eye she was gone from my world.

Every year thereafter, for over forty years, I wandered among the crowds unconsciously looking for a face, a look that might tell me that she was still there. Of course that face was gone forever, but I think because of the memories, I was more vulnerable during this festival than I would normally have been at any other time of the year. In any case, probably because of Miriamme, the time was ripe, and I was now open to see and hear.

The courts of the Temple at festival time were always filled with Jews and God-fearers (Gentiles who abided by most of the Laws of our faith but had not submitted to all of the ordinances, circumcision included, to complete their conversion). They came from all over the world, streaming into Jerusalem during these special days. The atmosphere was noisy and boisterous. The holy grounds teemed with moneychangers, sellers of birds and goats, teachers, philosophers and prophets alike. Milling throngs came to worship God during the holiday; they came to offer sacrifices, shop, or listen in the Court of the Gentiles to the teachers who gathered knots of people around them wherever they went. One such teacher that particular year was the man called Joshua ben Joseph, later to be known to the world by the transliteration of his name, Jesus.

Jesus, along with many other teachers of all persuasions, spoke in the Temple courts to large groups of people. Many of the listeners were young priests and young power brokers such as my son, John, and

Jesus caught not a few ears and hearts as he spoke of a new and loving covenant with our God.

Although I did not happen to see him then, I soon heard from my son and many others that there had appeared a rabbi from the north that taught like no other they had ever heard. When he spoke, it was with the authority (and the sometimes acrid tongue) of the prophets. Yet, with but a change of breath, he could mourn the cry of the poor and the lame. He spoke of the Law with a power un-granted by the priests, as if it was his Law to give, as if God himself had granted him understanding and the power to speak. Within a few days, he had attracted the attention of most of those who count, including myself.

My son John was captivated by this strange man and instantly became a follower. Our home was filled each evening with tales of miracles, of healings of both the sick and the lame. The younger priests were clamoring to hear Jesus and to talk with him. After all, he was new and different, young and full of fire—a challenge to the elders of my age. The crowds were growing about Jesus each day. The older priests and men of position, such as myself, were cautious and distrustful of miracle workers. The land was full of them; we had seen our plenty and needed no more.

We discussed this new, young rabbi from the north and decided that he was only worthy of mild attention if he stayed. We felt that after the holidays and the crowds stopped coming, he would just fade away into the countryside as had so many before him, no more than a wisp of smoke in the morning haze.

However, a haunting thought began to pull at the corner of my mind: what if the things my son said of Jesus proved true? Many talked of the Messiah, wrote about him, and expected him to come from the tree of David at any time to save us from the Roman yoke of overwhelming oppression. If there were the slimmest chance that this man could be the one for whom we waited, I had to know. Thus, I sought out this new teacher myself, for I was nearing the end of my years and had dreamed from the days of my youth that the Anointed One, the Messiah, would come and I would know him before I died.

You might think that I'd simply wander out into the court and listen to him at will, but I could not. I could not because of who I was. I was a respected Pharisee of wealth and position, a member of the ruling body, the Sanhedrim, and I could not let myself be seen trampling with the masses after some uneducated preacher—a miracle worker—a common tradesman—a Galilean at that!

I have learned much from our beloved Teacher, but in the beginning I was a terrible hypocrite, a stern judge of all who fell below my station. So, when I sought him out, it was in the shadows of the early evening at a private home where I thought I would not be known. I had ferreted out the time and place from my son at the noon meal. I then waited until John left that evening to see this Jesus, whereupon I donned a cloak and hood and proceeded toward the gathering where I knew he would be found.

I walked freely into the courtyard of the home. The doors had been left wide for visitors to come and go. I felt no threat. I was too powerful and self-confident for that, but I was nervous. I did not want to be recognized by anyone who could report back to the Temple and my friends—and thus I came in stealth.

My memory of that fateful evening is seared into my mind.

I lowered my head to keep within my own shadow as I made my way through the crowd, trying to get close enough to Jesus to hear what he was saying. He was facing away from me, but as I thus quietly approached, for no apparent reason I could ascertain, he turned. Through the circle of men standing around him, he focused on me, and suddenly my soul lay naked and exposed. He met my eyes and the seemingly impossible happened: my mind stopped functioning—went totally blank. Such a thing hadn't happened to me since the night I met my first wife, Awena, at dinner at the governor's house some forty years before. It is truly impossible to explain. I stood transfixed, mystified, as the power of this strange man exploded in my mind.

This happened in an instant, in the meeting of two men's eyes. In that strange, powerful moment, he knew me. He knew me to the very depth of my being, to the farthest reaches of my soul. And I realized, truly, he was the Special One, the One for whom we had been waiting.

I know not how long I stood there; a year, a second, it matters not. Nothing else was important from that moment on. I was his.

As I write this now, it is as impossible to explain the meeting as it was then. So in my frustration, I can but write down everything I experienced and heard about what he said and did. By doing so, perhaps I can clarify the mystery to myself first and then, should I be so lucky, to those who are to follow.

I have tried to the best of my ability to tell the stories that he told to us, as they came from his mouth, in his words, as I have heard with my ears and seen with my eyes. The remainder of my tale springs from my own knowledge and the words of his disciples, mother, brothers, and friends as they told their stories to me or as I heard them second-hand. Of the later, I cannot vouch save them as true, but include them for you to judge for yourself. I speak as one counted as one of his closest, and as one whom I believe is more knowledgeable in his secret ways than even the twelve.

This then is my story, the honest tale of an old man who had the privilege of knowing another far greater than himself, who walked the earth as you and I, yet came like no other before him. He was a man who gave us the example of his life for us to emulate throughout all the centuries yet to come. He was a man who taught us that the kingdom of God was not to be awaited; that it was with us, in us, around us then—and now—if we would but open ourselves to Him.

I welcome you to join me in my memories of an ancient time, the days of the Messiah's birth and early life; a time long ago when the world shifted on its axis and history changed its course.

Chapter 3

The World Changes… Forever

Behold, a young woman shall conceive and bear a son…
Isaiah 7:14

The little town of Nazareth lies well within Herod's grasp, as do all other villages, no different than Nazareth, in the rich land of Galilee.

Nazareth is situated right in the middle of Galilee and is separated from Judea by Samaria, which is also ruled by Herod. Nazareth lies in the wooded hills in the far north of our land. Here, from its airy loft, it gazes down upon the fertile valleys below, valleys that have contributed their share of labor and pain in Herod the Great's rise to power and wealth. But Herod is not in the minds of the people this day, for as I begin this story of my Master's birth (as told to me one evening by Jesus' mother), it is some 30 years earlier. It is summer, the busiest time of the year for everyone in Miriam's village. Work is everywhere to be done.

It had been a lovely warm day in this small hilltop community. The young girl, Miriam, barely twelve years of age, had gone about her chores with an easy grace and a light, lithesome step that could not help but reveal the happiness and contentment she felt inside. She was betrothed to Joseph, a strong, simple, gentle man; a man with a trade, a man she could love and care for and who would provide for the children that were sure to come.

Yes, Miriam was happy in her heart as she lay her head down in the cool of the evening, this night that was to change the world, this special early summer evening when she would learn of the Messiah's coming.

Slowly, the village sounds faded into the quiet of the night as the nearly full moon crept over the eastern horizon. The fertile valley stretched out below the village, and the cool, moist air rose to send its fragrance into the silver evening light. Softly, easily, Miriam drifted into a dreamless sleep.

Suddenly her breath quickened, then seemed to stop altogether as her eyes fluttered open to an eerily quiet room. She felt as if someone had awakened her by calling her name.

Slowly she looked about to assure herself that she was indeed alone in the small, shimmering, moonlit space. She could hear her mother's deep, rhythmic breathing as she slept in the adjoining room. Nothing else stirred.

Joseph was not with her to protect her, but she felt no anxiety, for a strange calmness and lightness had come over her. As she sat upright in her bed, transfixed in quiet wonder, knowing that she could never adequately explain what was happening to her, she felt—no, she knew—that she was somehow different; this night was unlike any other night she had ever known.

Then it came. It came in such a gentling way that there was no alarm, only a feeling that her heart was expanding and filling with love. It felt as if her very being was going to overflow in the overpowering grace that was all about her and that could never be spoken of in human words that she knew.

"Miriam," came the deep, soothing voice from somewhere within her mind. "Miriam, my handmaiden, I have come." Miriam sat bolt upright, then absolutely still, every nerve in her body alive. Her eyes drifted upward as the beautiful presence took her within, and she began to see and hear of a time that was yet to come. The scenes were within her, and of her, and love and lightness filled her to overflowing. It was impossible for her to tell when the voice was with her and when the visions were just unfolding without the need to communicate, but flow they did, and she watched, and the future was in her.

She saw the birth that was to be, and it was beautiful and sweet. She saw Joseph's and her son who was to come, she saw him teaching, and she saw him as one with the One whose name she could not speak. But it wasn't in words she heard. She saw it as if the events were happening right there in front of her eyes.

Then, as softly as it had come, the presence was gone. Miriam sat in the silence of the empty room; her senses awake in every cell of her being. She still felt as light as a feather, and in some strange and wonderful way she knew that she had been changed by what had happened to her that night. She knew that no matter what life brought her in the future, she would never again be quite the same.

Quietly, almost afraid to break the spell, she gently lay back on the bed to stare at the ceiling and wonder in those quiet, dark hours of the morning how she could be the one chosen to bear the child who would show the world a new way.

Silently, sometime before dawn, this gentle young woman drifted into sleep thinking, "I must watch him when he comes. I must watch my child for a sign."

As Miriam slept that night, another event was taking place far to the east, at Sippar in Babylonia. On the rooftop observatory the royal astrologers saw something unusual taking place in the early morning sky that filled them with excitement and awe. For nearly two hours they watched as Jupiter and Saturn met in brilliant conjunction, as if a single star, in the constellation of Pisces. The importance of the event was breathtaking in its magnitude, for it meant the end of an age and the beginning of another in its place. Pisces was the sign of the land to the west, of Israel, and to these men of learning, it meant the coming of the One for whom the Jews had been waiting since the time of David. The King had been conceived. The Messiah was to be born.

That same night the astrologers made plans to begin a journey to reach the land to the west nine months from that day. In their records they wrote, "We have seen his star appear in the first rays of dawn. To its source we shall journey. He has come!"

Miriam raised herself early the morning after the dream. She felt happy and excited. She could hardly wait to see her betrothed, Joseph, the father of her child, for she wanted him to know of the impending birth. She wanted everyone to know of her joy. But first she told her mother what had happened, told her of the child.

However, instead of the happiness she thought she would find in sharing the news, a cloud came over the older woman's face. As Miriam told of the wonderful tidings that she, a lowly young woman in this insignificant mountain village was to bear the child for whom all of Israel prayed—that she was to give birth to the Anointed One, the Messiah—her mother stood still as a statue. Her face twisted in anguish and turned ashen gray.

As Miriam finished her story, her mother raised her hands to cover her face and gave one long, grief-stricken wail.

What was wrong? Miriam wondered. She wanted to tell everyone the good news; she wanted to tell the whole world of her joy. She wanted to proclaim it from the rooftops: "I'm with child! I am going to give Joseph—nay, you, oh Israel—a child, the child for whom you have been waiting!"

But her mother's hands remained over her face. The shrill keening of loss and hopelessness grew in her mother's throat as she sank to her knees and began to rock back and forth as if Miriam had announced her own death—not life.

Miriam felt an uncontrollable chill. This was not the greeting that she had expected to receive. What had she said that was so wrong? What was going awry?

Slowly she backed away from the woman bending low to the floor before her. Miriam numbly turned and left the house. As she stumbled blindly down the street, her mind was suddenly seized by panic. She began to run—and run—and run. She didn't know where she was going. Tears streamed down her face as she raced through the narrow streets past the mud brick and stone houses that crowded in on either side. She was out of control—totally out of her mind with fear and dread. How could her own mother turn her back on her?

Down she raced along the path that led to the woods. She wanted to be alone. She wanted to think.

What had gone so terribly wrong? Confusion, hurt, and panic played with her mind.

She knew she couldn't go to Joseph's house as yet, for he was in a nearby town working and wasn't due to return home until later that day.

Why did Joseph have to be away on this most important day of her life? Where was he when she needed him?

Surely, the Lord would make it right with him. But if her own mother did not understand, didn't believe that Joseph's and her child was special, chosen by God, would Joseph? He couldn't deny her, could he? He couldn't deny their first child, could he? Could he?

There, in the dappled sun, among the trees, Miriam fell to her knees and prayed as if her young heart would break.

This was only the first disappointment for Miriam. For soon, instead of being able to share in the joy and the miracle of the child within her womb, she would be met with anger, rejection, and disbelief from the people of her village, her closest friends, and her loved ones as well.

It is said that God has many ways to test a soul and make one strong, and rejection is the loneliest way of all. And so it was that the handmaiden of God, so young, now dry-eyed and drained of any further emotion, finally stood, squared her shoulders, lifted her head high, took a deep breath, and headed out along the trail back to the village to Joseph's home. She was ready to face her fate alone.

Chapter 4

Trial By Conception

O Beth-lehem Ephratah, you are but a small Judean village, yet you will be the birthplace of my King who is alive from everlasting ages past.

Micah 5:2

After Miriam ran from the house, Miriam's mother gathered herself up and went straight to Joseph's home. There she was told that he had been away working in a nearby town but was expected back sometime that day. She settled in anxiously to await his return, quietly sobbing in a corner.

When Joseph returned later in the day, he unloaded his tools on the workbench adjacent to his house and hurried through the door to cleanup and eat. There, to his surprise, he found Miriam's mother huddled against the far wall. The woman instantly rushed to him and dropped to her knees before him, sobbing and wailing. She begged him not to expose her daughter, begged him to keep Miriam in spite of her condition.

He didn't know quite how to react when Miriam's mother first delivered the news, shrieking and pleading, clinging to his cloak.

As he heard the news that Miriam was with child, Joseph pulled away from the woman grasping at the hem of his robe.

In shock, a thousand thoughts crowded the mind of this simple carpenter who had never been confronted with anything more difficult than the span of a beam or the width of a door. His status in the village, though meager, was very important to Joseph. It was all he had.

"You fool, Joseph, you fool!" he said to himself over and over again,

"You should have waited."

Although the conception of a child during a formal engagement arranged by his family was not strictly forbidden or unknown, it was certainly frowned upon in this small, conservative village, and he would be mocked, or chided at the very least for his lack of control. And, of course, the innuendoes, the whispers, although never spoken to his face, would always be there: "Is he positive the child is his?" "I heard that Joseph..." "I saw Miriam talking to..." He would be forced to defend his honor over and over against the unseen enemy of the tongue, against which there is no defense save the truth, which he was not ready to admit.

Joseph was a good man to be sure; an honest man, a simple man, and he tried his best to keep the Law, which was clear on simple things. But this—this was totally beyond him. How should he react? What was expected of him? What did the Law say? Why did she have to get pregnant? Why?

This marriage was late, perhaps he should have skipped marriage altogether, he thought, trying to extricate himself from the problem that had been forced upon him.

Pacing back and forth, Joseph made up his mind. He was not an unkind man, but Israel is a patriarchal land, so he decided he would simply visit the rabbi and see if he could quietly dissolve the marriage contract. A man didn't need this kind of problem in his life.

With his solution in mind, he turned on his heels without another thought and immediately set off with resolve to find the rabbi, leaving Miriam's mother huddled alone in the corner of the one-room home.

When he talked to the rabbi, Joseph told him nothing of Miriam's condition. He carefully worded his probing questions, going over every aspect of the Law with regard to marriage so as not to raise any hint that he was just interested in pregnancy. The Law was clear. He could obtain a secret bill of divorce, a "git," witnessed privately and never filed with the authorities. It was the only way. No one would know; they would just think that he had tired of her or changed his mind, and Miriam would be free to marry again immediately if she could find a husband.

So, this was his solution—really his decree—for it needed no approval from anyone, least of all the woman. How could he be faulted? He had done the decent thing, hadn't he? He hadn't made a public display of Miriam. If she married right away, no one would know that she was already with child, and, best of all, it followed every jot of the Law, right down to the smallest detail. He returned home from the meeting with the rabbi to pace the room and await Miriam. As he waited, he once again began to feel the pressure of the situation pressing down on him like a stone weight. The misplaced anger of his own transgression began to boil within, seeking any outlet it could find.

Returning to the village, Miriam walked straight away to Joseph's home to see if he had returned from his trip and tell him of the news that they were about to have a child. Walking through the entry, exhausted and empty of any more emotion, Miriam looked up at her betrothed standing with his hands placed squarely on his hips, his face now dark with pent-up rage. Her mother, she noted, was there ahead of her, hiding pitifully in a corner of the room, her cloak drawn up around her small, huddled frame.

Spitting out the words—surprising himself with the harshness of their sound—Joseph told Miriam he was dissolving the marriage contract then and there. Her mother was a witness. He said it two more times to fulfill the law.

If Miriam could have felt anything, it would have been disgust, for she had done nothing wrong save give herself to her betrothed; and that involved the man standing in front of her angrily denying her.

She had done nothing to deserve standing alone having to endure the trial she was about to be put through by Joseph. But these were not her thoughts as she turned without a word and left Joseph's home, for she was dazed beyond feeling at that moment and could only vaguely understand what was going on around her. To her, the day felt like some horrible dream.

So it came to pass that what Miriam thought would be the happiest day of her life turned into a day of numbness that was beyond understanding.

No matter how Joseph tried to justify his decision, all was not well with him either, for, as I explained, he was not an unkind man, and his conscience was bothering him. He felt ashamed and sick inside. He knew the truth and it troubled him greatly.

There was no dealing with him. He threw the leg of a bench that he had badly cut clear across the workshop, cursing in a way that was most atypical of this gentle man. The stunted piece of wood narrowly missed one of the two apprentices who had already had two run-ins with Joseph earlier in the afternoon.

They didn't say a word; they just bowed their heads, avoiding his furious looks working with renewed vigor in hopes of getting through until nightfall without further mishap.

Late in the afternoon the rabbi came with words of counsel and a set of harmless but deviously designed questions, all aimed at finding out what terrible secret Joseph had refused to divulge. But Joseph was in no mood to field the rabbi's questions. He threw the old man out of his workshop most unceremoniously, which added further to the burning fire of shame and guilt that was now welling up within him.

He ate nothing that evening. Sick and confused, Joseph strode out the door; slamming it so hard it would wobble for months before he would fix it again. As Miriam had run through the streets earlier that morning, so Joseph walked aimlessly as the last light of day began to fade, not knowing where he was going, not caring. Out of the town he walked, as in the sleep of death, neither looking around him nor answering calls of greeting from friends he knew along the way.

A good hour passed before he sat down; darkness enshrouding him, exhausted and empty on the mountainside in the woods. He had no way of knowing that it was exactly here that his betrothed had cried herself into emptiness on that bright and shiny morning of her glory—and her shame.

Joseph unconsciously drew his cloak about him as the cool, moist breeze drifted up from the valley below. Shuddering in the chill, he pulled his legs up close and huddled himself into a ball. There, miserable and alone, his head sunk to his knees, and he fell into a sleep such as he would never know again.

Then he heard the voice.

"Joseph. Joseph, wake yourself."

Slowly, ever so slowly, he raised his head, trying to catch the voice he thought had emanated from the darkness now all about him. Evening had drifted into night. The moon had risen fully round over the eastern mountains, and the peaceful valley stretched into blackness miles away.

Looking around, seeing nothing, hearing only now the soft whispering wind through the pines, he pulled his cloak about him even tighter. Another shiver went up his back as the first prickle of fear entered his awareness. He could not see the source of the strange voice that had spoken to him, but someone had awakened him, of that he was sure.

Then the soft, slow, deep voice came again.

"Joseph, you have done wrong!"

Now his eyes grew wide with fear.

Unbidden, the voice continued, and Joseph trembled at its sound.

"The girl you will marry is my handmaiden, Joseph, blessed is she. I find no blame in her. She carries a child in her womb, a very special child, a child who belongs to the world—a child who belongs to me—your child, Joseph; your child to watch over, to teach, to see grow, a child born to die for me.

"Go this night, find your betrothed, take her unto you, take her this night as your wife, and know that she is good."

Joseph sat still for a moment that seemed interminable in the dark. There he waited, listening, not knowing if the voice within his being was finished, not daring to move or breathe.

All was silent again.

The soft whispering of the wind in the pines and the cold seeping into his body finally roused him to sit upright, then pick himself up, and stand. His muscles ached from the rock on which he had lain. His foot tingled with the pain of a thousand needles as his sleeping legs began to come back to life.

There was no question of what he must do. He had to find Miriam.

He began to walk back to the village from whence he had flown. Then something in the wind (or was it the darkness?) began to grip his being. It was that voice! Fear filled him; it coursed through his body in uncontrollable waves. His walk became hurried.

Then, without warning, terror took complete charge. It took him by the hand as he flew over the ground, the rocks, past the trees. His wild mind had frozen, locked in terror of the unknown. Nothing could save him from the voice—except Miriam. As he ran, his feet found their own way in the darkened streets, his robes went flying behind him, and his mind screamed, "Oh, Miriam, Miriam, I am so sorry. I am so sorry. Please forgive me, Miriam. Take the voice away from me... please!"

The sudden crash of a fist striking the wooden door so startled the occupants of the small mud and stone house that for a moment there was no sound, no movement at all from within. Then the sound of Joseph's hoarse voice up against the wooden plank door roused Miriam's mother from the frozen position she held, mending clothes by the fluttering yellow lamplight. She shuffled to the door and timidly opened it.

Joseph lunged through the door, slamming it closed behind him. A dozen eyes from neighboring homes withdrew from their windows as people began to whisper in their beds at the strange goings-on between the betrothed pair.

Joseph threw himself facedown on the floor, and then raised himself to his knees in supplication. Miriam's mother, in shock, stood silently by the door. Her hands trembled as she clutched a veil over her worried face. Miriam, sitting with her legs stretched out in front of her, sat on a ledge at the far side of the room, calmly lowered her sewing and stared at the blank wall in front of her.

Drained of any emotion by now, Miriam simply stared, refusing to acknowledge Joseph in any way. Her face was like that of a statue, carved in exquisite alabaster, flickering now in the dancing flame of the lamp, still buffeted by the sudden rush of night air that had exploded into the simple two-room home. She heard, but no emotion crossed her unblemished, young face, a face now strangely at peace.

Joseph was pleading now. "Miriam, please, Miriam, forgive me. Let us leave this place. Come with me, come to me, please, Miriam, please!"

Miriam slowly turned, lowered her small feet to the floor, stood, and walked silently, elegantly, over to Joseph. Her voice was quiet and controlled, carrying a cutting edge touched in ice, born of a new knowledge and strength.

Looking down at him she said, "Do you want me in marriage, Joseph? Is that what you are asking? Are you sure you want me in marriage?"

"Yes, Miriam, yes—in marriage. I want you. Please forgive me. I take you just as you are."

Without a moment's hesitation she ordered, "Tell my mother who is the father of my child, Joseph. Tell my mother!" Having been rejected earlier in the day, Miriam now spit out the words with a vengeance.

Silence fell like a leaden weight. Finally, unable to withstand her glare, Joseph cried, "I am. I am! It is my child she carries," he admitted. His head bowed, he cast his eyes to the floor, and silence fell again like a drape upon the three.

Miriam stared hard at him but didn't issue a word. Miriam's mother's eyes were wide with disbelief.

Again, unable to withstand the empty silence that lay between them, and with anguish written all over him, anger began to rise within him at her boldness. Finally he blurted out, "I admit it to you, and to your mother, Miriam. What more do you want from me?" He looked up into her eyes, his voice now husky, as he spoke in a low, warning tone.

But Miriam was not a coward. She brushed aside the challenge. She had not finished with him as yet, and thus she continued in the same icy tone that bespoke her newfound strength. Turning away from him, her back to his face, she asked, "Why are you here, Joseph? Why in the middle of the night? Why now, when this morning you threw me away?"

"I came because I felt I had done an injustice to you, Miriam." His control had broken again. He sobbed, "I could not live with myself. That is all."

Miriam abruptly turned to face him squarely, with such force and such a frigid stare that he felt she had seen everything within him, clear through to his soul.

"Is that all, Joseph? Is that the only reason?"

"Stop, stop, Miriam, I yield. I heard the voice," he started slowly, barely a whisper. "I heard the voice, and it told me you were the handmaiden of God. It said that the child in your womb is blessed, that our child is to be special. Oh, Miriam, please forgive me. I have wronged you. I know it now. Please forgive me. Come with me this night. Stay with me, be my wife."

Miriam would wonder later at the source of the courage she possessed to act as she did that night. Had God spoken through her? Or was it just that she had nothing left to lose? What had caused her to act with such authority toward the man she loved more than any other?

Yet, with all of this, she was not through with Joseph, not until she had dictated the rest of her demands.

"I will not go with you this night, Joseph. Go. Go to your home alone. Tomorrow you will make arrangements for the wedding. It will occur in ten days. Until that time you will not see me alone. Tomorrow my mother will bring you a list of things that you must do.

"And, Joseph," she added, as he raised himself to leave, "Remember this night. God has spoken to you, as he spoke to me. What is to come is holy. If you wish peace, never forget this night and what has transpired here."

Days and months later as Joseph worked in his shop or wandered the dusty road in search of work, he would wonder at this night. He would wonder if he had been a fool, if his conscience had gotten the better of him. He would wonder a thousand times whether he had really heard that voice. Had he dreamed it, or had he not? It had seemed so real.

Each time the voice of doubt came into him, as it must to everyone who has seen or heard God, it was followed by something sweeter, something far sweeter than any nectar of the vine. Each time he felt the pain of doubt and fear, he would shut his eyes, calm himself, and experience the lightness and joy that would flood his being, bringing with it a certainty that he had been witness to a very special happening. And with this experience came a certainty that this child of theirs would be special—very special indeed.

Since that night in June, almost nine months had passed. It had been a very difficult time for Miriam. Initially she told one or two of her closest friends about the impending birth, with an admonition not to tell a soul. However, the news seeped out, and this only added to the speculation about Joseph's enigmatic and stormy dealing with the rabbi. And, of course, there was the most unusual late entry into Miriam's home that night, the night of Joseph's vision. Even now, nine months later, there were still whispers, but the worst had passed. There were better items of gossip to occupy the townspeople, now that the months had worn on, and Miriam and Joseph both seemed to be content in this marriage that had started in such agony—and bliss. Most of the uproar only served to strengthen Miriam in her resolve and deepen her love for this special child soon to come forth from her womb; but the vicious gossip still hurt and would not soon be forgotten.

Before he became Governor, Legate to Syria, Proconsul Saturninus, Publius Sulpicius Quirinius had come to Syria at the will of Caesar Augustus to defeat Caesar's enemies. The Senator also had another mission: to ensure that taxes were fully paid by all the people of our land—to the north, to the south, to the east, and to the west as far as the sea and his army would allow—to pay for his upcoming campaign against the Homanadenses. To accomplish this task, he employed the offices of his Idumean tool, Herod by name, who decreed that each person must present himself, give count, and pay a tax according to his means, each in his own city. This was not the census that came a dozen years later; this was a tax upon Herod, who was thought to have become a slacker by Caesar Augustus.

Joseph had come to Nazareth two years earlier at the urging of his brother, who was working in the city of Sepphoris, a short hour's walk away from their ancestral home of Nazareth, where their father's father had plied his trade, and relatives abounded. But, because Joseph's own family home lay in the south, he had no other choice but to return to handle this taxing issue in the town where his small family property lay.

So, one fine, early spring day, Joseph took with him a donkey and borrowed yet another for Miriam, whose term was near. And from the hilltop village of Nazareth they ventured forth, setting their sights south to the ancient city of David—Beth-lehem—a short walk from the Holy City itself.

Slowly, they descended the wooded path from the hills of Nazareth to the spreading valley of Esdraelon below. The valley was rich with the coming of grain, now sprouting green in the early spring. The soil, rich and moist from the rains just past, smelled wonderful. The newness of the countryside and the coolness of the air lightened their hearts as they ventured south on their first journey together as man and wife. Miriam's heart was full of song as she walked with the pride of youth along the path beside her husband. She resisted Joseph's urgings to ride the donkey he had brought for her; after all, she was young, and she took pride in walking beside her new husband. Besides, she thought, the walk was good for her child—her child, her very special child.

After staying the night at the town of Esdraelon, Miriam and Joseph departed early the next morning to join the teeming crowds on the busy road leading north and south. They continued past the city of Scythopolis to cross the Jordan River and camp the next night at the hot springs, close to the town of Pella.

Joseph had planned to stay the night at the hot springs, as many did, and travel south again early the next day. They arrived late in the afternoon and set up their small camp before heading for the two sections of the springs—one for the men and another for the women. Just as Miriam began to step into the women's pool, however, she felt a strange tingling that began to hurt all over her body. She was so affected by this strange sensation, and even more so by a powerful foreboding, that she withdrew immediately and sent for Joseph, saying that she wanted to be away from this place, that it was not safe for the baby. Joseph had looked forward to this popular stop and tried to talk Miriam out of what seemed to him an unnecessary and ridiculous objection. But Miriam would hear none of it and pleaded with him to take her this night to the nearby village of Pella, just a few minutes' walk from the pools. Although Joseph disagreed and spoke to her of logic, he relented, because he was none too anxious to take any chances with his young bride and his first child within her womb.

The next day brought with it a warm, bright sun. Fluffy clouds drifted by in the deep blue sky. It was early in the year, and the air was cool and fine. Refreshed with a good night's rest, Miriam and Joseph set off again with renewed energy. They were both in good spirits for the day.

There were many travelers along the way, and there was much to talk about, many stories to tell, and many interesting people with whom to share. Thus, the trip went rapidly. They followed the Jordan River as it meandered south through beautiful farms and groves of date palms that lined the banks. The expectant mother hardly realized the toll that all the riding and walking was taking on her body and the child. The fifth day was the longest, and her body ached when they finally reached Jericho to spend the night with family friends.

They started out early the next morning, thinking they could reach Beth-lehem by nightfall. But as they traveled, Joseph became more and more concerned with Miriam's condition. By mid-morning she was beginning to show signs of pain. Sometimes she would turn ashen white, her eyes tightly clenched, as she held her swollen belly and moaned. Worried, Joseph slowed their pace slightly to give Miriam a chance to rest, since this leg of the journey was the most difficult. From the low Jordan Valley and the town of Jericho, they had a continuous climb up the hills leading to Beth-lehem and to Jerusalem not much farther to the north. By early afternoon he knew they would be still another day away from their goal, and fear for his wife engulfed Joseph as he sought a refuge for the night. He was sure of it now. She was going to give birth to the child early. He only hoped that by going at a gentler pace he could reach the town before her time came.

Joseph saw that Miriam's face was strained and worried. The jostling of the donkey didn't help, and Joseph was frantic with fear that he would have to deliver the child himself. This was his first child, and he had no idea of what to do should the baby start to come. Thus he did the only thing that he knew: he tried to comfort Miriam with words of caring and love. He told her that it was just a little farther, just over the next hill, and he asked her to hold on just a little longer. While he was talking to her, his eyes scanned the rounded hillocks and small, rocky cliffs for any sign of a village or a wandering tribe with whom he might seek refuge for the night. "Why didn't I take the well-traveled road up to Jerusalem, then cut over to Beth-lehem? Just to save an hour of time, I put us in this desolate valley," he moaned to himself as he hurried the donkeys along.

The new grass was a light yellow-green in the afternoon sun as they crested a high, rounded hill. Joseph gasped with joy. There, two hills to the west, he could see shepherds, their flocks feeding peacefully on the new shoots of grass.

Happiness overcame Joseph as he headed toward the men, pointing to show Miriam, now rejoicing too, that there would soon be help for her. Down the next hill they plodded, then up the next. As they crested the second hill they could see down into the small intervening valley. There at the base of the knoll stood a rocky cliff about the height of three men. Above the cliff the sheep grazed contentedly, and at the foot of the cliff lay a flat area that served as a camp. It was then that they saw the families of the shepherds they had seen on the hills above. He could count ten or fifteen women and old men, plus a large group of noisy children racing up the far hill, playing a game of tag.

It was late afternoon. The cooking fires were smoking, and the smell of food hung low in the valley, bringing warmth and joy to Joseph as he hurried down the near slope, leading the donkeys. Miriam held on to the rope reins with the last bit of strength she possessed.

As they approached, an old woman who had delivered many children in her sixty-plus years stood up from her chores and squinted at the approaching couple. Before Joseph had even entered the camp circle she was issuing orders to her two daughters-in-law to ready one of the caves, for she could see the condition of the young woman coming up the path. As Joseph walked into the camp, the old woman motioned to him to follow her.

"Come, my dear," she said, with a voice as old and as dry as the dust beneath her feet. "Lift her into the cave; she will be all right there." Once within the shelter of the cave, the woman clucked to Joseph, "Don't you worry, it's dry and warm in here. Just lay her down on the robes. She will be fine. I've brought more babies than I care to count into this world. Now go, shoo! Go out by the fire. Eat something. I will call you if you are needed." Sensing that she was finally in capable hands, Miriam relaxed. Joseph squatted by the fire and worried almost unto death.

Twilight had come. The men called the boys up to the hill to watch the sheep while they came down to take their evening meal. They knew strangers had arrived and a baby was to be born in their little camp, and they were all anxious to see for themselves. They had just arrived at the base of the cliff when they heard the unmistakable cry of a newborn child.

A sweet, beautiful, natural stillness fell about the shepherds as they noiselessly entered the cave. Hushed by the peaceful quiet within, the sight of the flickering firelight, and the sleeping child, they became aware of a rapturous presence that descended in their midst, wrapping about them and nurturing them there. Each unto himself, they felt the gentle presence of a soul such as they had never known. That night, they knew, was a special night. It was a night they would long remember, when each, without exception, felt the presence of God within the special child, and within themselves. Without a word, one by one, the shepherds came forward to silently kneel and reach out brown, work-hardened hands to touch the baby, lying so peacefully against his mother's breast. Then again in turn, the shepherds filed out to stare silently at the evening fire and watch the stars. The stars that had months before foretold of his coming and now held his future in their reading.

The next day, Miriam rested and nursed the child. It would be a few days before they would resume their journey to Beth-lehem, and she and the baby were the center of attention in this little cave just outside of town.

The women tended to Miriam's needs, and the simple men with their flocks peacefully grazing were just beginning to relate their experiences of the night before to one another. It was such a natural thing, this birth of a child in their midst, but somehow something was different. Each told how he felt the glow that seemed to radiate from the child. Reluctant at first to speak aloud of their feelings, the shepherds, one by one, recounted the extraordinary sensations they had felt within themselves. One said that it seemed as though an angel had spoken to him. Another, now emboldened by the sharing from the others, said that as he entered the strange quietness of the cave, it appeared that the cave was glowing and shimmering with an iridescence that seemed to fill his body with a newly felt love for the whole world and everyone in it. "Even the Romans?" one shepherd chided incredulously, while the others nervously chuckled. There was a long pause, then he answered, "Yes, even the Romans." There was no further response by anyone, for each was now deep in his own secret thoughts.

The children saw it first. From the hill east of the camp where they had been playing they could see a very richly adorned caravan winding its way up the road from the valley below. Upon hearing the children's shouts, the shepherds shielded their eyes from the low morning sun, and strained to identify the strangers coming their way.

From the trappings and the dress, they could tell these were wealthy men, and they wondered at them taking this road so far away from the better known routes north and west of them that led to and from Jerusalem.

At that moment in the caravan below, there was a unique man. This man was very wealthy, but not in his own right, for he came as a gift of a king. He had powers beyond any of his land—he was a mystic, a seer, a wise man without question, an astrologer; he was the king's most valued possession. He was the one who nine months earlier had gone to his liege with the story of a special child who was about to be born in the land of Judea. He had told his king the story of one who would rise greater than himself, one without peer in the land of Judea. And so his king had sent his wise servant to find this special one, with the admonition that he send word when he found the child so the king could send his own twin sons to witness the event for all time.

The seer had set off in the direction of the stars when they appeared for the second time in the western sky. He followed them to the land of Judea, to the Holy City itself, where he stayed unnoticed, awaiting the last sign.

The sign came on a cold night in December. From the roof of the Jerusalem home where he was staying he saw what he had been waiting for—the last conjunction of the stars. They lay just before him to the south. It fit. That was it! Less than two hours' walk to the south lay Beth-lehem. "Beth-lehem—that is where he will be born!" He rejoiced with great jubilation.

Knowing the scriptures, this strange wise old man from a country far to the east danced on the rooftop under his stars, and as he danced, he recited Micah to himself. Hardly able to contain himself, he recounted, "O Beth-lehem Ephratah, you are but a small Judean village, yet you will be the birthplace of my King who is alive from everlasting ages past."

His joy knew no bounds. That night he sent word through his servant to his king: "Send the twins. I will await them in the little town of Bethany in three months' time, and from there I will lead them to the child."

So this was how he and his royal companions came to be traveling up this little-used road leading to Beth-lehem, heading straight for the cave. He had left Bethany, his temporary quarters, the day before so as to meet the royal twins as they approached Jericho, and now, using his senses, he was leading them toward their goal. One of the twins would be king one day, and it was fitting that they should know that there was one born who was far greater than they.

The old seer had been feeling the approach of the caravan grow stronger for days as he waited impatiently for the small royal train to arrive from Babylonia. Now, after having joined the group, he knew they were finally approaching their goal; he couldn't explain it, he could just feel it.

Then, without a word, he pulled his camel to a halt in front of a row of three simple, unadorned caves, serving as simple homes for herders, their sheep, and families. He sat absolutely still for a second as if listening intently for something no one else could hear, then silently he slipped to the ground.

The gentle spring breeze murmured its way over the rocks that pushed their way through the lush green grass on the hills. Everything was still and seemed to be watching as this deeply moved, spiritual man gazed at the opening to one of the caves. Through tears of joy welling up from within and with gratitude to God suffusing his being, he headed up the hill toward the cave with a slow purpose and grace, a beatific smile upon his face. He could see the glow; he could feel the specialness of the moment as he effortlessly glided toward the light within the cave.

The awed and dumbstruck shepherds, their families and children alike, stared in disbelief as next they watched two identical young princes alight from their steeds and without a word follow this old man into the cave.

Miriam looked up from the child as the wise man entered. For a second the old man stood there unmoving, watching the mother and child, their faces bathed in the morning light, shining, radiant. Then he moved within, bowing as he went, ending on his knees. A look from the old man toward the two silhouettes at the entrance, and a welcoming smile from the mother, bade the two young princes enter. There, they too bowed low, and with the practiced grace that belied their position, they set before the child two identical boxes. Each box, wrapped in gold and beset with jewels, contained the rarest of incense, brought from India to please the senses of the new king.

Then as the man of wisdom bent low to see the face of the child, the child opened his eyes and looked up at him in return. The old man pulled back with a start. The eyes he saw were those not of an infant but of a gentle soul, seemingly fully conscious, aware and as probing as he. Jesus held the old man's eyes with his, and at the corner of his little rosebud lips played the barest hint of a knowing smile. The wise man found himself looking into the depth of the baby's soul, and the child into his, and in that instant the old man knew he had found the Messiah. He had come! "Oh Lord, the Messiah has come!"

The morning sun moved past the entrance as the three strangers sat to watch the babe in the darkening quiet of the cave. The old man looked deeply within, and there he found an enraged king, disasters, pain, and fear. And thus, he made ready to leave.

The wise man rose and went to the opening of the cave where Joseph was standing pressed against the rock, staring in wonder. Awe and fear of this old man of obvious power, wealth, and learning showed on his face. Miriam's story of this child's birth and the voice that had haunted him were hard in his ears: "She carries a child, a very special child who belongs to the world—a child who belongs to me."

The wise man bowed slightly to the child's father, and then using Joseph's native tongue, leaned near to whisper in his ear. "Go. Go far away," he said in a voice old and rasping, a voice with the timeless quality of fathomless understanding. "Go, take this special child, and flee into Egypt, where you will be safe. A great disaster will befall you and your little family if you stay. The king will follow you to the edges of his kingdom, and your child will be killed if you do not flee by Sabbath next. Heed my words, Joseph, I know your king and I know of what I speak. Take the jewels and precious gifts, for which you have no need, and sell them. Use the money to flee this land of mad Herod's greed."

That night the voice came again to Joseph and roused him, trembling, from his sleep, admonishing him to leave for the land of the Pharaohs, to flee before the beast.

Chapter 5

Abba

After they were gone, an angel of the Lord appeared to Joseph in a dream. "Get up and flee to Egypt with the baby and his mother," the angel said, "and stay there until I tell you to return, for King Herod is going to try to kill the child." That same night he left for Egypt with Mary and the baby, and stayed there until King Herod's death.

Matthew 2:13–15

In our Jerusalem home, sitting by our fire one cold, wet night, the Master added to the story of his youth by telling us of his first memories and of his sojourn into the land of the Nile.

Sitting there, watching him, listening to him in the firelight, I began to visualize how the incredible consciousness of the soul called Jesus had been slowly absorbed into the body and mind of the child. Much as any child, he was apparently only vaguely aware of his uniqueness at the time. But differences there were, for his mind, limited only by his undeveloped body and brain, was already working, loving, searching, and probing. I am sure that if you had been with him that night in our home as I was, if you could have looked into the depth of his startling gray eyes as I did, you would understand how special this man was.

"My first memory is of our flight to the Nile, of being so tightly bound to my mother I could barely move my arms or legs. I was wrapped in a carrying scarf, and from my position, tied close to her, all I could see was the bobbing head of the donkey—up, down, up, down—all day long. The unending rhythm made me very sleepy, and I would doze off, wake, nurse, watch the bobbing head, feel the gentle swaying, and sleep again—day after day.

"I can remember the campfires at night. I remember because I could understand everything the people said, but it did me little good because I couldn't speak a word. I was confused and anxious at first, trying to understand this new world that had been thrust upon me. But slowly, as time and world held sway, I lost my memories of the time before my birth, of who I was and why I had come. I lost them in the everyday life of my people.

"I was absorbed, as we all are, in the world of sound and sight: the woman next to us fighting with her husband, the donkey braying, the children screaming and playing, the heat of the sun, the dust of mid-day, and the loving of my parents in the same room where I lay. In these events I found my humanness, my love for my parents, my love for my Father, and most of all, my love for my people.

"We settled in the village of the Israelites, north of Heliopolis. There, father purchased a house made of mud brick, roughly twelve cubits on a side, with an enclosed yard of about the same size, which he used for his work. Father had taken the wise man's advice and sold all the gifts, save one, for our use on the journey. The coinage he received from the gifts helped to get us by, along with the income father brought in from day labor and his woodworking when that was available.

"Father was used to the soft woods of Galilee, but in Egypt he found that wood was a precious commodity, not used lightly for construction of large projects. It took him almost half a year before he received his first commission, and that was for a beautiful chest, not timber for wall or beam. When a man is used to working in rough wood, it takes time to learn the economy of precious woods. It also takes time to learn the new tools (expensive tools!) that are used to work the hardwoods, tools that were little used in the town of Nazareth. It takes a special patience to feel the grain of the timber, to take the most economical cut, to waste the least. It takes a special learning to understand the delicate jointing and joining of wood, the sanding and rubbing, the lacquers, stains, and paints. These things my father learned, but an artisan's soul is also needed to develop the patience and resolve for working on the delicate and small, and my father's heart still yearned for the bulky and the large. His work, in candor, was adequate but lacked the life that makes inanimate objects sing.

"I was too young to remember much now, but there are things that linger in my memory, special times for me, filled with thoughts that danced merrily within my mind. They amazed me and played with me when I had the time. For me it was a time to absorb, to watch, to hear, and to learn the ways and the feelings of my people. I could feel their hurts, their fears, their hopes, their desires, their jealousies, their loves and losses as well as their joys. These early years of my watching I will never forget, for they are burned within my mind and my soul.

"There was one event while we were in Egypt that made a lasting impression on my young consciousness, an experience that will stay with me until my last breath.

"We were living in upper Egypt, not very far from the city of Thebes, where there was a large Jewish population, and my father had been employed by a nobleman to prepare some items of furniture for a tomb. If my father wanted the work, he was told, he had to work there and no place other. So he packed what things he thought we needed, and we left our home in the north and traveled south to where employment lay.

"My mother, my father, my brother Jacob (who had arrived in the second year of our stay), and I traveled with our donkeys by foot and by boat south, up the beautiful Nile, far from our home near Heliopolis in the north, to the city of Thebes. There, father was assigned our place to live, which was across the river on a hill near the Valley of the Kings. The land there is only a short distance from the lush, fertile Nile, yet on the rugged, barren hilltop we were assigned, there wasn't a single living tree, bush, blade of grass, or shrub anywhere to be found.

"The sun is a vicious companion there; it is relentless to noblemen and lowly slaves alike—except the nobleman can take his rest in the shade of his tent, sipping a cooled drink. But for one who has no shelter, the sun is a constant enemy, tormenting him and driving him, until his will to survive can no longer urge him on—and it is precisely then that the slavemaster's whip holds sway.

"I believe I was a in my third year when father took us to this valley. I judge my age from what I remember of my then baby brother, Jacob, and the looks of the other boys there who were about my age. We lived along the top of a hot, barren, wind-swept ridge, looking down upon a narrow valley, which ran down to the flat land below. The valley was the working ground for the slaves employed by the nobleman to dig the cave, and on the hill were the living quarters, the tents set up for the craftsmen and freemen employed by him. Our tent was really quite large and housed our small family and all our goods with plenty of room to spare. Those who had employed father had set up a canopy and provided him with beautiful hardwood from Africa. Here it was that father worked from early morning until the sun dropped below the burning, barren hills. Toward the end of his employment, he even worked by lamplight to finish the furniture on time.

"I have so many memories of this time! I remember one morning standing by the corner of the tent when the nobleman himself came to view the progress of father's work. The nobleman was not at all pleased, since father wasn't working fast enough for what he had promised to do. I remember my father being as polite to him as he could, while all the time the man yelled at him and pounded on the worktable before him. The overseer translated the nobleman's words, but it was unnecessary, for his meaning was clear—the work was late! I remember the dirt and the stink of that hot day. I remember the terror that gripped my father, the sweat that poured from his body, for he needed the job, and we needed the money to live.

"I wondered at the difference between my poor father, doing his best, which wasn't good enough, and the poor slaves down in the valley working under the eye of the slavemaster and the threat of the whip, for my father had been whipped as surely as if his back had felt the straps.

"That was the first and only time in my life I saw my father work on a Sabbath. He worked out of fear; fear for his little family, fear for himself, and fear for who he was. A Jew never breaks the Sabbath! Only mother and I knew what that did to him inside—no one knew what it did to me. I watched as the other Jews who worked on the tomb turned their backs on father from that day on, and I felt the pain and sickness my father felt deep inside. His smiles stopped, and his laughter ceased from that day forward. I saw my father age ten years in the next three.

"On that Sabbath day, I knew that someday I would set them free. Not just the poor slaves in the valley but also my people, who were just as surely slaves to the Law as any slave I knew or could see.

"That stay in the desert was a turning point in my life. That was the point in time I discovered I was different from the rest. I would play with others of my age, but those times became rare, and this caused my father much concern. 'Go play,' he would say to me. 'Go play with the other boys. Kick dirt, throw sticks, and wrestle!' When one of them hit me he would say to me, 'Hit him back, boy. Don't let them do that to you!' I couldn't. They were mean because I was different. They made fun of me and taunted me because I wanted to be alone. There were other things brewing within me, and their taunts just drove me even further within myself.

"I found the silence and peace I sought when I could get away from them, and it was in this silence that I first heard the voice. It came as soft as a gentle whisper—so alive that I turned my head to see from whence it came—but there was no one there. It was in the desert, in the land of the Pharaohs, that I found my Abba, my true Father, my beloved guide within. It was a voice, a vision, a light, a knowing and a presence that came about me, and with it came the change.

"I was still a child however, and I thought as a child in so many ways. I remember thinking, 'If only I were grown, then it would be different. No one will make fun of me then. Someday they will see how different I am. In the meantime, I'll play the game. I'll go play with the children when I have to. What a bore!' I would think, 'I'd rather be with my Abba, my dear Father within.' I loved Him so, even then.

"When I listened to my father and the other men talking among themselves, I heard them recite passages from the Law; the Law that has been all-important to us since the time of Moses. The Law that gave us rules to live by for every aspect of our lives. Yet somewhere deep within I knew there was more. I knew there was something infinitely more ordered, more compassionate, more loving, more understanding than any of the laws I heard repeated over and over again. The Law was used as their justification, their comfort, their excuse, but none of them talked about that feeling, that voice, that something that whispered to me so clearly in the quiet and aloneness of the desert. That strange, unfathomable presence lay within me and became a part of me.

"I remember thinking that if people would just stop talking long enough and find a silent place, they could hear Him too. I thought that if they just tried to listen, they would find that the pains and pleasures they held so close were nothing. If they could but turn within, there they would find Abba waiting with open arms for them, and all else would fade from importance. All the problems of man were but mere feelings—not reality—things that could be loosed and set free in the sea of His radiance and caring.

"I tried to tell my father about the voice once, at the supper table, but his mind was on his work and our struggle to survive. So it was with some feeling of sufferance that he kindly brushed me aside with a hint of ridicule and mocked gravity. He gave my mother a wink and said that if I didn't want to play like other boys, then I should do something constructive, such as helping my mother clean. With that he let out a hardy laugh and tweaked me on the cheek.

"I was sitting across from him at the time, and my mother was behind him at the cooking fire. I looked around him to my mother, and pouted the minute I caught her looking at me. In her eyes I saw the hurt, the hurt for my feelings, and in her eyes I also saw the question, 'Who are you, little one, who are you?'

"But who in any family listens to a little boy, save his mother? She would hold me by the hand, or tightly in her arms, and I would feel so very close to her. I loved her so.

"There was a strange thing between my mother and me. She knew when I was deep in thought; she above all others honored my time alone, but her deep eyes were always probing and asking, 'Who are you?' From my earliest memories I can remember her holding me in her arms tightly and hearing her whisper, 'Are you? Are you, little one? Are you He?'

"Often were the times that I would find a quiet place in the shade where the boys couldn't find me—but she did. With her eyes, those probing eyes, she would always ask the same question, 'Are you?' I can remember thinking, 'Abba, help me. Abba, help me to know. Who am I? Look at her; she's watching me for some reason. Father doesn't do that, he's busy, always busy working, trying to please someone, but she does. I wonder if all fathers are like that? Yes, mother, I am different; I feel it, but why? Why? Oh, Abba, teach me. I'm just a little boy—teach me. Why am I the only boy who wants to sit and watch everything, learn everything? Why don't I just want to play like the rest?'

"I had an insatiable thirst to know everything about the country we were in—and beyond. I knew that there was more than just the dry, desolate land of strangers where we lived; I knew there was. I felt them calling. Just who was calling I didn't yet know. I was born to do something, but what? 'Abba... Abba... Abba,' I would wail. I would chant it over and over again, rocking back and forth, eyes closed, until

He came."

When Jesus was in his second year, word was received that the terrible King Herod was dead, but Joseph hastened not to return to Judea, for fear still gripped his loins. To understand why Joseph and so many others still feared to return to our country you must understand the tyrant and king called Herod "The Great." Words cannot describe how terrible this hated man was.

Even now a plethora of stories abound about the Master; some true, some exaggerated, and some fanciful. His childhood is no different. It was said that Herod butchered all the children in Beth-lehem to prevent him from growing up and challenging the king. To slaughter all the young children in a village would mean nothing to Herod; after all, he had commanded his mercenaries to butcher entire villages before. What did it matter if he killed a few dirty children—especially if it meant safeguarding his kingdom from a rumored new "king"? Did it actually happen? No, because I would have heard about it, but perhaps you can understand the character of the king if you realize that people could believe that he would.

As Herod's reign wore on, he became so hated among our people that he could find few he trusted in his army, and certainly no one in all of Israel to serve him as his personal guard. He relied on mercenaries: Germans, Gauls, Africans, and Thracians to do his bitter bidding. His sick and fetid body was a just dessert for a life spent spreading horror and pain to households in every corner of his kingdom. On many an occasion, if a man incurred his wrath, Herod would order the entire family annihilated—butchered. This included everyone from the youngest child (the "furthest branch") to the most distant relative (the "deepest root").

Herod's own family, friends, and loved ones were spared nothing in his insatiable lust for wealth, power, and safety of person. He killed two husbands of his sister Salome, whom he loved; the only wife he truly loved, Mariamne, whose death haunted him to his grave; and two of his own sons, namely Alexander and Aristobulus. In fact, just days before his own death he also caused to be killed his eldest son, Antipater; his brother–in–law, and his mother–in–law; and who knows how many more?

Shortly before Herod died, he erected the golden eagle of Rome over the entrance to the holy Temple itself. When two learned scholars, Jehuda ben Saripha and Mattathias ben Margoloth, and their students pulled it down, Herod burned the two scholars alive like human torches in front of all the people. The remaining thirty or forty followers he had hacked to small pieces by his men. It was said truly that he "ruled like a wild beast" and was hated by all who came within his shadow.

Because of these misdeeds, God visited upon Herod every manner of horror and pain known to inhabit the body. His once lean, hard body became obese to the point where he could hardly haul it about on legs and feet swollen beyond recognition. It is rumored that his genitals rotted, worms lived in the mortified flesh, and near the end of his days, part of his member fell off. He lived in constant, horrific pain.

He gained an incredible appetite, which only fed the pains in his bowels and stomach. Immediate cramping and convulsions seized him for the better part of an hour after each intake of food. Even after the cramping stopped, the burning fire within never gave him a moment's peace. As he spoke, waves of putrid stench emanated from his interior, so that only the hardiest of souls could control themselves and keep from retching while close at hand. Even as terrible as this is to contemplate, there was more, for living sores continually oozed and caked upon this grotesque, living beast.

Just weeks before his demise, this mad creature, not done with his people even unto his own death, caused all the leaders of the nation to gather in Jerusalem and there be shut up in the hippodrome under guard. He ordered that upon his death the soldiers slaughter each and every one of the leaders, sparing none. Thus, the death of Herod was to be grieved throughout the nation Israel and beyond, wherever Jews resided. Fortunately, before the king's death was made known, Herod's sister and her husband released those shut up in the hippodrome. But knowledge of the plot did not escape the people, and their fear of the Herodian line grew daily.

Now, in the land of Egypt, the news of the events transpiring in Israel did not go unnoticed. Daily, the caravans were met with trepidation and excitement to hear the news. King Herod was dead! It was certain now, his evil presence was gone, but who was to rule in his stead? Herod's will had been read, and his son Archelaus was to be king. This was a change, for Archelaus' brother, Antipas, had been his sole heir until a few months before his death, and we all knew that he was quite mad by then. All Jews held their breath, waiting to see whether Rome would uphold Herod's last will and what kind of a king Archelaus would be.

Without the approval of Caesar Augustus, Herod's will was in doubt, for Herod ruled only at the whim and will of Rome. Knowing this, and knowing too that Rome honored rulers who could control the masses (and add to Rome's coffers), Archelaus attempted to consolidate his rule before going to Rome for confirmation. Thus, he tarried for more than a year before going to Caesar for approval. In the meantime, without a formal king, sedition and war spread throughout many parts of the land, especially in the north. Many there were who set themselves up like kings, or passed themselves off as messiahs, gathered bands or small armies (some containing thousands of men), and made war on the armies of Archelaus and Rome.

While these things were happening away from Archelaus' center of power, in and around the city of Jerusalem, Archelaus was busy trying to consolidate his power. This was not as easy as it may seem. It is true that Herod's armies pledged their loyalty to Archelaus in Jericho immediately after his father's death, but he also desired to win the favor of the people at this time—without force—for he wished to proceed to Caesar with the leaders of his country behind him. He needed this because of questions about his father's will raised by others in his own family. Some of the people believed him and were willing to curry his favor in hopes that the favors would be returned when he was officially declared their king. However, more remembered his father and looked upon any in Herod's line with deep suspicion. Seeing that Archelaus' position was not secure, they sought to bring him down in any way they could.

Thus, as Archelaus tarried, insurrection spread throughout the land. Starting in Galilee in the north, it raced south toward the capital itself. At last, Archelaus could allow no more. On Passover he sent a regiment of a thousand men to control the throngs of people demanding justice for the murder of Jehuda ben Saripha and Mattathias ben Margoloth, and their students.

Archelaus loosed his army upon the people. The foot soldiers killed those they found in the Temple. His horsemen followed, killing those who had escaped and those in tents around the Temple area that thought themselves safe. When the killing was over, thousands of souls lay dead. Thus the reign of Herod's terror continued even unto his son, and the people of the land lived in constant fear.

As word spread of the butchery, Archelaus and his relatives left for Rome to plead their case; but now fueled with even more hate, rebellion spread throughout the length and breadth of our land. Before Varus, the Roman governor of Syria, could stop the chaos, there had been no less than ten thousand battles, ending in Jerusalem itself, where Varus set up crosses along the road and crucified two thousand of our people who had opposed him.

Thus the people ended their fight against Herod and his kind; some lived in fear, and some in their hate, but all waited for the promised one—the Messiah—to come and free us from our despicable plight.

Perhaps you can now understand why Joseph and his small family tarried so long before leaving for home.

But, this begs the story my Master was telling in the living area of our home that night. Let me resume my recounting of his tale as I remember it.

"I was now four at the time father finished his work on the furniture for the tomb. I remember it as if it were yesterday. Father was packing up the donkeys. He was done with his work, and we were all glad to be going back to our home in the north. Father had been paid that morning, but the nobleman was still far from happy. Father had done his best, but it just wasn't good enough. I remember looking at him as he received his pay and for the first time thinking that he looked incredibly old as he silently bowed his head and took the verbal abuse along with his pay. I loved him then, his skin dark from the sun, his wrinkled brow that gave him an air of dignity I had not remembered in the past.

"After the men of Egypt left he stood silently for a long moment, just staring out over the sand, across the Nile to the east. His vacant eyes spoke to me of our beloved homeland, our Israel, which he missed. Then he shook himself as a great sigh emanated from his depths. We all held our breath. I watched then as some great load was lifted from his back. He straightened, turned, and looked toward me, a splendid smile coming over his face. The wrinkles at the corners of his eyes deepened as he picked me up, threw me about in the air with a great shout, then hugged me to his breast with his great arms wrapped about me. He swung me around and began to dance. My mother's eyes lit up with relief and delight at the sight as she watched with my brother blissfully happy in her arms. Never had I seen my mother looking so young and pretty, and never had I felt such warmth, joy, and love from my father as I did that day.

"I was overjoyed as my father set me upon the donkey's back. We were off to join the caravan, the slow caravan heading north to the lush delta region of the Nile.

"We headed back to our home near the house of Onias and father's shop, which awaited us. I knew now that this place where I had spent my early years wasn't our true home, for I had seen father's vision of what we had left behind in our homeland of Israel. But our house in the north of Egypt offered warmth and safety and, with the exception of the short sojourn south, it was the only home that I knew. I couldn't wait to see my old friends whom we had left behind, like Lazarus, whose family, like our own, was just one of many displaced by Herod, who also awaited their return to the Promised Land.

"As we traveled north, my father's thoughts were of going home, from whence we had fled. After all, king Herod was dead, thanks be to God, and we could afford to go now. Father had worked for the Egyptian lord just shy of a year, under terrible conditions in the desert, but the pay was exceptional, so we had the ability to make the long trip back, yet we did not.

"We stayed in Egypt for almost three more years after we returned from the tomb work on the upper Nile. The tales of rebellion and war from those who were traveling through, or who sought refuge within our communities between the great cities of Alexandria and Memphis, along the mighty Nile, kept us away. Many there were living here in exile, afraid for one reason or another to return to the land of their fathers, Israel.

"We found during that time of our continuing stay that the emperor Augustus had finally decided to divide Herod's kingdom into three parts. The hated Archelaus was appointed ethnarch over Judea, Idumea, and Samaria. His land stretched from the border with Egypt on the south to the border of Galilee on the north, from the Jordan River on the east, to Mere Nostrum in the west. Nazareth, the town of my mother's birth, was spared the rule of this beast of prey and was granted, along with all of Galilee and the land east of the Jordan, to Herod Antipas. Although Antipas would not tolerate the least threat to his portion of the kingdom, at least he did not turn to the slaughter of innocents as a means of control. The last son to outlive their monster father, Philip, was given the newly settled lands of Batanaea, north and east of Galilee, which were sparse of men and beasts, and certainly of Jews.

"Finally, after nearly three years of riot and war, we heard that a tense peace had settled over the country, and once again thoughts of home entered the people's minds."

As Jesus spoke, I mused that these years since king Herod's death proved unique in all of history. God took Rome, the unchallenged, cruel master of the world (with her imperial talons in the flesh of every man, woman, and child of her kingdom) and bonded her to an oppressed people: totally, inexorably dedicated to God's will, and holding to a messianic fervor never before seen to such a degree in all the history of the world. He located them both at the same place, at the same time in history, at the crossroads of the civilized world—and there He sent His Anointed One. One who would do His will without question, who would bear humiliation and hate, yet teach His people about Him, and about His love.

Jesus continued: "To this day, the earth has had a peace administered through fear, hate, hope, and waiting; but now," his eyes met mine, "now, dear Asher ben Ammi, now is the time, that one time in history when all things come to pass. The heavens have opened to humanity—no man can hold it back. There will be no other time such as this for eons. We must leap with joy at the opportunity our Lord has given us. It is now! Do you understand? This is the good news I have been trying to get those that follow me to see—the time of heaven has come. Now. Don't look for some time in the future. It is now. This is what I have been trying so hard to help all of you to understand. Take it now within your heart, and never let it go. This is the peace that surpasses all understanding. This is a peace administered by love, joy, sweetness, and compassion. The kingdom of heaven is here, dear Asher." His eyes moved to my young wife. "And you, Miriamme, do you understand? Go within, dear ones. Go within. Open your hearts. In the silence that follows, he will speak to you—he will love you so."

By now our hearts were tearing, and tears of devotion for our beloved teacher moistened our faces. My dear wife, Miriamme, left her place to sit on the floor at his feet. There she placed her head on his lap. He stroked her head, stared again into the fire, and continued his story.

"Now, with a degree of sanity returning to our land, father finally felt that it was safe enough for us to return. Father knew my mother's heart and how it yearned for the companionship of her family, her friends, and the village she left behind. I think this was what finally drove him to decide. He used to watch her at night, as did I, and see the yearning in her eyes. Although she never said a word to him, never complained, just supported and honored him in every way, he knew her most secret desire. And so the day came to pass when father could stay her heart no more from the land she loved: the peaceful hills, the tall trees, the rocky meadowland, and the people, the people who made it home. And so we made ready for the long trek back to our homeland—Galilee."

Chapter 6

By Firelight His Youth

When Herod died, an angel of the Lord appeared in a dream to Joseph in Egypt, and told him, "Get up and take the baby and his mother back to Israel, for those who were trying to kill the child are dead."

Matthew 2:19–20

Shortly after I met Jesus, I had an occasion to travel to Jericho with my son, John. After my first encounter with Jesus, I knew in my heart that he was unquestionably a man of God, but I hadn't as yet let anyone know my true feelings.

As yet I still didn't know what it was about him that attracted me so, for by all standards and outward appearance he was nothing but an illiterate, itinerant craftsman from (of all places) Galilee. But, even though I thought him to be beneath my station, there was something drawing me to him. So, unknown to anyone, I made the trip a necessity. I knew that Jesus was at the house of a man called Jonathan, and I would be welcome there. My son knew of him being there too, but as is usual with fathers and sons, being men, we let not each other know our true feelings. And so, in separate worlds, we traveled the very same path, on our way to see (as Peter often called him) the great fisherman.

As we rode along, side-by-side, I glanced over to catch a glimpse of my son, the man I loved and of whom I was so proud.

Cantering down the dusty road together, against the flow of the holiday throngs streaming to Jerusalem, I wished with all my heart that I could share what had happened inside me, inside my heart, with my son. But, of course, my lofty male pride, the forty-two years that had passed between us since his birth, and my social standing had worked their subtle ways and made this father's feelings inaccessible. Later, Jesus would break down all the barriers and rules I held so dear; but that is about me, and I wish to tell you of my Master, my Lord. I tell this story now because it was here, under the fruited trees, that I heard him first tell of his growing years.

He was seated on a garden bench, within the vine-covered garden walls of Jonathan's home in Jericho. There were perhaps fifteen or twenty others, spread out around him, sitting on the ground.

Jonathan was a genial host, and his wife, Ruth, kept us well supplied with fruit and drink as the day wore on. I remember thinking, "I have never felt so welcome, so surrounded with love, as I do here." This was my first real meeting with him, and unused to his power to move me like no other, I fought tears and emotions the entire day as I sat at his feet to listen. I didn't want to speak. I didn't want to eat. I didn't want to do anything that would take my eyes or my ears from him.

By the end of the day, my head was reeling as if from drink, and that night, as my son slept, I wrote. I wrote everything that I remembered that this man said. I prayed, "Oh God, may you give me the power to tell those that read these words how this man affects my heart and soul. Let me tell his story in a way that they too can feel his presence as I do."

The next day Jesus continued his teaching, casually answering questions and joking lightly with the friends that surrounded him. Someone in the group asked, "Master, tell us of your youth, tell us of your growing up in Galilee."

Jesus grew silent, as I was later to see him do on so many occasions when he was about to tell of himself.

With a soft, gentle look in his eyes, he began, and our world dissolved into his.

"I will tell you of my trip from Egypt after having been away many years.

"We traveled in a caravan from Egypt, until we reached Joppa. There, the caravan broke away from the coast to head south and east, up the foothills to Jerusalem. Father dared not go there, for although Herod was dead, his sons lived on, and this was the land of Archelaus, who turned out to be the most vicious of all those who came from Herod's loins.

"From Joppa we also headed east, but by the route that heads north through Samaria. I had heard nothing good about the Samaritans from our people, because, I was told, they broke from the true religion of our fathers. They were apostates. But I tell you, I remember nothing but kindness from these people; kindness to us, to my mother, my father and me, my brother, Jacob, and to the babe, Joses, my second brother born shortly before we left. I loved them for that. They did not turn us away, but took us in and treated us as their own.

"The closer we got to our home, the more excited we all became; all of us except mother, that is. For me, there was so much to see and hear. I had never experienced anything except palms, flat green fields, the river Nile, sand, barren soil, and rocks. But here in Israel was the beautiful sea, the rolling fertile hills, and trees unlike any I had ever seen. You can't believe what joy there was in every step along the way for this wide-eyed boy.

"I will never forget the day before we reached Joppa. We made camp overlooking the sea. A band of heavy gray rain clouds rolled in toward us from the west. My father stopped me along the road. He said nothing, but just held onto my arm and looked to the east. As my eyes followed his gaze, the setting sun, colored a molten gold in all its rain-cleansed radiance, broke through the clouds in a shaft of light, and I saw a sight I will never forget. Atop the deepening, purple hills shone a brilliant golden jewel. Shimmering and glowing in the heavenly beam was the most radiant sight man would ever see, the Holy City itself—Jerusalem!"

Here Jesus stopped for a moment. I am sure he was still recalling in his mind the sight that had so impressed him those many years ago. He painted such beautiful pictures for us when he told us stories that in no time at all we were also seeing them in our minds. So when he paused, we too saw the scene and were lost in the same warm reverie of his past that he was experiencing.

After a moment, a little sigh escaped him. I learned to expect this little wistful sigh, and then a quick sheepish grin, whenever he paused in a story or got lost in the past of his memories. I loved this special part of him that only those close to him ever saw. And so, with his delightful grin the tale of his journey home resumed.

"I mentioned that the closer we came to our new home, the more agitated my mother became. Something was bothering her. We had all long forgotten the vicious gossip that had accompanied my mother and father's marriage, but the closer we came to home, the more she worried about our reception. No one in Egypt had known her or the strange events accompanying their betrothal and my birth, but she knew that the villagers wouldn't forget, for villagers never do. The inhabitants of the little village thrived on gossip. The years since the uppity workman and his pregnant wife left without a word of good-bye had not gone unnoticed. Oh yes, they had heard the stories of kings and seers who came from countries far away and left expensive gifts for Mary and Joseph's son... but really, Joseph, the builder? Who would expect anyone to believe that! And what was that about the stars? Rumors. Stupid tales. No one in the village had seen any special events in the sky, and even if they had, what did that prove?"

With these candid revelations, Jesus had us completely within his grasp. He was leaning toward us now, his blue-gray eyes, wide with pretended alarm, flashing back and forth with mocked earnestness and hurt. Wide eyed with pretended alarm (his hand cupped the corner of his mouth as if someone outside our group might overhear), he whispered the most damning revelation of all, "Some said that my mother had a bastard son!"

The whole group gasped! This was too much! For if it were true, all in attendance knew the consequences, we shouldn't even be listening to him—especially me. This was such a damning charge, for he had been teaching in the temple and the Law stated, "A bastard may not enter the sanctuary, nor any of his descendants for ten generations." We were aghast at the idea that anyone would think that this special man was a bastard! The people rose as one, anger flashing in their eyes, their faces growing crimson as their blood rose rapidly to a boil. They demanded of him to tell who had said such a thing.

Jesus, a master of the moment, held the hurt look for a split second, just enough time to see us rise to the bait. Then, unable to contain himself any longer, he rolled back upon the bench and doubled up with laughter. As we stood there, dumbly looking at each other and wondering what had happened, he roared with delight.

When we realized that he had been purposely playing on our sensitivities and emotions, teasing us, the group broke into nervous laughter, still feeling a bit unsure, sheepish, and self-conscious. Jesus looked at us again, and then continued to laugh uproariously. As his mirth infected us (and how could it do otherwise?), real, joyous laughter, the likes of which I hadn't heard for years, poured from us too. It was useless to go on with his story after that, so with a promise that he would continue soon, we followed our hosts into a supper they had prepared in their Master's honor. It was delightful. There was such joy in these simple people, a joy I had never experienced! I couldn't say why I felt so good. I just did whenever I was in his presence.

That was the first experience I had with Jesus' wry humor, but it wouldn't be my last. He could tell stories about himself that would embarrass us terribly, and then laugh at his own absurdity and stupidity. I didn't understand then how our beautiful teacher could ridicule himself so in front of us, and more importantly, in front of strangers brought by us to be shown his wisdom and grace. I didn't understand how this man of God could show us his weakness one moment, then his unique strengths and singular gifts from God the next. It took me a long time, but with his help, I did understand, and in time, loved him all the more for it, for each story had a moral and each gift a purpose. I put my tale of him in plain language, although when in a crowd he often spoke mysteriously in story and tale.

Jesus taught in so many ways. Once, after a time such as this, I brought a Pharisee such as myself, to see him. He was an old friend, a man of great learning and importance, a man I wished Jesus to impress with his unequaled knowledge of the Law. I briefed my friend ahead of time to expect finesse in the interpretation of the Law, the likes of which he had never witnessed.

This was to prove a day of lessons for me, however, not for my friend. For my comrade stayed only long enough to hear my Master confess one story, then left in a huff. I held my breath, for as Jesus spoke his first words I immediately sensed my mistake. Jesus was not speaking with the refinement of manner and tone of which he was capable, but rather, he portrayed the heavy, guttural accent of the north, and I knew this would not set well with my Judean friend. Not well at all.

The story Jesus chose to tell showed himself up to be an unlearned soul and additionally, the tale fell hard about a certain unnamed man of the Law, a Pharisee. His moral struck far too close to home and my friend bolted in a rage. "What a waste of time!" he snorted. Looking back, he wagged his finger at me and sputtered, "Bring me not again to hear your Galilean friends, Asher. Spare me the effort, bring me not again."

Nothing escaped the Master's eye, and thus, after he had finished teaching he came over to me, put his strong arms around me, and hugged me. Knowing the hurt and burning embarrassment within me at that moment, he held me at arm's length to look deep into my eyes. It was just as he had done the very first time I had seen him. There was magic in those eyes. He said, "Asher ben Ammi, I love you." He said it with such simplicity and such feeling that I couldn't help the lump from forming within my throat.

"Do you believe in me, Asher?"

"Yes, Lord!" I said, surprised at the question.

"Then do you think I would embarrass you without a reason?" He knew I couldn't answer. "No, you know I wouldn't. Then why did I send your friend away and hurt you? I did it for a reason, Asher. I did it to teach you and all of them here that we cannot judge. We cannot judge anyone. First, your friend came to judge me, and then he judged you, then after he left you judged me. Dear Asher, only God knows another man's heart. Neither you nor I can presume that we have that knowledge of another.

"Why do I tell stories on myself, Asher? Why?

"I do it to let you see that the least shall inherit the earth, Asher, not the greatest. For in my Father's eyes, the least is first, and the greatest is least. Don't you see? The great have already reaped their reward on earth; they need nothing of Him. But, Asher, there are so many poor souls in this world who give nothing but love. They give everything they have and receive so little. These are my people, Asher; they are mine. For them I feel. For them heaven will be opened. There is nothing I do that the least among them cannot do. I am no better or no worse than they, and it is by example only that I must show them this. Lofty words will not do. They feel humble and unworthy of me, Asher. I must show them it is I who am humbled. It is I who am honored to be in their presence."

My, how I learned from him that day. He spoke with such feeling, love, and pain in his eyes that I wanted to slink away. I was so ashamed. I was wealthy beyond measure, and in my life I had given so little and had humbled myself before none. The pain in my chest was overwhelming. It was true that my friend came not with an open heart but to find fault with my Lord, and to show him up as a fool. And I, I was worse. I brought him here knowing he came to judge. I brought him here to show Jesus off. Woe unto me, for I was judging worse than any. How dare I presume to judge this man of God by being embarrassed by him—for him! This man, who for our sakes made himself the lowest among us. Oh, how this man could touch that something special deep inside me. Oh, how this man could teach!

It wasn't for another year again, at Passover, with the city full to the brim with people, that Jesus took time to rest awhile with us and tell us more of the story of his youth. Although I heard more details later, while with others of his disciples, this night was special, and I want to keep its telling apart. It was at supper. We were lying about on couches. Though the dining room was large enough for a sizeable party, this night only Jesus, my son, our two wives, and I were there. He came to our home alone, without any of his followers, as he often did. This night it was in answer to my dear Miriamme that he picked up the thread from where it had lain that lovely day in Jericho and continued telling the story of his youth.

"First, my dear Asher, I ask you to understand that our worlds are far apart. You, all of you, are Judeans, and I am a Galilean. We are not the same. You were raised with the Holy City all about you. You are the most educated, the most honored of the Jewish line. Coming from a small town in Galilee, however, one is not favored with such luxury. Here, you profit by association with the Temple; in Galilee we feel only the sting of its taxes and the priests' contempt for our very existence. Here you coexist with the Romans in an uneasy peace; in Galilee we suffer with whip and chain the slightest whim of the lowest Roman or Greek. For you a good year is measured on a tally sheet of profits and losses. For us a good year is measured by whether we had food enough to spread on the table each night to eat.

"I say these things not to be cruel, not to make you feel better or worse than me, but to help you understand my story, and my people, the people who surrounded me as I grew. I tell you so that you understand all people in the future as they come to you for help, as they surely will. When I am gone, your home will become a refuge, a gathering place for those who are seeking after me and are lost. Each of you in this room is special to me, so special, I wish you only knew. Each of you lies cradled securely within my heart, and in our Father's mansion, there I shall reserve room for you."

Jesus had a way of filling our hearts to breaking. He taught us lessons (some of which were very hard to take), and then he filled us with the love that passes all understanding. In his love, somehow, the medicine became not quite so bitter, and our resolve to meet his expectations became, as he intended, a burning desire within. He saw us as shining beings, and that was what we wanted to be. We wanted to be to others as our Master had been to us; and even if we fell short, as we often did, we made the effort, which was more than we had done before. And Jesus, as a mirror of his loving and gentle Father, showed us in his own kind-hearted ways, and in his deep forgiving eyes, that we were special, that we too could attain the heights of love he demanded of us.

And now, dear reader, it is your turn to forgive, for I have rambled on with my comments and left our Master far behind. Please let me go back to his story, the story of his growing as he told it that night.

"While in Egypt mother had heard from traveling friends that the stories about her and father had grown while we were gone. And sweet as she was, she felt anger and fear inside, for the gossip had been mean. Our welcome, however, was exciting and wonderful for me. The whole village turned out to see us as we arrived. They hugged mother and father, and then turned their attention to my brothers and me. My mother was so proud of us. I looked up at her and adored her so. My father was the biggest surprise of all, however. He was smiling, and for the first time that I can remember, I noticed he had lost some of his teeth. It makes me laugh now to think that this is one of the things that I remember most clearly about that important day so long ago.

"As the day wore on, I came out from behind my mother's legs and began to watch the people, some of them gathering into small groups, thinking that no one was watching or could hear. It was then that I understood my mother's fears, for the welcome from many was a false one. Now there would be more stories for them to spread. And who picks up cruel stories faster than anyone? Why, the children, of course. So my life in the village started with taunts and name calling once again, as it had in Egypt. It drove me more and more within myself, where I found and explored my difference.

"Our home was just as mother had pictured it to me in her stories while we were away. It was one of many mud brick, and stone houses that lined the streets. Our house was built right to the edge of the dirt pavement, which was wider than some of the streets in town and proved most helpful when my father brought lumber into the yard. The house itself was one story, up against the side of a small hill, which, by digging, had been made into a vertical cliff. The house had only one room, which was of fairly good size. On the side of the house built into the cliff, a wide bench had been carved. The bench ran along the full length of the house. Here father placed two wooden partitions, centering them, to separate the two platforms on either side for the children's sleeping spaces. Mother and father then used the small space remaining in the middle for themselves. I loved these cozy little rooms, for the partition, which was at the foot of my bed, was made of the most beautiful wood, finished in the way father had learned in Egypt, and had the most magnificent shine. On the side of their enclosure that faced the rest of the room, mother hung a curtain for their privacy. To my way of seeing, our house was the most wondrous in all the world.

"The rest of the room contained a large wooden table with two benches on either side and two chairs at either end. It was here that the family lived, ate, and entertained our guests. At the back of the house against the other stone wall was the fire pit that mother cooked in, which also heated the house. The oven was in the work yard, outside. Because the house was very dark, father built a glorious wooden louver wall between the house and his work area adjacent to the house. At just the right time of day, the light would flood through the crossed slats and cascade through the air to land at my feet. Years later I would remember my brother Joses playing in the light and shadows as if they were real. To my mother's distress, he would kick up all the dust he could, so as to make the shafts of sunlight into solid bars of living light.

"The work area outside the house was backed against the hill on one side, the house on another, and a low wall surrounded the last two. Over the entire work area was a canvas canopy, held up by vertical and horizontal poles. In later years, although I never wished to make for myself the life of a builder, I did come to love this cool, light, breezy work area most of all.

"With his small family settled, father turned his energy to making a living, and to my education. He took me to the little synagogue in the village, a large square building, hardly distinguishable from any other house along the street. Here he entrusted my education to the old rabbi, who had a face etched with deep rivers of time and a long, unruly white beard that was sprinkled with just a touch of black around his chin. He carried five thousand years of our history lost in the corners of his mind.

"The only thing I can remember of this holy place is the darkness, which spread into every corner of the room, and which, to a young lad, was very mysterious indeed. The only light came from a square hole in the roof, where a brilliant shaft of light streamed into the room. It provided enough light for the seven or eight of us studying to see and read the Torah, which is why we came. I used to love to listen to the old rabbi tell us the stories of our people. By the time I was ten, I knew them all by heart, and most of the Torah as well. He was a Pharisee and believed with all his heart that the Messiah would soon be coming to save his nation Israel from the Herods and the oppressing Roman conquerors. Those prophecies he could find in the Torah that told of the Messiah's coming he would read to us with tears streaming down his face and a far away look of longing in his eyes.

"It was in that small, dark room, listening to the old man drone on, that the thoughts of my special being first entered my mind. It is so hard to explain now, so many years later, but it was like having an idea flit on the edge of your consciousness, or like seeing a figure in the mist coming off the lake. There is something so familiar about the image. The way they walk or hold their head perhaps. You hail them, but there is no response, and a great uneasiness descends upon you.

"I knew I was different. From my earliest memories, I knew things that others didn't, but even to myself it was incomprehensible. It was an awareness just beyond my consciousness, something unsettling and uneasy, something just out of my grasp, something I had to know! But what, I did not know.

"It wasn't just dreaming of becoming the Anointed One, for every young boy in the village had at one time or another dreamed that he would grow to be the Messiah and save his people from the tyrant Rome. Every young lad also thought that he would become the long-awaited warrior-king. But for me it was different. I did not play at being a king, for there was something inside me that said they were wrong. Somehow I knew, and that knowing is so hard to explain. I just knew that when the Messiah came he would save his people with love and grace, not with pain and war.

"The Father whom I found within was the Father of all people, and he had given nothing to me but love, compassion and grace. So, when the boys took turns playing at being king, I would turn away. I would go to my quietness when work was done. I would go to the hills, the mountains, the lonely valley, or sit by a stream. There I would watch the animals, the flowers, and the trees; there I would still myself and know that my Abba and I were One. It was a very special time, my youth. In solitude I found my Godness, and that is where I was and what I was. There I began to understand that the slaves I had known in Egypt were no different from the people of our land, nor from you or me today."

He was staring at us now, as he demanded with his expression, his eyes, his being, that we truly understand the core of his teaching. We knew that he was communicating with us—his soul to our soul—as he continued, his voice husky, pleading that we grasp his teaching.

"Freedom comes from within, and when one finds freedom there, no Roman, no Herod, no landlord, no man can ever take your freedom away from you again."

Jesus paused and looked almost desperately into each of our eyes, one after another, to see if we understood, to see if we felt what he was saying. We did.

He turned back to the fire, stared at the dancing flames, paused a few moments, and then continued his tale.

"My day started early. While father ate his morning meal I straightened up the workshop, sweeping up the wood chips, scraps, and shavings, saving them for my mother's fire. After I finished, I would come inside for fruit and bread before I ran off to my lessons with the old rabbi in the synagogue. When my lessons were through, about midday, I'd return home, where my mother would have a bowl of porridge and goat's milk waiting. Then while I ate, she would busy herself at the cook stove, for she had to cook for my father's workmen too. My new baby sister—my third brother, Simeon, had been born a year earlier—would be slung to her breast nursing, yet she never missed a step. I remember sitting there at the great wooden table watching her and wishing wistfully that she would look at me like she used to do before the other children came. That was when she had more time, when her eyes would ask me, 'Are you, son, are you?' And I felt so special! But those days were gone forever, lost in the business of everyday life. How important to grant oneself time away from this, to find the quiet place, to still the harried soul, to just be still, to find His healing peace within.

"When I finished my meal, I would once again go out to the work area, clean up whatever mess there was, and put away any tools that were left about. This chore I did as rapidly as possible, for if I finished cleaning before my father took the midday break, he would sometimes let me walk to the synagogue with him, where the men gathered to talk and debate. I always found a spot where I could see and hear without being in the way, for the men didn't like playful little boys who raced through the dusty street and were full of endless noise. On fine warm days, the men would gather in front of the synagogue in the open square, or under the shade of the broad, spreading trees where benches for the old men had been placed so long ago by my grandfather. There was no other diversion in our village except the news of the day and, of course, our religion, which they loved to debate endlessly. I sat quietly, never moving a muscle for fear the men wouldn't let me stay, just listening and watching. It was here that I learned of the hope, the desires, and the pain that lived within the soul of the people, Israel.

"Our village lay close to a military road from the north, and although it was not used with great frequency, the legions and troops from Rome and Antipas would sometimes storm through the town. I learned early, as did every other man, woman, and child in the land, to stay out of their way if possible and to do their bidding rapidly and well when you could find no escape. They took what they wished and feared no law save their own. After they had taken what they wanted, they passed on with a great flurry of bravado and grit. It was then that I would race to the synagogue where the men of the town would invariably gather to scream their vengeance and lament their lot. It was in watching the incredible force of the imperial eagle that I realized that a new way to freedom must be found, and somehow I knew that its new form was within me, waiting only for the right time to be born.

"Rome may have conquered the world, but not in the minds of the Jews. For in the minds of our people, we were the chosen of God, we were the center of the universe. Our people were converting the world with our religion. In Cyrenaica, Syria, Asia, Galatia, Macedonia, and even in Italia people were circumcising and becoming Jews; and if they didn't circumcise then they became God Fearers and joined us too. We may have been the poorest of nations at home in our own country, but we were seeding our finest throughout the empire—it was the time and place for a Jew. I was a Jew, and as a child, I absorbed the consciousness of our people. We were special, we were God's chosen, and God said, 'From my body Israel must come a child, and that child shall become the savior of the world. He shall spread my word and spread my name.'

"Thoughts such as these raged within my soul. There was a hunger there that needed to be fed. No, there was fire, and the more I fed it, the more it raged. I was pent up and yet could speak of this to no man, no woman, nor with any other whom I knew could I share what was held within me. And so, before I came to manhood, I had been prepared, and when the time did come, I could do nothing but follow the path laid out for me. I cried out to my Father, 'God, oh please, tell me when it is time, show me a sign!' And He showed me a sign, and the sign was the Baptist, John by name. He reached forth from the river Jordan to touch my forehead, and my skull exploded in wonder and ecstasy—my God had finally come!"

Jesus stopped, for I think my mouth was agape with astonishment. I had never heard the story of his awakening, and it was all a bit too much for me to comprehend. I know he was reading my mind, which had filled with a dozen questions all at once, for he said, "Why the look of surprise, Asher? What is it that you cannot understand, what is it you find so unusual?"

Unusual! Unusual wasn't the word, for I was speechless. My Lord had revealed himself in such a touching way; so intimately that I could do nothing but sit in dumb silence while my eyes filled with tears and I experienced the most intense loving I had ever felt.

Chapter 7

The Temple

When Jesus was twelve years old he accompanied his parents to Jerusalem for the annual Passover Festival, which they attended each year. After the celebration was over they started home to Nazareth, but Jesus stayed behind in Jerusalem.

Luke 2:41–43

By now the hour was late, so we left our repose at the dinner table and gathered once again in the large living room to sit near the fire. I knew the servants were ready for their beds yet had to wait to clean up the dining room from our supper. I, too, would normally have been trying to adjourn, lest I offend our guests by yawning in their faces—but not this night. This night was special, more special than I knew at that time, and I was awake with an alert eagerness I hadn't known since my youth.

How rare it was to have our Lord alone and all to ourselves without the ever-present crowds about him, or even his disciples. Without the threat of spies from the Temple, from Rome, and from Herod, Jesus could relax. He didn't have to guard every word that came from his lips. How rare, indeed, that he could speak in plainness and understanding and not in parables.

Jesus, too, seemed caught up in the telling of his youth and made no attempt to end the evening as long as we seemed eager to listen. The dining room lay between the cooking and the living areas, so, after rising from the table, it was but a few steps through the small door at the rear of the room into the large, comfortable living room beyond.

There had been a cold northern wind blowing all that day, and the warmth of the blazing fire was welcome against the howling intruder outside. I guided Jesus to the couch nearest the fire, and we all relaxed, hoping that he would continue from where he last left off.

Jesus leaned against the couch and let out an easy sigh as he sat staring at the orange flames dancing in the fireplace before him. His eyes drifted into the past as we watched the flames reflected in those eyes that seemed wearier now than when we had first met him. The fire cast long shadows, tracing the lines of his lean, weathered face.

Once settled, he eased back comfortably and took up his story.

"In the afternoons, if there was no work for me to do and no errands for me to run, I would often go up into the hills to be alone. Mother didn't have much time to spend with me now, as she had the other children to care for, so my focus tended to turn within, rather than developing a dependency on her.

"We had an old woman living with us at this time to help with running the household, but that never stopped mother from working as hard as ever; she tied the latest child to her, as she had done with my brothers and sisters before, and continued her tedious tasks. My time was generally taken up with watching and listening at the synagogue, doing my chores in my father's workshop, or being alone in the vastness of my Father's land.

"As I sat on the open hill I could feel the warmth of the earth beneath me, the grasses, the flowers, the plants, the blue sky above, the drifting, formless clouds that showed every color of my moods. And it was here that I knew I was One with my Abba. I would sit silently, looking out over the rolling hills to the north and the vast valley to the south, feeling the gentle breezes in my upturned face. I would smell the air, and a feeling of exhilaration would course through my veins. When I was alone in this way, I felt my specialness with Him who was somehow my life and my searching. Alone, I could talk to my Abba, and although there was no voice in answer, somehow I knew he was with me, and everything was all right. I felt so calm and sure. I had a knowing that my time was coming, if I could only wait. I could feel His presence as I slowly, silently walked backed to the village in the evening's deepening shadows, cast by the last rays of the rapidly sinking sun. As I was maturing, my time was coming.

"How can I describe the feeling that was growing in my breast? How can I say in words the aimless anticipation that surrounded me? All these things I kept in my heart as I worked through the days, waiting, always waiting. At times I was overwhelmed with the feelings that flooded my being when I looked into a person and knew compassion for them beyond understanding, for at that second I truly was that person! How I struggled with these feelings when I found myself helpless to express them in this body of a small lad, not yet of age. The frustration was swelling each day. I felt like a volcano as the pressure of my youth met the germinating awareness of the spiritual being who was developing within me at the very same time.

"I was twelve years old, and unbeknownst to me, my life was about to change in a way I could never have foreseen."

Listening to Jesus, my attention sharpened at this point, for I had met our Master's mother before and had heard some of the stories of his youth from her. Now, hearing from our Master how he saw himself during these formative years, I was enchanted. His mother described him as a strong, silent lad, with a consuming need to have his time alone. She had told me that sometimes he seemed like a moody young boy who didn't get along very well with his peers unless they were of his ilk. He could be raised to passion by incompetence or slowness in others, and in a fit of temper he could lash out at them with little warning, so that he was often ill tolerated by other children in the village. He was far above the understanding of others his age—or any in their town for that matter—and his frustration knew no bounds. Time and age were his enemies then, although it seemed in listening to him that as a lad he knew not why.

When I had spoken to his mother, she noted that his greatest struggle came when presented with man's injustice to man. Galilee is, and always has been, the core of rebellion within our land. There he was raised, and there he heard his countrymen cry out against the injustices perpetrated against them by Herod, Rome, and we Judeans. Since the time of his earliest memories in Egypt, he had been determined that the downtrodden of the world would be lifted up, and he, in his youthful ways, was impatient for the righting to begin. His mother, Miriam, wished, as I suppose all mothers wish, that she had spent more time with this youth to counsel him in patience, softness, and understanding, but her young household was growing, and all of her brood needed their mother's touch as much as he.

As it turned out, however, over the years our Master changed, becoming the softest, most understanding man I have ever known, and it was hard to picture him in any other way.

Asked about his schooling, his mother had said that where the other children studied by rote, Jesus absorbed, analyzed, and critically understood the Law that made his people the nation Israel. So it was that the old rabbi in the town filled with pride when he heard that his student was to visit the Temple in Jerusalem with his parents for Passover that year. He sent with Jesus a letter that he was instructed to keep unto himself, introducing him to a bright, young, ambitious priest, Nicodemus by name.

As I would find, it was far more difficult than I could ever imagine for this special man, this special soul, trapped in a body of a boy, locked in the little town of Galilee. The people of Galilee were known by we Judeans as "am ha-arez," a denigrating term connoting uneducated peasants. I was constantly amazed as I watched Jesus rise to prominence as he gained the respect of all those who would bypass their prejudices long enough to hear his words.

"Passover was approaching," Jesus continued his story, "and my parents were making ready to go south to Jerusalem as they had many times before, but this journey was to be different from any they had taken. This time my father had told mother and me that I too was to accompany them to the Holy City where I had yearned to go for so long. I was a man now, father said, and it was time I visited the Temple and made myself clean through immersion and my first sacrifice—an unblemished lamb.

"This wonderful news brought great joy to me, and I ran to the synagogue to tell the old rabbi. It was here that I felt for the first time the full impact of this great man's caring, he who had been so tolerant of me during my years of growing. I will never forget it. He sat me down, and with tears forming in his eyes, he handed me a note, written on skin, with instructions to present this to a certain priest of the Temple proper—none other would do. Then he hugged me, swore me to silence, even to my father, and after assuring himself I had stowed the missive properly and understood my directions correctly, he showed me to the door.

"Jerusalem was beautiful! It was a city such as I had never seen. There were people by the tens of thousands; so many, I could not grasp the immensity of it all. The sights and colors, the smells of animals and spice, of wood smoke, incense and sacrifice; the sounds of voices and the horn of the ram erupted and mingled into a dumbfounding, dreamlike state within my mind. The days of preparation ran one into another, with only patches of clarity to mark their passing.

"When we arrived, we took up residence in a tent of sorts. Our tent was one of thousands like it that had been set up around the Pool of Bethsaida to the northeast and within a few steps of the great Temple itself. The closeness and color of the tents and lean-tos that surrounded us with their multitude of occupants astonished me. But if I was astounded by this, it was nothing compared to what was waiting for me within the Temple walls.

"The following day we stumbled our way down the circuitous path shared by both man and beast in the haphazard placement of this city within the City, until at last we found ourselves walking directly under the very fortress that housed our powerful captors. It was in this tent city that Herod Archelaus, not so many years before, let loose his dreaded horsemen upon the people. From these mighty walls overlooking the Temple, built by Archelaus' father, with stones larger than I, the Romans watched everything and everyone that came and went into the confines of the Temple.

"We entered through what was called by many, 'Death's Gate,' for it was through this passage Archelaus' soldiers rode to attack this same camp of pilgrims a few years earlier.

"An audible gasp issued from my throat. I grabbed for my father's hand as my knees buckled; the awesomeness of the Temple so close in all its glory with the multitude seemingly all pushing toward a single goal brought terror in its wake. My mind made a vain attempt to sort out and catalog the scene, but it was useless. Clinging tightly to my father, we picked our way through people of every kind: small and tall, dark and light, wealthy and poor, ignorant and bright, those with golden tongues and those who were dumb. All whom I saw seemed to be crowding and aimlessly milling about in a totally incomprehensible manner—or at least so it seemed to this country lad of twelve.

"At the south end of the Court of the Gentiles, father exchanged our Roman coin and bought an unblemished lamb for sacrifice. I was amazed and confounded at the noise and clamor from the vendors, each vying for our coin so that we could be about our Father's business. If you could have seen me, you would have seen a boy's eyes wide with wonder, surprise, fear, and absolute delight."

Jesus turned to me and said, "Why, Asher, I might even have seen you there that day!"

I blushed, aware of our Master's well-known feelings toward those Sadducees and Pharisees (such as I) who profit at the well of the Temple gates. Although in my defense, I hasten to add, I make my living as an honest tradesman and not as a tax collector, moneychanger, or profiteer. But, as much as I would like, I cannot deny that my well-paid connections in and about the Temple have served me well.

As you can discern, my Master, always ready to teach those who were willing, and knowing all there is to be known about me, could not help delivering the painful jibe, yet with a sly grin and a twinkle in his eye. And, as usual, the result was exactly to his liking, as my wife Miriamme began to snicker, and my son and his wife met my embarrassment with outright laughter. At first my blood ran hot as my pride rose to defend my lost honor, but moments later we were all laughing uncontrollably as I threw up my hands in total surrender.

As we somewhat belatedly controlled our mirth and threw more wood on the fire to keep the chill from the evening, we assured our Lord in the most forceful tones that we wished him to continue. His eyes sparkled in the dancing light as he looked my way and asked if I was recording everything. I assured him I would write everything on the morrow so as not to forget anything that he had said. Thus, seemingly satisfied, he continued with his memories of his first trip to Jerusalem.

"For the next two days leading up to Passover eve, father and I cleansed ourselves daily in the living waters of the pool," Jesus started again. "We then walked the Temple grounds, stopping here and there to listen to one rabbi, priest, lawyer, or teacher of one persuasion or another share his knowledge of the holy books. I found that father, like most of those from our town, loved to point out a weakness or add a point to an argument whenever he felt that he could contribute anything meaningful to the discussion. However, to be a Galilean, I was to quickly learn, meant many things, not the least of which was that we had heavy accents, and those of Judean background would stare at us or give us surly looks. They even mocked my father openly on more than one occasion. Because of this, I began to listen very carefully and found that our language, the language of Galilee, was quite imprecise, as it had lost many of the subtle sounds that made the language so rich here in the south.

"I remembered back a few days before," Jesus said, "when father was buying the lamb for my first sacrifice. My father asked to purchase a lamb, a seemingly simple request. Instead of complying, however, the Temple merchant sneered at him and said, 'You stupid Galilean, do you want something to ride on? Or something to drink? Or something for clothing? Or something for a sacrifice?' My father blanched, realizing his lack of education. His embarrassment was made all the more painful because of his son's presence. He could only point at the small lamb to make himself clear. He wanted me to be proud of him, and he had been belittled because of something he couldn't help, because of the way he was raised and the simple words that he spoke. I suppose he couldn't know it then, but I tried to show in my eyes that I adored him and was more proud of him there, standing in front of that merchant and all the others watching, than I had ever been before, for he was doing this for me."

Jesus affected me on so many levels—he moved me so. All he had to do was caress a memory, and remembrances of my own welled up within me—and within each of us who heard him. Every father who has ever lived knew of the father-son relationship of which Jesus spoke, and of the burning pain of shame at being embarrassed in front of one's son; being made to look less than one so desperately wished to be for him. And each of us in the room with him knew the language difficulty that faced our brothers from the north. To a Galilean, the subtle differences of intonation in the word "lamb" were meaningless; but to us (like the Judean merchant who belittled Jesus' father), the way he pronounced the word it could have meant "donkey," "wine," or even "wool" as well as "lamb." Of course the merchant knew what this Galilean wanted, but he decided to mock him first before taking his money.

Jesus turned from the fire to look at us with eyes that seemed to say a thousand things, that seemed to be looking at all of us, and at the very same time into each of our souls separately, always loving, never judging. This time I could see in those eyes that he was offering, by way of this story about his father whom he dearly loved, an apology, an apology for all the times he knew he must have embarrassed us by slipping back into his local dialect while in our land of Judea. He was so incredibly humble, and I was again so incredibly ashamed. For I had been embarrassed on many occasions by his Galilean ways, and now I realized again, on hearing this simple story from his childhood, how wrong it is to judge another without walking long and hard in his steps.

The small, sheepish smile came over his face as expected, and he continued once again. "I can still see that day in my mind, as if it were happening all over again. I was standing in the long line, awaiting my turn to approach the altar, the young lamb slung over my shoulders as I had seen the others do, and once again my emotions began to overwhelm me. The sounds of the animals bleating in fear hurt me so terribly. I had never killed anything before, and the thought of killing this little trusting creature wrapped around my neck sickened me. Yet, the overwhelming pageantry I felt from actually being in the Temple, next to the Holy of Holies, seeing and hearing the throngs of people, made me feel small and insignificant and proud and brave all at the same time. I was, at that moment, one with my people, Israel.

"When my lamb had been prepared and parts of it burned upon the altar, I felt something pull at me, not on the outside, but inside. I felt as if my Abba had touched me, as I had felt him on my distant hillside, and I knew that this sacrifice too would be somehow changed in time.

"With the ceremony over, my father slapped me on my back and we rejoined my mother, who was watching from the Women's Court just outside. Everyone was in a joyous mood as we retreated to the tent that father had rented for us to stay in. After a meal and time to rest, mother dragged father off to visit the many marketplaces, permanent and temporary, where goods of all kinds from around the world were laid out in a feast for the eyes. Such a scene could be found in the city only at the time of great celebrations. After much begging, I convinced father I wouldn't get lost, and he let me go to the Temple alone, with many admonitions not to annoy anyone nor get in the way. I was elated! Now was my chance to carry out my secret mission—to find the elusive priest in the temple.

"Nervously, I patted the letter that I had tucked securely in the pocket on the inside of my beautiful new robe. Oh, how special, how puffed-up, proud, and manly I felt to be entrusted to carry this secret message to an unknown priest in the very confines of the glorious Temple itself. My imagination knew no bounds when it came to guessing its mysterious contents. Perhaps a conspiratorial message from a rebel leader to an accomplice in the Temple, I imagined. 'What a wonderful trick,' I thought, 'the Romans will never expect a lad to carry a message of this magnitude.' I had wondered agonizingly as to its contents all during the week of our trip south to Judea.

"As soon as my parents were on their way, I headed straight for the Temple and continued past the outer walls directly toward the Holy of Holies, just as the old rabbi had instructed. It wasn't hard to slip past the guards at the gates into the labyrinth of hallways and rooms that made up the Temple complex since there were so many people asking questions and directions.

"My heart was pounding as I followed the rabbi's instructions, walking quickly and silently through the labyrinth, until finally I stood in the hall before the screen. I sat down cross-legged, tucked back into the corner where a column met the wall, and tried to calm myself, expecting at any moment to be arrested and thrown into prison.

"It happened quite unexpectedly. I guess I had learned to block out more of the outside world than I knew, for the first I was aware of anyone else's presence was a gentle hand upon my shoulder. I looked up with a start into the eyes of a kindly man with no anger on his face. He looked down at me, I think equally surprised to find a boy in these sacred precincts, and told me I would have to leave. Without a word, I reached into my inside pocket and drew out the letter I had guarded so carefully and handed it to him. With a quizzical look on his face he slowly broke the seal, unfolded the small piece of parchment, held it up to catch the lamp light, and read its contents. When he was through, he studied me very carefully, as if he still hadn't made up his mind whether or not he should take me seriously or most unceremoniously have me bodily thrown out of the Temple precincts.

"After what seemed like a long time, I could see that he had made up his mind. With an air of finality, he grabbed my hand, turned on his heels, and with robe flowing gloriously behind, took me in tow, retreating down wondrous stone corridors to a destination I could hardly guess. All I knew for sure was that I was following as fast as my feet would allow. We first went down a long hall, where at several locations I caught sight of the altar and the people lining up to offer their sacrifices outside. Then, with a jerk of my arm, up a flight of stairs we went.

"It was getting darker in this part of the building, and I was becoming more than a bit apprehensive. Finally, after what seemed like an eternity of passageways, halls, columns, and rooms (some with priests and scribes and some without), we entered a medium-sized space with maybe four or five men huddled in a group. My 'guide' approached one of these men, who I would guess was about my father's age. He leaned close to the man's ear and whispered.

"The man had jet black hair, a peaceful face, and wore the robes of a Pharisee. The first man left us at that time, and this new charge motioned me to follow once again. This time we entered a small room next to the one in which we were standing. Here, he arranged himself on a rug, pulled up a low table in front of him, and unfolded the letter I had brought.

"After several minutes of reading, a smile creased his face. Leaning back against a large pillow, he looked up at me standing there before him, my hands hot and sweaty. 'So!' he said, his immense teeth and gums showing as his smile grew larger. 'Your rabbi has sent you to me?' I nodded my head yes. 'Well, he says that you are some kind of scholar.' There was a mocking tone in his voice. 'He says that you know most of the Torah by heart. He says that not only have you memorized it, but also that you understand it! Is that true, boy?'

"Again, all I could muster was an affirmative nod. 'He says that he wants me to make you my ward. He wants me to talk to your father and arrange for you to stay here in Jerusalem to study under me. Is that what you want, boy? Is that what you want, too?'

"The very idea of it was too immense for me to grasp all at once. Of course, I had dreamed of coming to the Temple and learning, but I never imagined that one day it would actually happen.

"My tongue finally found its way. 'Yes,' I stuttered. 'Yes! Oh, yes, I most assuredly do.'

"That was all it took. In his mind it was settled. He would see to it that all the arrangements were made. He held the old rabbi in deep respect and owed him a debt of great weight that he had feared he would never be able to pay. So finally, in this request, he had found his opportunity to return some measure of gratitude to his benefactor of the past. He was quite delighted to find in me a way of satisfying his obligation of love to his old Galilean friend.

"That afternoon was one of the happiest in my young life, for my new guardian priest, Nicodemus, took me completely under his care, spending the rest of the afternoon showing me what seemed to be every wing, room, and corridor of the Temple complex. I saw the doors, some of them eight times the height of a man, as one after another we passed, many of them covered with gold, silver, and bronze. I saw the finest rare woods (reminiscent of Egypt), intricate carvings, rich cloth, and vestments stored in the closets. And, as if that were not enough, my mind reeled at the vast storehouses under the dirt and stone courtyards above, filled to overflowing with coins and gold and silver implements of every kind. Riches beyond my imagination, all obtained from the offerings of our people, far and near, rich and poor, to our God, the God of Israel.

"I was lost that day most of the time—and completely loving it. 'Imagine me,' I thought, 'Me, a builder's son from Nazareth touring every nook and cranny of the Temple. Even if it ends here, it will have been grand.' Before I left that day, Nicodemus admonished me to be sure to have my father attend morning prayers in the Court of the Israelites; he would find us there and speak to my father then.

"As you can well imagine, I could hardly sleep that night. I tossed and turned so much that in the middle of the night my father could stand it no longer, saying, 'What's the matter with you tonight, boy? Either you stop thrashing about like a sick kid or I will throw you out on your ear!' I knew he didn't mean it, but I made sure to lie quite still after that.

"Finally morning came. I thought we would miss prayers altogether, it took him so long to get ready. He seemed to be enjoying my discomfort immensely.

"I tell you, it was quite a sight to see when Nicodemus picked my father out of the huge crowd and told him he would be pleased to see him after services. Can you imagine?" Jesus said with a merry laugh. "Can you just imagine the look on his face when everyone around him turned to stare at him, wondering why this obvious Galilean had been singled out and honored by a Temple priest?

"Father was sweating from every pore, although I remember the morning to be quite cool. He looked down at me as if to ask if I could possibly know what this was all about, then thought better of it. What could his young son know about anything so important as this? Thus, he turned his attention back to the service, churning within himself for the rest of the hour until services were done. I am sure he didn't know whether he was to be honored or flayed behind the immensity and majesty of those doors."

Jesus glanced at us and said, not unkindly, but just stating the facts of the matter, "You, being of the Temple crowd, having education, wealth, and influence, know nothing of the mystery, fear, and awe with which the country folk hold the men behind the gates of the Temple seal."

I understood what he was trying to convey, for I had seen farmers, shopkeepers, and many others who had traveled to Jerusalem from the far corners of our country shake with an excitement long lost in youth by those of us raised within sight of the City. I have seen men go mad and throw themselves upon the altar in ecstatic fits. I have even seen men loose their bowels in fear when a priest or scribe singled them out for some reason and approached them. These things my jaundiced eyes had seen, so I knew of what our Lord spoke about his father, and my heart went out to him. I gave him a reassuring smile as he continued his story.

"Father left me behind and cautiously approached the door that had been pointed out for him to enter. I know he was petrified; his simple life had given him no knowledge of Temple protocol at all, and yet he wanted desperately to please. Several men who had been nearby waited close at hand to see if they could pick up some small bit of gossip or intrigue to carry back to their friends and families. As for myself, I was just as nervous, but for a different reason. I wanted more than anything to be allowed to stay here in Jerusalem.

"I didn't have to wait long. Father must have come to a rapid decision, for I soon saw him returning down the long marble colonnade that had been built by Herod in his ill-begotten attempt to buy the loyalty of his subjects. Father's face was white and somber, and he seemed shaken by his experience. He put his arm around me and said with great gravity, 'Son, let's find someplace cool to sit.' I followed him out of the Temple building and into the outer court, where we found a bench under a portico and sat.

"'My boy...'

"That was all he said for what seemed an eternity. His eyes were blank, deep in some mist-shrouded thought, and I was dying with anxiety. 'My boy,' father finally continued, 'something great and wonderful has happened. Something has come about that I do not understand. That priest...' he paused again. 'That priest you saw approach me'—words were coming hard for him here and I saw him fight back tears—

'he wants you to stay here in Jerusalem and study under his direction. He thinks you have the makings of a fine rabbi.' He paused again, then said, 'Before I say any more, I think that since you are now approaching manhood, it is time I tell you all that I know about you, about your coming, about your birth.'

"Father then proceeded to tell me everything he knew or remembered about the voice he heard when I was born, about the astrologers and young twin kings, about all these things that he had held within himself all these years. He ended with the story of how the priest Nicodemus had talked to him this morning; how he had singled me out and decided that I was worthy of his teaching. I could tell that father was decidedly honored and perplexed by being singled out by Nicodemus, and I was nearly beside myself waiting to see what my father's decision would be. Could I stay or not?

"Finally, after a long pause he said, 'I have decided. It is all too much of a coincidence, all that has happened in your life. You must be a man now; the Lord has special plans for you, of that I am sure.'

"'What, father, what is your decision?' I wanted to yell at him.

"'I have decided you will stay!'

"I shrieked with delight as I jumped to my feet, drawing the attention of several men nearby. My father, already more nervous than I had ever known him to be, put his hand to his lips (looking fervently to each side of us in hopes no one was watching) and pulled me down to the bench by the hem of my robe. 'There is just one thing more,' he said. 'You must not tell your mother—you must not let her feel that there is anything amiss. We still have two days here; I will determine a way to tell her in my own time. Is that agreed?' Of course, I agreed. This was the happiest day of my life. Imagine me—me—studying at the great Temple in Jerusalem. What would the boys back in Nazareth think when they heard the news?

"The Sabbath came and went, and still father had thought of no way to break the news to my mother that her son would not be returning home with her. As we walked and talked together over the next couple of days, exploring the shops and seeing the city, mother and father spent long hours (long hours for me, at least) together, all to no avail. He was no closer to telling her on the last day than he had been on the first.

"All during this time I kept looking at him, staring at him, trying to make him say something—but nothing seemed to work. Mother was happy and singing these last days, with no thought of father or me and no knowledge of the imminent problem we had between us, and father found it impossible to break into her mood. Father had bought her some beautiful cloth to be made into new clothing for the family and a large new pot for her to use in cooking for her growing brood. We even stopped to have some sweets prepared by a crazy roadside vendor on the way back from the market streets. Sweets, however, were hardly what was uppermost in my mind at the time. Although he started to tell mother that I wouldn't be returning with them several times, each time he became afraid or stumbled over the words, changed the subject, and finally let it slide—my frustrated, infuriated skulking to no avail.

"When the evening after Sabbath ended and mother was packing our belongings for the trip to begin the next morning, I could wait no more. I pulled father outside the tent and asked in a very exasperated voice what I was supposed to do. It was then that he concocted the most bizarre scheme to allow me to stay and yet again forestall telling mother what was going on. 'Tomorrow morning I want you to slip quietly out with your things. Do not awaken your mother, or we will both pay dearly. I will tell her you left early with my permission to travel back with Joshua's family. Once we are on our way, it will be impossible for her to refuse what is already done.'

"This was the first time I really focused on how powerful my mother was when it came to something she considered important—like her family. On this trip I gained a new respect for her power within our little clan that I would not soon forget. In the future I was to consider her feelings and influence to a much greater degree than before. In fact, only a few days later I was to get yet another warning to heed her dominant position, and this time I vowed I would never forget again.

"I had just been settled into a room within a rock's throw of the Temple and started into a routine of discourse with the teaching elders, listening and reading, when straightaway my mother burst into a session with the teachers of the Law, my father trailing sheepishly behind. It was such a breach of etiquette that all mouths, including mine, were agape—this was no place for a woman! Mother strode right up to me, her little feet echoing through the great hushed hall, looked me square in the eyes, and said, 'Why have you done this to us? Your father and I have been frantic, searching for you everywhere.'

"I was shocked to my roots. I stammered, 'But, didn't you know that I would be here in the Temple? Didn't my father tell you that I would be in His house?' Mother missed the double entendre in her agitation, as I thought she would, but father hadn't, and unexpectedly I found anger rising within me. I stared straight at father, my eyes flashing with rage, as I realized he still hadn't told her!

"Nicodemus was not there when my parents arrived but was hurriedly summoned, and he met the three of us on our way out of the hall. He was able to quiet my mother, but no arguments he could make, nor statements as to my unique abilities in rendering the holy books, and my special understanding could avert her insistence on my return with them to Nazareth. She judged me far too young to be away from home and her supervision.

"So it was with sad heart and resentful spirit that I once again headed north to our home in Nazareth. A trail that had once been bright with promise now seemed dark and lonely."

Dawn was drawing close, and the last glowing embers of the fire were dying when Jesus seemed to weary of his memories. He ended this most incredible night with two sentences that covered the next four years of my Master's life.

"It was almost a year later before my constant insistence finally persuaded my mother that it was hopeless to try to keep me away from my inner calling, and my parents once again sent me south, entrusting my care to the patient and loving Nicodemus. It was then I began to study from the most learned men of the time, Hebrew, Greek, and Hindu alike."

That last statement intrigued me. I knew little of the Greek's pagan beliefs, and I knew absolutely nothing at all of Hindu people and their even stranger faiths. But my curiosity was going to have to wait, for Jesus was bidding us all a fair night (what was left of it), and this was not the time to bring up another subject, for we too were bone weary and needed sleep. Yet sleep would have to wait for me, as in these early morning hours, while the rest of the household slept, my Lord took me apart and taught me the mysteries—the mysteries that even now wait for you.

Little did I know that this was the last opportunity I would have to hear of my Master's life in my home and from his own lips. I think that he had divulged more to us in this one evening than he had shared with anyone else in the almost three years of his teaching, and I was honored beyond words. I wondered if it was because he knew that I would write down all that I could remember of the evening?

The following week I pieced together the little more I was to learn of this period of our Lord's life directly from Nicodemus himself. Nicodemus was now an old man like me. I knew him from the Temple.

Chapter 8

Nicodemus

After dark one night a Jewish religious leader named Nicodemus, a member of the sect of Pharisees, came for an interview with Jesus.

John 3:1

Is there a single one of us Jewish rulers or Pharisees who believes he is the Messiah? . . . Then Nicodemus spoke up. (Remember him? He is the Jewish leader who came secretly to interview Jesus.)

John 7:48 & 50

I heard Jesus slip out of our home quietly sometime before dawn as he headed back across the Kidron toward Bethany. I tried to continue sleeping but I was too excited. I wanted to put into practice what my master had taught me a few scant hours earlier. He told me that the easiest time to reach out for our Father was in the silence just before dawn. So, with but a couple of fitful hours of sleep, I slipped out of bed, leaving my sweet young wife sleeping peacefully. Her beautiful raven black hair was spread over the pillow like a gossamer veil as I crept alone to the rooftop. Shortly before the sun stole its way over the far horizon I closed my eyes and turned within to our Father, as I had now been taught. As the sun slowly spread its warmth upon the earth, it engulfed me in its radiance, filling my body throughout with a warming light that permeated the depths of my being and matched the loving splendor I experienced within. The sun is indeed too bright to behold, but it dims to a pall beside the iridescent resplendence of the one God whom Jesus taught us to find in the depths of our souls.

Refreshed and renewed, I looked about at the new day. Down the hill below my rooftop perch, the city was coming alive. In the distance I could hear an occasional dog barking as his stomach told him that there would soon be scraps from the table for him to eat. When I listened very carefully, I could hear the first of the shopkeepers setting up their wares at the foot of the western Temple wall. I took a deep breath of the crisp, clean morning air, filling my lungs with the cool breezes that were coming up from the Valley of Hinnom, bringing with them a scent of the sea far below and to the west.

Walking down from the roof, I silently slipped past the family's sleeping quarters, then down the outside stair into the beautiful protected inner court, kept always green with the royal palm from Egypt and our own native fig. The court was also filled with a myriad of wonderfully blooming wisteria and other climbing plants clinging to the white walls with splashes of living, brilliant colors. The plants were placed in this sheltered court to give splendor to the eye as they gathered the warming rays of the sun, reflected from the surrounding two-story stone walls. Here the plants were protected from the frost that would not be long in coming—autumn was close at hand.

I loved autumn, for it meant that the Feast of Tabernacles was approaching, and the Feast of Dedication was soon to follow. The weather was magnificent and invigorating at this special time of the year. I crossed the courtyard with its beautiful mirrored pool and slipped into the room where the servant girls were busily baking bread and preparing the meals for the day. I sat to chat with them for a moment as I ate some fruit and bread, cold now, left over from the day before. I didn't want to wait for the fresh bread baking in the inside oven at this chilly time of the year, for I had set my sights on meeting Nicodemus this morning, and it was quite a walk to the Baths where I knew he would be.

Jesus had left for Bethany the morning after telling us of his youth, and for two days now I had been completely occupied with affairs of business, knowing there would be precious little time during the holidays. But now, with all of that in John's hands, I could find nothing more important than to find my old acquaintance Nicodemus and ply him with questions of my Lord.

The walk was invigorating; even though it was mostly downhill, it was some distance, and it did me good. I thought I should probably do this every morning, then chuckled aloud to myself as I dismissed the ridiculous thought as rapidly as it had come—just another one of my good intentions never brought to fruition.

Herod built the Roman Bath, or Thermae as the Romans called it, in his mad attempt both to curry the favor of Rome and to spread the influence of the Greeks and their combined culture throughout his kingdom. Later, when his son Archelaus was banished, the Romans enlarged and completed the Bath to suit their needs. Actually, the custom of public bathing thought to be a heathen activity by most of my countrymen had many adherents among the leading families of the city. On several occasions I found it quite a profitable and convenient place to consummate a transaction with business acquaintances.

Approaching the Bath, one isn't impressed by anything about the building but its size, for the outside is less than spectacular. But once inside, a visitor cannot help but be awed by its opulence, rivaled only by the Temple itself. As one enters, one passes through a colonnade into a beautifully landscaped garden, then into the building proper. The first room is a wonderfully arched hall about which the remaining rooms are all symmetrically placed. Using the Roman convention, the hall itself has at its apex a dome more than thirty cubits high, held in place by massive walls, and Egyptian granite columns of two colors, themselves twelve cubits in height. These in turn are topped with white marble entablatures. The mosaic floors contain geometric patterns of incredible beauty, and the lower walls are also lined with marble from all over the world. There are three baths, each of a different size and temperature. The largest is a pool of naturally cool water called a Frigidarium. The second bath is of slightly warmer water (which I prefer) called a Tepidarium; and the last is a very hot bath called a Calidarium, which is housed in a most impressive domed room with clearstory windows of translucent alabaster interspersed around the top. Not only is the water heated in this room but hot air also comes from the walls.

Reaching the Baths, I unclothed in the changing room, placed round me a large towel provided by the attendant, and headed for the Sudatorium, or dry sweating room, where I thought Nicodemus might be. True to form, I found him there and was greeted with warm delight. He, too, was in good spirits, delighted to converse with someone of his own persuasion, and he was even more agreeable to talk about the young boy Jesus, sent to him to learn so many years before.

I told him some of what Jesus said about how he came to be Nicodemus' ward. As I expected, this was all it took to get the old man started. I have to chuckle, for I too am his age and can ill afford to call him "old."

"I will start where he left off with his story," Nicodemus said, "but first I must tell you that, as you have probably already guessed, Jesus was a most unusual boy.

"The first thing I did when I read the note from my old friend, the rabbi from the north, was to ask a few questions of Jesus. These I made progressively more difficult until I asked him a question concerning the Torah that baffles even the wisest of our scholars today. I doubt if what I asked made the slightest impact on the boy, so well versed was he in the Law. But, Asher, it wasn't just that he had memorized the Law, and the commentaries, of our fathers. It was different. It was almost as if he had written them himself. For his answers, even though they were short and youthful, were at the same time pointed and accurate. He displayed such a compassionate understanding of them that it was all I could do not to expose him to everyone right there on the spot. Why I didn't, I do not know. There was something inside me that kept me from it. Mind you, Asher, I wasn't old and feeble-minded like you in those days. I was sharp and bright."

I had not been around Nicodemus for some time, and I had forgotten his quick wit and jolly manner. Once again I was beginning to enjoy his way of telling a story, as much as the subject matter itself.

We both laughed until our sides hurt, then, feeling weak and a bit giddy from the steam and heat, we pretended we were thirty years younger and jumped headlong into the cold waters of the Frigidarium. It had an amazing effect. I actually felt as though the years had melted from me. Arm in arm we climbed out of the pool and chatted as we wound our way into the Unctuaria where we entrusted ourselves to the masseurs. They were slaves who were honored and treated with great respect for their special gifts of kneading and prodding, tender ministrations that worked miracles on old, tired bodies such as ours. As we lay in flaccid peace, our sore bodies being treated like those of kings, Nicodemus continued his story.

"I knew I had a find! For before me I had a young man with a brilliant, supple mind, one who, with proper training and deft handling, could be molded into the most extraordinary priest Jerusalem had ever seen. He would need a great deal of training, I knew, for his Galilean background served him ill for what I had in mind for him."

The masseur rolled Nicodemus over with a grunt, and then started working on his toneless girth. Settled again, Nicodemus closed his eyes and continued. "I was mistaken, though, for I had no idea at that time just how headstrong and bright he really was.

"The first step was to keep him in Jerusalem under my tutelage. In that regard, his father proved no obstacle, for he was in mortal fear of me and the unfathomable power I represented to him. Alas, the mother of the lad proved a worthier adversary. Not impressed in the least with the uniform of pomp, nor the use of rhetorical logic, nor even the threat of the Lord (forgive me), she whisked him away and out of my grasp for almost a year.

"It took this long to get him back, but come back he did, thanks to my good mentor in Nazareth, some backbone left in his father, and the lad's own persistence. He stayed here in Jerusalem then for the next three years. Three years wherein he received the highest wisdom and teachings there were to be had from holy men of learning in three of the richest cultures known to man.

"May the Lord forgive my arrogance and pride, for during the entire time he was with me, while I supervised his growth, I let not any of the hierarchy know of his gifts. Because of my birth, I had no way of becoming close to the power of Annas or Caiaphas. Lord, how I resented them and their structure in my youth. But my brilliant young student, Jesus, was indeed a different story. You see, I checked his genealogy, and although of simple birth, I could follow his line back all the way to David. Imagine, Asher, all the way to David!" The masseur asked him to stop at this point, for Nicodemus was gesticulating and shaking his arm so violently it was impossible to hold him to the table without physical restraint.

"Calm yourself, Nicodemus, old friend," I cautioned. "You could stroke right here on the table, and wouldn't that be a pretty mess." The thought of it, for some bizarre reason, brought a tickle of a smile to the edge of my lips, and then I found I could fight the urge no longer. The twitch became a smile, the smile a barely concealed chuckle, then outright laughter overwhelmed me again at the thought of seeing the old man in death, his hand upright and his finger extended to the sky in righteous indignation. I thought, "I shall stuff him and install him in the Temple for all to see!"

Oh, what a picture. Lord, I was laughing, holding my sides in merriment. Nicodemus, with finger and arm still straining at the ceiling frescoes above, his face frozen in righteousness, alone in his world of the past, slowly became aware of my uncontrolled chortling. The first things to change were his eyes, refocusing from their lofty, distant visage. Slowly coming to gaze upon another sight equally as incongruous: a half-naked old man doubled up with laughter on a narrow slab of a table, teetering totally out of control, with two masseurs staring at each other in confusion and disbelief.

Still holding his godlike pose in the body denied its rightful pomp, the ends of his mouth, too, began to form into a sheepish smile.

"Sorry," he said, and slumped limp back onto the table. When I gained my composure, I assured him that I also had launched into a pet speech or two in my time, and now I knew why my family invariably laughed themselves silly while I flew into a rage. I apologized for laughing, reaching over and grasping his arm in friendship. I think from that day on we shared a special closeness—both in each other and in our friendship with a very special man.

It was only after I made a solemn oath never to reveal this conversation to our colleges in the Temple that Nicodemus consented to continue his story.

"Anyway, Asher," he continued, giving me a wary sidelong glance, "I sought to teach the boy to my ends, not his. I planned to teach him far beyond the wisdom of any then in the service of the Temple, beyond even Hilled, whose wisdom was legendary; incidentally, he was also of the line of David. Then, at the propitious moment of my choosing, with the Essene's marginalized as to be no longer relevant, I expected to bring Jesus forth to rightfully claim the inheritance stolen from the people. However, my plans were not his.

"As he grew in years under my tutelage, he grew into manhood, and with that growth, he also grew headstrong and impatient. He saw through my scheming and ended my plan, which, in looking back, Asher, I realize was from the start a foolish and self-deluded one.

"By the way, I understand that your son, John, has become an open follower of Jesus. From your questions, might I deduce that you, too, are a follower as well?"

Although I knew Nicodemus fairly well, I did not know him as a confidant, and his question immediately put me on guard, as rightfully it should. For in the politics of the day, a careless slip to the wrong ears could mean financial ruin and loss of influence for perhaps years for me, but it could be far worse, far, far worse.

He had just told me, in so many words, that he had once had hidden designs on the High Priest's position. What did I know of this man's ties to the inner circle of power? I myself had no ambitions in that regard, since I had gained entrance to the ruling body not on religious grounds, but by wealth. However, I was cautious because there had been rumors, which I tended to ignore (perhaps inadvisably), about Caiaphas' concern that Jesus was becoming too compelling among the masses and that he might cause trouble with the authorities, meaning the Romans. I knew Jesus well enough, I thought, to know that he had no designs on the Temple power, nor Rome's, for that matter, so I dismissed any danger as being ridiculous.

Nicodemus, on the other hand, was a shrewd, observant politician. He read my hesitation perfectly, and as we moved into the Unctuaria where our hair was shampooed, our skin scraped with a straggle, and our bodies anointed with oils and unguents, he waved his hand to dismiss his own question to me and continued himself instead.

"Never mind, Asher, you should not answer that question without knowing me and where I stand on this matter. Did you know I just saw him recently, a few days ago, privately? Did you know that your son, John, was the one who brought me to him?" He could tell by the surprised look on my face that I did not. I was flabbergasted.

"I saw him for the first time in twenty years," he continued, with a strange, distant look in his eyes. "I had to see him again. I had to be sure that this Jesus, who was teaching in Galilee, was the same Jesus I had taught so many years ago here in Jerusalem. It was he, Asher, it was he!

"Asher, my dream has come true. He has wisdom far beyond our understanding. I have been unable to sleep these past days, for his teachings have burned their way into my mind. He spoke to me of so many things, especially of a new birth for our people, one that I am only now, with great reflection, beginning to understand. I tell you, he knew me so well, and although I endured the sting of subtle reproach for my past deeds, in truth, it was milder than I had prepared for, and love was at its seat.

"His teachings were as mysterious as the source of the wind, for although I knew not of what he spoke that night, it is just now coming upon me like a gentle breeze in the dark hours before dawn. I know that he is unique, Asher, and I feel that I am being reborn, not to woman, but reborn in my soul. My spirit sings a new song, and I know I must seek him out and learn from him more; no longer will I be the teacher and he the seeker, but the other way around. If I were but younger and stronger and had more of the courage of my youth, I would stand for him, Asher, I would drop everything and follow him. And in that vein, dear fellow and friend, I ask you to warn him. Warn him that even now Caiaphas' men are watching him at every quarter. They report almost daily of his activities, and they in turn to Herod, of his sayings. Please warn him to be most cautious, lest he slip and say what he is not yet prepared to say."

Now finished and feeling like new men, we stepped out into the bright new morning and the carefully groomed gardens. We walked silently around the manicured lawns, each lost in his own thoughts, until I motioned Nicodemus to a seat in full view of the radiant and warming sun. Looking deeply into his eyes I said, "Before we part this day, dear friend, I wish to thank you for sharing your morning with me, and for being so candid in your speech. However, I came to find out about those years that you did have him in your care. Could you tell me anything about those three years?" He smiled a gentle smile now, and he seemed to settle a bit as he stared deeply into the depths of the shallow mirror pool that lay at our feet. And thus he drifted back into memory.

"In our own faith, Asher, I instructed him as far as I was able. Every Law of our fathers he was taught, and of the Perishaiya, every oral tradition and each sacred rite. Even unto Hillel I led him for a month, to absorb every subtlety he could discover with his probing mind.

"Then when I judged him to be complete in Jewish Law, I led him to the Greeks. I had made many contacts, and many favors were owed in kind, so into their schools I enrolled him to learn everything he could, both myth and fact alike, to learn of Socrates, Hippocrates, Hermes, Homer, and more. The ideas of the Greeks were foreign to our young lad, and like his people before him, he fought against them with a vigor I had not before seen displayed so early in youth. But the amazing thing was, Asher, he learned their lessons well, and unlike we who merely turn our backs, threaten, and cajole, he turned their own weapons of tongue and mind against them, and with pure and unadulterated logic he put them in their place. Pride is not limited to us Jews, however, and after one particularly strident session wherein Jesus showed the pompous scholar to be a fool, he was asked in no uncertain terms to leave the school. I tell you truly, I have heard myself and heard reported the things that he says and the things that he does, and I think that he unwittingly absorbed perhaps more than he would care to admit."

Nicodemus continued, "When I had just turned twenty, I had occasion to come upon a man of strange looks and even stranger demeanor. I had been sent to the port of Joppa to deliver a message outbound to Alexandria, and on my way back I strayed from the path set for me to see what promised to be a most spectacular view of the sea.

"I rounded a small hillock and ventured down a path, settling on a flat patch of dirt in front of what appeared to be a little cave. I had just pulled from my bag some bread and unwrapped the fish I had purchased in the market that morning, when I nearly died of fright. From behind me came a roar of laughter, which, when magnified by the acoustics of the cave, sounded to this poor soul as though a giant were about to devour me. In fact, it turned out to be a most fearsome but gentle man, dressed in nothing but a loincloth and a simple leather thong that was slung across his chest and under his arm. He was a fright to see, what there was of him. A man shorter than you, Asher, slight of build; he had the most amazing beard, for it stretched down to his waist, then looped up over his shoulder and wrapped around his neck again. He wore no cover on his head save the unruly, dirty, gray mop of unshorn hair careening down his back, but his eyes were more vibrant and friendly than any I had ever seen.

"At first I was so petrified that I could not have issued a sound if I had tried. My eyes grew wide and round and my hair stood on end like a cur. I couldn't have run to save my life if I had wanted to, for my legs had turned to stone and my bowels to water. I thought I had found a devil, come to haunt me from his grave! Later I would be thankful for my failure to escape, for in less time than it took me to regain my composure, his gentle voice and warm demeanor had convinced me to stay. Thus, with trembling hands I ate my fish and shared some strange hot dish that he brought out for me to dip my bread into. This old man lived until just a year ago, Asher, and I visited him each week during the last months when his health began to fail.

"This extraordinary little man had come from India, a far-off eastern land, once conquered by the Greek Alexander. He was full of a strange wisdom that I learned, if not to agree with, at least to respect. Incredibly, he spoke the perfect Hebrew of our fathers, which he said he learned at his father's royal court, in a place called Punjab State. He came to our land many years ago on a trading mission and never found reason to leave. He washed himself but once in ten days on his trip to the ocean below and spent the rest of his time there in that small cave contemplating the manifestation of his gods from the Atman, the One unknowable being.

"It was to him that I brought Jesus last, and although I thought highly of him, Jesus would say little, but I think from him he learned much. Jesus did not have to learn to speak to God, for he already had the wonderful, uncanny ability to talk to his Father directly (whom, as you know, Asher, he calls Abba, a term only a child would use, which in truth bespeaks of his total childlike trust). This intuitive facility to know our Father directly, I could not fathom, just as I could not understand that he and his Father were One. However, that fact was unshakable in him even at this early age.

What this wise little man was able to show Jesus was a special way to retreat within himself, a practice of breathing and concentration that he made Jesus do over and over each day. I know of this man's ways. They are subtle, very subtle, and while this young lad of fifteen argued, stomped, and stormed at being made to practice these absurdities, he was changing ever so slightly each and every day.

"I remember one afternoon slipping quietly into the little two-room house I had acquired for the two of them to live in within the city walls. Jesus did not notice my presence, so overwrought was he, pacing back and forth, waving his now strong young arms to emphasize his point to his teacher, who was sitting placidly on the floor against the wall with a look of extreme peace, contentment, and pride on his face. Yes, there was just the slightest look of amusement, too, at the corners of his eyes—a twinkle I could recognize. For an aroused Jesus was quite a sight to see.

"'Why? Why do you insist that we must come back over and over again? Why?' our young lad asked, looking intently at the small, quiet man in the corner. I stayed silently in the entrance shadow, enjoying the play unfold just as the old man had desired. He had been working with Jesus now for over six months and had confided that his training was nearing an end. He told me that in India students trained for tens of years at a master's feet and still could not come close to the depths this young man had reached in so short a time. 'The philosophy of belief is unimportant,' he would tell me, 'it is the wisdom of the soul that counts.'

"The old man finally replied quietly to Jesus' shouts and accusations, without a ripple of agitation. 'Because, my fine young man, you have many lessons to learn, and it would be quite impossible for you to learn them all in one lifetime. It is quite apparent, for example, that you haven't learned patience.'

"Jesus bent over to within a foot of the old man's face, looked at him sharply for a long moment, and then with a shrug of futility shouted, 'Patience! I've been here six months and what mysteries have you shown me? You tell me that I come back over and over. But where is the justice of it all? Look at the people; they are poor! What good is it? What possible use does this knowledge have for my people? What can I do with it? I'll tell you what I can do with it—nothing!'

"Jesus was now pacing back and forth, a wild-eyed youth with pent-up energy that we both knew must soon find its escape. His arms were clasped behind his back, in the posture of his elders (how subtle the influence of our breeding, I thought).

"'There are poor people everywhere, soldiers everywhere!' Jesus continued. 'The priests in their beautiful robes don't care! No one cares! I ache for justice. There must be justice, but where, where can it be found?' He cried to no one in particular, yet everyone, for there is not a man alive today who has not heard this cry of our people. I knew the teachings of the old man, and I remembered too the urgency of my youth. In Jesus' youthful mind, everything was immediate. I could see that he needed time to ripen. The teachings of this master took time, and Jesus could not wait.

"Then as I silently watched, Jesus suddenly stopped his pacing, and his head slowly bowed and cocked to the side as if he were listening to some inner voice that only he could hear. He was strangely silent for the longest period; there was not the slightest sound in the room, as his teacher and I watched this wonderful young soul mature, ever so slightly. Jesus finally began to speak in a low, slow voice. As he did, the old man turned his head toward me, and in his eyes I read his thoughts:

'The time of his teaching is over.' I knew then that I had to let him go. My plans for him were ended.

"My attention turned back from the old man to our young charge. Then, with a peculiar look etched upon his face and in a voice quite strange, soft, and otherworldly, Jesus said as if to no one in particular, 'Karma takes time... and I approve it anyway.'"

Nicodemus looked into my eyes; his own eyes pleaded with me to grasp the mystery he had so recently penetrated. "I tell you, Asher, I didn't understand what he meant then, but I do now. When I sat with him the other night, Asher, I knew. He is the One for whom we have been waiting.

"Asher, he is the Messiah!"

Chapter 9

First Warning

See, all your angry enemies lie confused and shattered. Anyone opposing you will die. You will look for them in vain—they will all be gone. I am holding you by your right hand—I the Lord your God—and I say to you, Don't be afraid; I am here to help you. Despised through you are, fear not, O Israel; for I will help you. I am the Lord, your Redeemer; I am the Holy One of Israel.

Isaiah 41:11-14

During the days of the Feast Jesus would walk each day to the Temple. However, after the celebration of the Feast, I noted that Jesus immediately took leave of the city. There had been a terrible confrontation with the priests over a manifestation of God's power that he instigated on the Sabbath, a thing I too thought he should never have done. Oh Lord, so much I had to learn! When the trouble arose, I immediately warned Jesus of what Nicodemus had said about trouble brewing, but it seemed to have no effect on him. This man operated from an inner guidance, not one that any of us who followed him could know or understand.

Once Jesus left for Galilee, I began to listen much more carefully to the Temple gossip, which through practice I had learned to ignore in the past since I thought it petty. Now, however, I found new reason to hear, and thus newly attuned, I found great cause to grow uneasy for the safety of my Lord. I became so concerned that I took it upon myself to ride with my servant to the north, to Galilee, to warn Jesus of what was transpiring in dark corridors and behind locked doors.

I am ashamed to say that I still took great care to let no one know that I was a follower of the man called Jesus, the Galilean. I justified it in my mind by saying that he needed a hidden follower in the Sanhedrim to keep him informed of the treachery being hatched with ever greater vigor each day, but we both knew that was not really true. I was simply afraid of losing everything that I had worked so hard for: my position, my wealth, and, of course, my image in front of my peers. I thought that I had much to lose, but for those who were not followers, there was even more to lose. There was far too much at stake for those in power to allow some "pretender to the throne," as they would say, to arouse the passions of the people against them, against Herod, or—Lord forbid—against even the Roman Eagle itself.

The remembrances of the massacres and excesses that took place when the great Herod died were still all too fresh in the leaders' minds. They had lived through insurrection and wished to avoid it happening again at all costs. So they bided their time, waiting and watching, knowing that it was only a matter of time until Jesus would make that fatal slip of the tongue, and then they would have him. I might add, in humble honesty, the leisure and wealth we enjoyed in Jerusalem depended on the peace of our little nation, such as it was, and on how well we were able to get along with our masters from afar. We were truly just pawns and spoils of war.

In any case, it matters little what I say in my own defense. You will judge me as you will. I know I was weak, but I have been harsher on myself than on any other, so I am able to continue and share with you if you will allow. Because he taught me by example to open myself to others, to expose myself to others, no matter the risk, no matter how much of a fool I appear to be, I will tell you of my life with him in hopes that it will help you to understand him. I do it willingly. He used to plead with us to hear, if we had ears to hear and, to see if we had eyes to see. I ask you to do no less.

Jesus was a soul who suffered more and loved more than we can ever comprehend. Come to Galilee with me, the Galilee he loved, and see him as I saw him, talk to his disciples as I talked with them, open yourself to him through an old man's heart and eyes. You have probably already heard many other stories, some true, some not, I suppose, but these were special times I had with Jesus that I thought you might like to share.

I found Jesus in Galilee without trouble. It was never hard to find him anymore, for wherever he went there were crowds, whether in the towns, on the lake, or in the hills—even in Judea I could find him, if I but knew the general area. So, when I arrived at the lake in the afternoon, at the mouth of the Jordan River, we simply rode westward, then north, following the shore to the northern end of the lake. We rode around Tiberias (Antipas' newly built capital). This was a city Jesus would not enter because Antipas built it upon a cemetery, and thus the land would always remain unclean.

Once past Tiberias we began watching the low-lying hills hoping to spot a crowd of people.

The Sea of Galilee (or the Sea of Tiberias as it was beginning to be called) was one of the most beautiful areas in all the land. In late fall, as it was then, it was most pleasing indeed—neither too hot nor too cold—for Galilee is the most gentling of places to be. The sun shone brightly that day as we skirted the edge of Tiberias by hugging the hills to the west. Once past Magdala and Gennesaret we dropped back once again along the shoreline and found the lake absolutely calm, like a piece of polished glass, reflecting the pastel pink-gray clouds from above the eastern hills. The closer we got to Capernaum, the lighter my spirits became, and as we rounded the north end of the lake and headed east, I could barely keep from singing with joy, for this was his country, and I knew he would be close at hand.

A bit west of Capernaum we spotted the group I had expected. Numbering nearly fifty, they gathered at the top of a small rise, a short distance up from the shore. I urged my lathered steed up the hill, carefully guiding him around the large black basalt stones that littered the hillside and hid in the tall grasses, stones that could lame the unsuspecting man or beast walking unwarily off the beaten path. The stones, which were common all over the area, had been spewed about the landscape in ancient times by a long-forgotten volcano from a time of fire and fury long before man ever set foot here, and they added an unusual quality to the otherwise beautifully peaceful countryside.

Jesus watched us approach. He could see us coming at a far distance from his vantage point on the hill overlooking the shore and the placid waters below. As we came close enough for him to recognize us, I could see a smile spread over his face, for he was genuinely delighted with our arrival.

Afraid of disturbing those who had gathered, we dismounted a distance away and closed the gap on foot. Jesus waved to me to come close, then bid me come through the crowd to sit by his side. With a gentle smile on his sunburned face he clasped my arm and pulled me down to sit upon a robe that had been spread upon the ground for him to rest. His eyes hesitated just a moment in mine, and I could see the smiling laugh lines that were being etched upon his sun-darkened face, so much outside was he in those busy days. In that moment's pause, a love passed between us that would have made a trip four times as far well worth the effort.

Still smiling, he turned to the people seated about him, enjoying this scene of welcome for an old friend of his, and introduced me by saying simply, "This is my beloved disciple from Judea. He has come this far to see me." The crowd was warm and relaxed, and murmurs of welcome could be heard from them as he continued. "He has come to warn me of the trouble I am in, haven't you, Asher ben Ammi?" I was startled to hear him discern the cause of my trip before I had time to even say a word in reply to his greeting.

Before I could question him, he held up his hand for silence and cocked his head, listening.

The crowd heard it too. It was the sound of a rapidly approaching rider atop thundering hooves, apparently hidden from our immediate view by a row of bushes and trees up the hill to our rear. Because Jesus and I were facing the water, I had to turn to see who came this way alone, off the normal road. Without turning, Jesus addressed the small crowd around him in a low voice that carried a sense of authority, control, and a total lack of fear. "Listen carefully, all of you. No matter who rides this way, I wish you to remain calm. Watch me, not him, and listen to the words I say."

No sooner had these words escaped his lips than I saw a surprised rider pull his steed to a halt as they came around the row of trees and onto the mass of people sitting in their path. The horse, not expecting the crowd, shied as if it had come across a lion.

With nostrils flaring, the beautiful beast reared and pawed at the air with powerful hooves. Its bit tore into its foaming mouth, and its reins jingled taut as the owner pulled back violently to keep from being thrown to the rock-strewn ground.

The rider soothed his high-spirited horse with expert hands, then, holding tightly back on the reins, he slowly pranced the nervous animal the rest of the way down the hill to where we sat. There he stopped, looking down imperiously from atop his horse at the seated man of no apparent means who held the assemblage tranquilly in his hand. All the while, Jesus, impassive to the commotion, calmly kept the rapt attention of the crowd with easing words meant to soothe the troubled and worried among them. Because I was the only one, save Jesus, with my back to the rider as he came upon us, I was the only one turned completely about when Jesus asked us to ignore the newcomer. I turned my attention away from the rider, but not before I identified him in my mind for later use.

The rider was a Roman of very high rank, judging from the cut and colors of his tunic and the quality of armor he wore. This ominous intrusion was of the most dreaded kind, for one never knew what a Roman might do in such situations, and common sense dictated that no one should provoke him in any way. Our very presence was cause enough to bring about his fury. The faces of the people, however, rather than being wide-eyed with awe or fear, showed no immediate reaction of any kind, so commanding was Jesus' presence on them.

The Roman's name, I was later to discover, was Placidus, a Tribune, elected to uphold the rights of the plebeians against the patricians.

I met him some months later in the Baths, wherein he approached me, saying that he too recognized me from the one chance meeting on that lonely hill in the backwaters of Rome's far-flung empire.

Placidus, if not a follower of my Master, did become an admirer of his and later wished me to tell him all I knew of "the man with the strange eyes," as he called Jesus. Placidus so impressed me with his sincerity that I subsequently met him on several occasions in Jerusalem just to share what I knew of the man he accidentally ran into in Galilee that day. It was thus, in meeting with him quite by accident, that I was to hear his point of view of the chance meeting that afternoon in Galilee. The story, as it tumbled from the lips of this Roman, showed me once again what an incredible effect our Master had on all those who came into contact with him—both friend and foe.

Placidus was on his way to Jerusalem, but instead of going directly there from Rome, he landed instead in Tyre three days earlier, for he carried instructions to the Tetrarch Philip, son of Herod the Great, from the emperor and the senate. He had ridden hard all the first day to reach Caesarea Philippi in a timely fashion. He then spent the rest of the day and all the next consulting with Philip on matters of state. He had enjoyed the mild day in Caesarea and wished he could have stayed longer before heading south, but duty called him to Jerusalem.

While in the newly built and beautiful city, however, he was determined to make the best of it. In the afternoon he rested in the spacious quarters provided to him for his use. And in the cool of the evening, before the dinner in his honor was to be served, he enjoyed walking the terraces with one of Philip's daughters. The terrace below his room overlooked the sweeping plains of Gaulanitis and hung suspended directly above the tree-lined banks of a beautiful stream, meandering its way rapidly to the Sea of Galilee in the south. Philip had constructed the city of Caesarea atop the Greek city, Panias by name. He named the new city in honor of Caesar Augustus and spent quite a bit of his time in this lovely city. Built on a grassy plain spread out from the foot of a large bluff, it was the northernmost fortification of Philip's kingdom and the center of his government. From the base of the cliff sprung clean, pure water, as if from a magical source. The water flowed with a delightful gush into pools below. In the face of the cliff, just above the pools, was a cave dedicated to the god Pan, and several rock-cut niches still housed statues of his nymphs.

But no matter how lovely the city and the company, Placidus had come to this land to accomplish a task, and thus the following morning he was up and on his way before dawn.

Placidus started down the easy slopes toward Capernaum, feeling the wind in his face and, under him, the powerful steed that carried him easily on its back. The Roman felt happy and curious about this land of which he had heard so much.

As he loped the morning away, he took bread and meat from his leather bag and sipped at the wine in the skin.

On and on he galloped. He told me his mind wandered to the people and the land he was in as he descended down the hills into the valley to the south.

"I wonder what these people are like?" he mused. "I read that they're a stubborn and excitable lot. They don't accept us even yet, after all these years and with all the autonomy we have given them. Strange.

I hear that we conquered them, yet in their own minds they are free. Strange qualities, these Jews. How can they say we've never conquered them? They are under our fists, aren't they? Already I don't understand them—but I will—by the gods, I will!"

He was quite a storyteller, and although I cringed at the words he used and his perceptions of my people and our land, I showed it not; nor did I voice any objection, for he was Roman and I a Jew. Had it not been for the teachings of my Master, I would not have been able to listen to the arrogance of this man; even though he meant nothing by it, it cut deeply into my skin. To him, Rome was the world. So, I rendered unto Caesar his due and, taking a deep breath, opened my ears to hear him continue his tale anew.

He said that he made a slight change of direction as he left the well-traveled route and struck out across the open hillside to skirt just north of the town of Capernaum, along the northern ridge. He didn't want to be held up by any minor functionary in the border town that marked the line between the two tetrarchs Philip and Antipas. Insignificant officials were always trying to court the favor of Rome by being nauseatingly accommodating to anyone of rank who happened their way, and he wanted none of it.

His horse carried him along the high ridge overlooking the lake that now spread out before him like a blue, mist-covered jewel. Breaking past a fence line of dark black basalt stones, he turned his steed downhill toward the water. As he cleared the last small hillock and carefully guided the horse through the rock-strewn field, he whipped his horse into a gallop, seeing his day's goal, Tiberias, in the mist-shrouded distance far down the western side of the lake.

As he broke past a heavy line of trees, seemingly out of nowhere, there appeared a gathering of about forty or fifty people sitting on the ground before him. The unexpectedness of this find frightened his horse, which reared and pawed at the air, threatening to throw its rider from its back. But Placidus, an expert rider, having spent most of his adult life on the back of a horse, instantly soothed and stroked his horse as the great beast nervously snorted, pranced, and sidestepped in wide-eyed terror, fighting against its new owner's practiced, calming hand. Placidus slowed the horse to a walk, and then sidestepped him dangerously close to the seated crowd below him, affecting all the grandeur that his Roman presence commanded and expecting an immediate subservient response.

I remembered the event from my own perspective sitting below that powerful beast. I could smell its lathered body and actually feel its breath close at hand. I recalled the rough jingling of the horse's reins and his master's armor and weapon slapping against each other and the leather they both wore.

From Placidus' perspective, he couldn't believe his eyes! No one in the crowd moved, not a single soul. Their attention was riveted upon a man, roughly thirty years of age, seated on the ground before them. This man, who from all outward appearances was no different from the rest, was speaking in such a low voice that Placidus could not hear his words.

"They're not paying any attention to me!" he thought. "How incredibly strange; we bring fear wherever we go, but I have no effect on them whatsoever. That's some power the young man has over them," he admired. "I am Rome, and yet they are all ignoring me, and so is their leader." As he jerked his horse's reins to stop its pacing, he studied this young man more carefully and thought with startling humor, "He uses a lot of hand gestures; he would make a good senator."

He watched the young man in the center of the crowd for quite a while. Nothing was said. He just watched. Placidus told me that he felt compelled to just sit there and stare; he didn't know why. It was as if the man had cast a spell. Jesus never slowed his speech as his head started slowly to turn in the stranger's direction.

Then it happened! This Jesus, a simple man of no means, a quiet man, on a quiet hill, in the fall of the fifteenth year of the reign of Tiberias, met the Roman's eyes—and held them.

"By the gods, look at those eyes!" Placidus' mind roared. "He's possessed! I have to get out of here. There's no fear in those eyes. His eyes are burning, burning into mine! Move! I must leave this accursed place. I must go!" His mind was now screaming at him. But he couldn't move, for Jesus' eyes were slashing their way into his skull—into his soul.

I too remembered that day as if it had just happened. The air was electric with the tension.

Then, as suddenly as it began, it ended. Jesus slowly lowered his eyes to the people seated about him, each of whom (including me) held his or her breath, not daring to breathe, let alone to chance a glance or a guess at what was about to happen.

Suddenly free of my Master's will, the Roman wheeled his horse about and spurred it into a headlong run for the freedom of the sea. "I will find you again, my man," he yelled back across his shoulder in Greek. "I know not who you are, but someday I will find you again."

As the dust settled, the sound of the galloping horse was lost into the valley beyond, and the peace of the hill returned. You could hear an audible sigh from the crowd around Jesus as they let out their breaths in unison.

Jesus once again turned his attention to those who awaited him, enraptured and terrified by what they had just witnessed. Never before had anyone seen a Roman flee before a Jew.

In hidden whispers behind hands, in quizzical looks from one to another, and in all of their minds, the people began to ask themselves who this man must be to perform a miracle such as this. But Jesus, sensing that they thought to make him a leader of man against man, sought in a subtle way to change their minds by example. For the people still looked for a warrior king, and I knew enough of our Lord by now to realize that his kingdom was not one of this earth. Not this man.

Jesus spoke to them in a soft voice filled with concern, his brow wrinkled as he tried to express what he needed them to understand. "The Romans are like beasts of prey," he said. "So I ask you, if you are cornered by a beast of prey, do you show fear?"

He stopped, waiting until he knew they were all following him. "No. If you do, he will attack. He will sense your fear and attack. I say to you, look them in their eyes, face your tests with calmness and no fear, and they will not attack. The Romans, as you have seen, and those like them are wild beasts let loose in the world today. You must learn to live with them, you must not fear them; they are not of our world, for our world is with our Father, and He watches over you with love, beyond your understanding.

"If you lived in the forest, and it was there you wished to stay, but you found the forest filled with wild creatures of the land, then you would have to learn to live with them in harmony and peace. You would learn to give them space; you would know not to antagonize them. You would learn their ways, and you would learn to avoid them. Yet in this forest there can also live the hunter, who lives to curse and kill the animals of prey. He lives to struggle with them, and he misses the sweetness of the day. You can live in the same realm as the hunter and in the same forest with the beasts of prey and yet be touched by neither of them. Do as I have taught you if you are confronted. Did you see what just happened with the Roman? Did you understand? I ask you, did he stay? Did he hound you? No, he rode his way!

"I am the way. Do as I do. I will teach you a better way: a way to live, a way to love, and a way to be free. Loose the thongs that bind you. For too long the scribes and the Pharisees have bound you to laws of fear, my brothers and sisters; loose them, and throw them away!"

Jesus was sitting cross-legged, bent forward and holding his arms upright and out as if he had just been cut free of his imaginary binding. His expression was tense, his eyes pleading. "Don't you see? You can be free. Loose your spirit, for God is only love, and He loves you. God loves you as He loves me. I am not different from you. I am you. Do as I have shown you each day. Loose the thongs that bind you and you shall be free!"

Some of the people were smiling now. A mixed look of relief and peaceful ecstasy had found its way across their faces. The strain and fear so real a few moments before had vanished. Some were quietly crying, tears silently rolling down the brown, weathered cheeks of these simple people—his people. In some magical way, this incredible man of peace was touching everyone there.

"Lift your eyes to your Father; look about you, He is everywhere. He loves you as you love your own children. Look there," he nodded toward a young woman who was holding a precious child fast asleep against her breast, a child who had slept peacefully through the life-threatening confrontation of the moments before.

His voice lowered and softened to a compassionate whisper. "See that woman with her arms around her child? Think you not that our Father loves you much more than even she can love her babe? I say to you, He can and does. He cries with you, He loves with you. He has given you life; He breathed it into you. Think you not that He rejoices in your living of it fully and warmly?

"Throw down your burdens. They are worth nothing. Seek your Father above all things. He will provide for you in all things. Lift up your eyes to the high places and let your hearts soar to the mountaintops.

I say to you, take my hand, step with me into the starry night sky. Let me be your guide, and we will fly. We will fly, as the angels do. You shall have no fear. Your Father in heaven is a loving God, not someone to fear. He is a part of you, even now as I speak."

Then, pausing, Jesus looked at a man who sat a little way down the hill and off to one side. "Look too at that man with his son, the son who sleeps quietly in his lap without a fear, without a care. Become as a child; trust as you did then. Curl up in your Father's arms and He will surround you with His light and love.

"I say to you, love one another as I have loved you. You feel my heart; you know my love. Feel His love, which is greater than mine. Go to Him in the private places of your heart. He will be waiting."

There was silence then, as each in our own way thought on his words, thought of our own lives, thought of our own fears, hopes, and aspirations. And I loved him.

I simply loved him.

"It's time now," Jesus said with a tone of finality that meant we were coming to the end of his time with us this day. "It is time that I go, my Father calls me. It is time that you, too, go back to your work, back to your villages, to your husbands, your wives, and your lovers—but know in your heart that God is your only true love.

"For those of you who have lovers now, think on what I am about to tell you, and for those of you who have known no lovers for a long time, remember back. What pleases you more than anything when you are in love?" He paused to look from one to another. "I will tell you." He gestured for emphasis. "It is doing something wonderful for your lover, something that will bring him or her happiness.

"God is your lover. He can find nothing that brings Him more joy than to bring you happiness. He does not shut the door; He seeks a love affair with you. Open your door at sunset, in the calm of the evening, or in the quiet morning hours before dawn. Open your door and find Him waiting there. He will bring you the purest of love, beauty, and happiness that you can imagine.

"Go now. Go in peace. I will be with you always."

The crowd slowly began to rise, the older more slowly than the young. After sitting for a long time, I understood their plight, for my joints had become stiff and sore—the riding I had done hadn't helped either. Jesus rose as well, brushing and shaking off the dust, grass, and dirt clods that had been thrown on us from the horse stopping so near.

He walked a few steps over to where his disciples were standing in a little knot talking among themselves, said a few words to them, patted Peter on the back with a smile, and returned to me. "Asher, you rode a long way to be with me. Let's go."

With that, he abruptly turned and headed west down the hill away from Capernaum. I turned to find my horse, only to see that Peter had grabbed its reins and was leading it and my servant away in the opposite direction. I turned back to Jesus, who was now striding rapidly down the hill ahead of me. "Wait, Lord!" I cried, and hurried my short old legs down the hill after him.

When I caught up to him, I was out of breath and had to stop, bending over with my hands on my knees, panting and gasping for air. Jesus leaned over to look at me, his mature muscles in their prime, hardened by years of work, lifting and plying wood and stone, and now over a year of walking in the open countryside of Galilee. It surely made me wish for my youth again. "I am sorry, Asher," he said, "my mind was occupied with a thousand things. I will walk more slowly." With that, he sat back on his haunches, waiting for me to recover.

No longer in a hurry, he stared out upon the placid waters, now showing the deepening, warm yellows of the late afternoon sun. In a wistful voice, still staring out over the land he loved, he reminisced. "I used to be able to come here alone. No one came nearer than the foot of the hill. From here I used to watch man and beast making their way to and from the mixed blood of Capernaum; and alone, I could find time for my Father. It was here, in the beginning, that I gathered strength. But peace is no longer mine. It seems I can't find it anywhere. Unless I leave far before dawn and climb high into the hills to seek my Abba, my beloved Abba, they will find me and hound me for miracles. Miracles, that is all they want! Cannot they see, Asher, I seek not to give them a meal, I seek to teach them to fish the plentiful waters themselves. I seek to take them to their Father who provides all things."

Looking up into the deepening blue of the sky, he intoned, "Oh, God, You have taught me in such a loving way. You are in me—I feel your presence like the softest dream. Never do I speak without feeling you as One with me. Oh, beloved God, I am caught up in you and in my Oneness with you. I gather them to me to teach them, to help them feel your touch, to make it as real to them as you are to me.

"But, it comes so slowly, dear Father. Do I have time? Month after month I try, and with most of them, those I will have to depend on, I seem no closer to opening them than I was the first day I found them. Dear Father, talk through me I pray, help them to see you and know you as I know you. Help them to see you through my eyes, hear you through my ears, feel you through my body."

I had never heard Jesus sharing the intimacy of his heart and soul this way. I felt almost as if I was eavesdropping, hearing him pray to our Father this way. I didn't know if in this strange mood he remembered that he wasn't alone, that I was standing by his side as he squatted, staring out over the placid waters of the sea. I had not experienced this closeness with him before and knew no one who had. This glimpse of my teacher was so rare, so precious, that I didn't dare move. I scarcely wanted to breathe. I felt so honored to be here with him at this extraordinary time, and I felt so sorry for him. He was always giving, never taking in return, and yet in Judea, there were some who wanted him out of the way… permanently.

Of course now, as I sit to write, these many months later, I know that the greatest cruelty of all was yet to come.

Chapter 10

The Time of Waiting

Then one day Jesus came from Nazareth in Galilee, and was baptized by John there in the Jordan River. The moment Jesus came up out of the water, he saw the heavens open and the Holy Spirit in the form of a dove descending on him, and a voice from heaven said, "You are my beloved Son; you are my Delight."

Mark 1:9-11

When my Lord finished praying, he sat forward on his haunches, arms wrapped about his knees, staring at nothing I could see. Then he blinked and kind of shivered, as if a chill had run through his body. He smiled at me with that sheepish little grin, then stood up and slowly stretched the whole length of his body. It had been a long day, from before dawn until now, late in the afternoon, and he still wasn't done. He couldn't rest because now he had me.

He turned toward me. "Ready?" he asked. I nodded my head yes, and we headed down the hill toward the water once again, but this time in the leisurely manner that leads to an easy communication between two friends who share a special love.

"Did you talk to Nicodemus, Asher?" Jesus asked, as we slowly approached the shore and turned west away from Capernaum, toward Gennesaret.

"Yes, Lord, I did. He was very helpful to me. He told me everything that he remembered, up to the point of your leaving Jerusalem. He was the one who set me to listening and watching in the Temple for any plots the priests were hatching against you. I have also employed two others I trust to do the same in my absence, Lord. I will get word to you as soon as possible if I feel it is important."

He didn't say anything, just sadly shook his head, then bent down to pick up a flat stone and skip it across the water toward Tiberias in the distance. "I used to love to do that as a child," Jesus said. "There were such few good stones like that in Egypt, so it was a rare find indeed, for there was mostly sand and more sand. A rock like that was not one to be wasted on oneself, but savored for showing off to a friend."

Once again we just walked quietly along the shore. I felt that there was something he wanted to share with me, but I couldn't pry, so I waited quietly. After walking the better part of an hour, we approached the outskirts of Gennesaret. He motioned to a large black boulder near the water's edge and there invited me to rest. We put our backs to the large, timeworn stone, and finally my beloved Master began to speak.

For me, hearing his voice was like hearing the angels sing. Unlike his younger disciples, I was far too old to worry about position or place with him, nor could I walk with him on the long, hot, dusty roads between towns as they did. My only joy came during the quiet times with him. But, dear God, these were the finest hours of my life, for at these times he, too, was relaxed and introspective, and in a sharing mood. I was simply a friend he could trust. I was not one he had to prepare to send out among the wolves. I was simply one to listen to his thoughts un-couched in parables and aphorisms that kept him safe from Herod's spies.

As if he read the feelings within me, Jesus said, "The quiet times are most important, Asher. Make sure you are your own best friend, so that you fear not being by yourself and going within. I had to learn that again, Asher, after returning from Jerusalem. I had to learn to be alone all over again.

"Asher, do you know what it was like to come back from the Holy City after three years of study with the finest minds in the land? Three years of intellectual straining and growth—then Nazareth—a carpenter shop—and nothing!

"I almost went crazy. This was truly my time for growth and testing. Others think the testing of my will and strength comes now, but I tell you, this is no test. The testing is past. Now I see the end, and there is nothing this world can throw against me that will stay me from that light. Please, Asher, let me tell you of that time between heaven and hell, the many years of waiting."

I felt a sense of urgency in the way he spoke, as if he needed to tell someone and relieve himself of the burden before he could get on to his other work. The telling itself didn't take that long. It was the feeling that came from him that utterly overwhelmed me; and as I retell his story, I pray you put yourself in my place, along that same rock-strewn shore, at the softest time of the day, and hear his words the way I did that day.

"When I returned home I was sixteen and considered a man," Jesus told me. "I took my place in the synagogue, and I took my place in my father's growing home. There were now four brothers, the last boy being named Judas, and a sister, Sarah, with one more yet to come, and all had to be clothed and fed. That was the year I met a girl in Cana named Julia, and although I saw her only once, it was love in my heart that I felt for her from that day on. It was six months more before we went to visit relatives again in the village, and all the long days as I wrestled with the wood and learned my trade, the thought of her was what kept me alive, kept me at my work in the shop.

"When I look back now, I am sure it was God's hand that gave me this time. For I know also that I would have gone mad with boredom and run away if it had not been for the thoughts of winning the hand of that maiden, who in my heart loomed larger than anything I had learned in Jerusalem. In my wonderfully imaginative, youthful mind, I dreamt of becoming the finest craftsman in all of Israel, earning fees from the wealthy and powerful so that I could make for her a home. It was she who kept me at the bench all the long days after my return.

"I think it was God's hand too that held me from going back to the nearby village of Cana for so long. For had I gone back earlier I would have found that she had been betrothed shortly after my first visit, and it was not meant to be that I would know her touch or feel her arms around me when I needed to be held. The fire within me burned strong and bright, then died as quickly as it had come. As time went on, I was to understand that if I had not wanted this woman more desperately than I had wanted anything before, if I had not known how the thinking mind can lose its sway, if I had not yearned for her in every way a man can yearn, I would never have been able to understand those same feelings in another.

"But I do understand, Asher, as it is with you. Your beautiful Miriamme is less than half your age, for which you have taken much abuse, yet when I look at the two of you I see only the true love that binds you." I looked at Jesus, and in his eyes I found the incredible understanding and deep love he was capable of. He judged me not that my sweet wife was a girl of twenty and I an old man just over sixty, for I did love this woman with all my heart, as she did me.

I wondered at this simple man named Jesus, who could share a part of himself and make each and every soul who heard him feel that the sharing was meant specially for him or for her. I say her because he taught there was no difference between men and women in God's eyes and so, even though it was far more difficult for women to seek him out, they did so in surprising numbers, some even following him from place to place, which was a cause of angst among his closest disciples, but he never turned them away.

He sighed deeply, and then leaned back against the stone. Fearing that he would stop, I begged him to continue, if it wasn't asking too much. He turned his head toward me again, smiled a smile of yielding, and continued on his way.

"After Julia, nothing meant very much to me for a long while. I did what was expected of me, but I fear that my father was at his wit's end with me. Nothing that he or any of the family could say brought me joy. I am ashamed to say that I reveled in my unhappiness, and I fear that I learned to enjoy the attention I derived from it. I had become an insufferable, self-centered, brooding young man. I also developed a religious snobbishness that was unconscionable. I knew I was better than any in our little village, and in the synagogue I showed my knowledge of the Law with smugness, to everyone's distaste. I was not sharing what God had planted there for all to see—quite the opposite. I was using my knowledge to make them realize their own stupidity. I was worse than the worst of the Temple priests.

"Now, Asher, do you see why I lash out at them when I have the opportunity? I see in their smug priggishness, me."

Of course, I recognized what he was saying right away. We Pharisees had a way of making everyone think that we were better than they were. We had started our sect to make the Law of the Sadducees more livable for the common man, but ended up making more laws than man could ever live with. And for the "uneducated of Galilee" we even made special dispensations; otherwise, none of them could have entered the Temple "clean."

Although he told the story on himself, my conscience burned with the lessons learned. I am also sure that my Master knew all this, even though one would never know it from his look or the way he spoke. Jesus had difficult lessons to learn in his youth, but learn them he did, for this man was now a soul of infinite love. Yet the other side of him was certainly not unknown, for when he felt that it was necessary and due he could deliver a tongue lashing like no one else I knew.

But, I digress again, so let me continue. It was about here in his narrative that we watched the giant red orb we call the sun slowly come to rest over the hills to the west approximately where Nazareth lay, then sink into the very hills themselves, as if being absorbed in some magical way.

"My father became very sick when I was eighteen years old," Jesus continued, "and lingered ill and unable to help until I was twenty-two, when I became the head of the house—a position that ill suited me. It was this event that caused me once again to reevaluate my life. I loved my father terribly, and to see him wither away in my sight, day by day, had the most sobering effect on me. For this, too, I give thanks; for it was in my love for my father that I learned to lose myself in someone else's pain. It was through the love that he had poured into me that I was finally able to see that truly it is in forgetting ourselves that we find ourselves in the end.

"Lessons come so hard for us all, Asher; we add them one by one, and the hardest lessons of all are probably the most lasting.

"In the long years that followed, I learned that each lesson was like the leaf of a tree. With each lesson, we add a leaf to the branch that is us in the lifetime we are experiencing. Once all the leaves of a lifetime have been added and the life is complete, we add the limb to the trunk. With each life then, we continue to add new limbs to the trunk of the tree, until someday we become complete: the beautiful, full tree that God intended us to be. And the most beautiful tree of all, Asher," he said, with a large smile on his face, his arms upraised in a gesture of humble supplication, "is God!"

He reached out to pull me to my feet. "Come," he said, "you are my guest for a change, and a feast is being prepared for you tonight."

I smiled with heartfelt gratitude toward this man of miracles and held out my hands to meet his. He lifted me to my feet with one easy motion, for I was but a feather to this strong young carpenter from

Galilee. We started walking back eastward toward his city, but we did not hurry. As we walked, we stayed close to the water's edge, where its lapping on the stones made music in our ears. As we walked I asked him questions, for there were many holes in the fabric of his life I was weaving.

"Lord, I know much now of your growing up. But tell me, these last ten years or so, what have you been about? And what took you so long?" I added with feigned reproach. "If you had started ten years ago, I would have been young enough to enjoy you more!"

My Master stopped dead in his tracks, and then with a howl of delight said, "You'd better start running, old man, lest I throw you in the water this night!" With this admonition, he made motions of throwing me into the lake; I for my part started to run as if for my life. "You had better run, you old fool," he shouted after me in a mocking manner, shaking his fist. "If I had come ten years ago," he yelled, "you would have been too busy counting your money to have even seen me to your door! And I, old man, I would have thrown you in the lake!" He took a few leaping steps and was on me. The look of mock rage had melted into a bellyaching laugh. He dipped his hand into the lake and sent a cascade of water into my face.

As I wiped my face with my robe Jesus gave me a heartfelt hug, then together, arm in arm, we walked back into town.

There were no more serious discussions that night, for Peter and his family had provided a scrumptious meal, delightful company, and the most wonderful sleeping mat I had ever slept on (or so it seemed to me that night). Perhaps I was just tired, and, having reached my destination, could finally slacken. I didn't wake in my little room until far past the hour of work. Upon entering the family room, I found everyone had gone except Peter's mother and John, son of Zebedee, whom Jesus had asked to stay behind and wait until I woke.

Counting this day, which was the day of Sabbath eve, I stayed nine more days. These days of warm, sunny weather and cool evenings still remain with me, for it was during this period of time, away from family and responsibilities, that I relaxed and listened, watched and waited. Each afternoon save two, Jesus walked back to town with me alone from wherever he was teaching that day. I was also able to spend much time with John of Zebedee, and I learned much about him. He turned out to be my watch-mate for I was not as young and energetic as the young men surrounding Jesus, nor Jesus himself, and my Lord made accommodations for me by way of John. I would rise when I felt refreshed, and after my morning fruit and bread, John would guide me to Jesus that day. I found John to be young enough, and I old enough, for him to be open and totally honest with me about his understanding of the teachings of Jesus and his feelings toward him, especially because of John's special place as a disciple—one of the twelve.

As these beautiful days wore on with Jesus, I gained more and more insight into this special man whom God had sent here to us to teach us of His love. Our leisurely afternoon walks gave Jesus time to clarify for me much of what was rolling around in my mind and help me with some of the concepts that I had been wondering about as well.

It seemed that he was almost compelled to tell me of his life, in a way that I never heard him speak when he was with the crowds, nor even when he was alone with those that traveled with him. It was as if my age and years of experience afforded me a special vantage point, a certain perspective with which to look upon his life.

One day as we walked back to Capernaum from the countryside of Bethsaida, he hung back with me to be out of earshot of the rest, then began to speak to me in such earnestness that I had to take particular note. As he spoke, I felt that he had a special need for me to understand him. It was as if everyone who was close to him (his followers and disciples) were so awed by him that he could not truly have a friend—just a friend—to share both his joy and pain alike, without pretense or judgment. At this particular time in his life, I was humbly honored to fill that role, for although I was impressed with the miracles, I came not for that reason and paid them little heed—for I came to find his soul.

I could tell that he was already deep in thought as we walked along, for suddenly, without looking up from the dusty path we traversed, he opened the conversation between us almost in mid-thought, saying, "I had to fill that empty hole in my soul!" He looked at me as if pleading for me, for anyone, to hear and understand him.

"Can you understand, Asher? It gnawed at me like a wild animal, a wild animal never able to satisfy its hunger. It almost drove me insane. No one I knew had that gnawing pain, that hunger inside—for God, or woman, I knew not which. I only knew that there was a yearning in my soul, a fire that needed to be fed, and the more I fed its flames by living, the more the fire grew, until it raged within me without ceasing. And

I was pent up and could speak of this to no man, no woman. With no person could I share what was hidden there within me. There was no one I could talk to! Not my mother, who loved me but could think only of caring for my sick father and feeding our large family; nor did my brothers or sisters care to understand.

"The weight of providing for the family was overwhelming to me at that time. I wished to flee the wood shop whenever I had a chance, yet my guilt for not doing just a little bit more for my family, to earn just one coin more, wore on me more and more. Fortunately, by the time father died, my brother Jacob was able to do everything that I could do (and quite a bit better I might add), and Joses wasn't far behind, although, like me, he wouldn't ply the trade once full grown. Then in the next ten years, Simon and Judas grew into the trade, and my load was lightened considerably, until finally I was away more than I was there."

We stopped. This time it was I who pointed to a place to sit and talk, for I wanted to give my Lord my undivided attention, which I could not do while we walked along the rocky path. He seemed more than willing, waving on the others when they looked back to see what made us tarry. I spread my robe on a grassy knoll, and in his supple, easy manner he dropped down to the ground and lay flat out on his back looking up unto the heavens, the heavens that he tried so hard to share with us but as yet only he was able to see.

"I know that God put me in my particular family," Jesus told me, "without a wife, and without position, so that I would yearn mightily for Him, so that I would desire Him more than my life itself. And I did. I knew I was the One who was to come, Asher. I don't know how I knew, I just knew, and that is a terrible burden to carry. I knew of all the Scriptures that foretold of the coming, I knew them all. Yet there were so many missing pieces yet to fall. I felt my chest constrict with the pain of constant waiting. I would pray, 'When? Oh, God, please tell me when. Show me a sign, dear Father, show me a sign!' I pleaded over and over, night after night, month after month, year after year.

"And when my lessons had been learned, and I proved myself strong in His ways, he showed me a sign—and the sign was John. He was howling in the desert, and from that desert wild, I could hear him whispering my name. I heard him—no, it was more—I could feel him. I could feel him pulling me, and I had to drop my tools and go to him.

"I headed south and found him near Bethabara.

"As I approached the crowd lining the banks of the river where John was baptizing people, it was as if they were not there, so centered was I. I saw only John. I walked slowly toward him. The crowd began to part in front of me, I know not why, and slowly into the unhurried, hip-deep current I waded.

"When I stepped from the crowded shore into the water and started to wade toward John, I was already in ecstasy. My whole life had focused on this point in time, my time of initiation. Every cell of my being had prepared for my time of opening. At this appointed place, at this tiny green strip of land along the river called Jordan, the whole of the universe stopped for an instant as God reached down through the heavens to touch one simple human soul, me, a poor Jew of no import; and in that instant, his son and He became One.

"John saw the crowd parting and saw that they were watching someone approach. Mysteriously, one by one, the noisy voices silenced as I stepped down into the water. It was then that he recognized me. I had to be opened. He reached out as I neared him and touched my forehead, and my mind exploded with light, love, wonder, and joy! And as I told John later, I saw what appeared to be a brilliant light, descend. It was a light like I had never seen. My beloved Abba had finally come. He finally came to me!"

At the edge of Jesus' voice there was the same hint of incredulity and wonder I had detected when I first heard him tell the story of his earlier life, before the warming fire in our home a few months prior. It was as if he still had difficulty believing it had actually happened to him. As for me, I had no trouble believing it at all, for he was the most wonderful person I had ever met.

He shook his head again at the marvel of it all, and then continued the most astonishing story I had ever heard.

"From the banks of the river He then sent me into the wilderness of the desert wastes, and there I lay entranced in paradise, day upon day, so many I lost count. It was there He told me of my future, and He told me of my past. He showed me my people, whom I had so carefully trained, and He told also what I must do. And as I lay there, I was grateful, and I cried, 'My God, my God, you have finally fulfilled me. I am finally whole!'

"He gave me my task, which I pursue; a mere outline only, and He gave it to me to fill in the gaps as they appear before me, to use my senses, my knowledge, my feelings, my memories. It was then that I finally knew what I must do, what I had to do to fulfill the prophecies.

"Then, as mysteriously as it started, it was suddenly over. I raised myself as from the dead. For the first time I noticed the total barrenness of where I had been. I was black from the long days in the relentless sun. I was parched and needed drink, but my mind had a singular clarity in its purpose, and so I set myself upon the path He had given me. And each day since then I have followed the course as it was set before me—and I will follow it unto the end."

There, on a distant shore, I sat next to the most holy man our one God had ever made—and I wept. I wept for the feelings of my Lord, for the feelings that were now mine. I wept because on that special afternoon in late fall in the land of Galilee, I, too, found God. I found him in the words and feelings of my Master Jesus. I sat there and wept. Jesus watched me intently as I sobbed uncontrollably, and then unexpectedly he reached out and hit me a blow to my head.

I fell back against the ground, dumbstruck and unable to move. And there, I now too found rapture in Him of whom Jesus spoke. I cried within, "Oh, God, why me, an old man, my life gone to waste?" And it was then, in a state of ecstasy, that I also knew what I must do.

It is in the sharing of this period with Jesus and his words with you, before my own time comes to an end, that I am finally able to honor my love for our Father, my Master and Lord—and also now you.

Chapter 11

Miracles and Message

"Tell everyone to sit down," Jesus ordered. And all of them—the approximate count of the men only was 5,000—sat down on the grassy slopes. Then Jesus took the loves and gave thanks to God and passed them out to the people. Afterwards he did the same with the fish. And everyone ate until full!

John 6:10-11

Jesus replied, "The truth of the matter is that you want to be with me because I fed you, not because you believe in me…" They replied, "You must show us more miracles if you want us to believe you are the Messiah. Give us free bread every day…"

John 6:26 & 31

I mentioned earlier in this story of my Master, that one of the reasons I felt that Jesus and I had become so close was that I never sought him out for the miracles he brought. The reason I sought him out lay within him, not without; but to my distress, I was soon to find that was not true of everyone... including me. And in this lesson that soon came, Jesus once again found a way to bring his missive home for those of us who had ears to hear and an open heart to accept the wisdom within.

For two days after Jesus had awakened me, changed me, by the shore of Galilee, I was in a blissful state of ecstasy. I had seen the Lord God in all His brilliant light and felt His compassion total and complete. During these two days I could function little and think none at all. I allowed John to take me to and fro, but my consciousness was not of this world. I drifted in a shimmering haze of resplendent, luminous love that filled me completely, and I knew evil not during those days. When I looked upon the Master, I saw only the most dazzling, shimmering light. And some of the people, when he spoke to them, would begin to glitter and beam and glow as well, as if they too by heaven's light did know as well as I the mystery of which he so often spoke. So powerful was this man who but slowly grew toward his destiny.

The thought came to me that I would never awake from this beatific dream, but upon saying this to Jesus, he only smiled knowingly and laughed at me in a kindly way, saying, "Just wait, Asher, just wait." So it was. On the third day I arose to find the world once again as it had been. But it mattered not, for in those days that I had walked His path, I had learned much, and I had changed. I had truly changed inside.

But then, just as I thought I had all the vision-sent answers to the problems of the world, I found that I was to learn more, more than I knew or understood at the time. For this was the day of the loaves and fishes. And the day after that came even more.

We left early; I along with the rest, for Jesus wanted to cross the sea in time to teach along the pilgrims' path. There he taught the morning through as the crowds gathered and grew, until by noontime the crowd had become largest I had ever seen come to hear him. I stayed on the outside of the gathering to let others come close to see him, some for the first time. And too, I wanted to talk to some of the people arriving and tell them to hurry to his side and also learn from this most amazing rabbi. This was a new experience for me, not hiding my discipleship but rather displaying it in the open, and I was finding it exceedingly joyous indeed.

As midday came close I wondered if he would break to allow those who had not brought food to hurry on to Tiberias or back to Magdala to find their meals. Then as I started to work my way through the throng to get close enough to my Lord to offer up my purse to feed the lot, I saw at once that Jesus had already started to distribute the few loaves and fishes his disciples had rounded up amongst themselves. Then to everyone's amazement, the basket holding the meager supply kept circulating, back and forth, row after row, back to where I was standing. As it came, the wonder of everyone there grew. With my trader's eye, I tried to discern where the food was coming from, and although I found that some souls shared what they had already brought tucked away in their tunic or robe, this in no way could account for the total lot. I, along with the multitude, looked in wonder at the miracle my Master was performing; and with joy in my heart, I foolishly called him "King" along with the now unruly mob.

Such a ruckus was being raised that Jesus realized any more teaching was out of the question that day. In fact, the people pressed in upon him so hard that I began to fear for what the crowd might do. They were screaming now hysterically; some wanted favors granted, some wanted the healing that they had heard he could perform, and others carried the idea of "Messiah-Savior-King" to the fore with more vigor than he could allow. Then, as I had often seen him do when things were not to his liking, he bid his disciples to hold the crowd at bay. Then he retreated, taking with him only Peter to walk with him awhile to protect him from any who would persist by stealth to follow.

We thought that he would return in the early afternoon, but as the day wore on and it became clear that he would not come back in time for them, the crowd became restless, some even angry. So, while some stayed behind with one of the boats to wait for Jesus, I joined the others and headed back to Capernaum, for I was weary to the bone. The wind was also picking up, and the locals were saying a storm was coming from the south, which I wanted to avoid if I could. Being caught out in a small fishing boat in a gale was not something I wanted.

When we reached Capernaum, it was almost dark, and the impending storm could be seen fast approaching. It appeared as a solid, foreboding, dark, gray wall in the twilight, coming across the lake toward the north. As the others pulled the boat safely upon the shore away from the now choppy water's edge, I walked to town along the stone path rising from the shore. The light was beautifully eerie as the last rays of the sun streaked through the black, gathering clouds in brilliant shafts of gold and gray-pink light. Once inside the house, I nervously watched through the small window as the cloak of night silently settled in around the houses. Soon the first pellets of rain spattered against the dusty ground and the storm slipped moaning in upon the land.

We all worried for the remaining boat that stayed behind alone, waiting for our Lord. As for me, I could not rest; as the storm struck with wind-swept fury and howled about the house, all I could think was that I had left my Lord for my own comfort. I was self-found guilty of thinking of no one but myself.

Finally, I could stand it no longer. I pulled a heavy, warm robe about me and headed out and down to the shore. I didn't actually think that I could do anything to help, but it was one of those times that I just had to do something, anything, to ease the ache of worrying within me.

The rain was not falling as hard as it had first seemed, for as I picked my way down the path to the water's edge, I noted with gratitude that I wasn't getting as soaked as I had expected to be, for the rain had now settled into a heavy mist. The wind, however, was gusting with great force upon the water, and a dense fog had descended, bringing intermittent swirling blackness and an eerie silence with it, making it even more dangerous to be at sea. I could see that vision of more than a short distance would be impossible until the storm let up. I knew that storms of this nature were not unusual and often blew away as rapidly as they came, leaving no trace of their vengeance and fury in the calming wake. The only thing that made this storm different was that everyone who lived near this inland sea knew enough to stay off the lake when the winds approached. Jesus and his disciples were out in this storm, and in the convoluted path human minds take, I wished that, instead of Jesus, it had been me lost in this night's black sea.

As my mind whirled in a murky world of worry and self-pity, I lost track of where I had been walking. Realizing that I had been out for quite some time, I stopped and tried to get my bearings. The only sound I could discern, beyond the wailing wind rushing around my ears, was the crashing waves breaking at my feet along the rocky shore. The murky, swirling mists were flying about me like a nightmarish dream when suddenly the clouds parted for an instant and it looked as if, about twenty paces distant, a lone man stood in front of me. I was so taken aback by fright, so fearful of the apparition that I could scarcely breathe. There, in the black and blue-gray vaporous haze, stood my Lord, looking intently out to sea. Then, as a gasp escaped my throat, Jesus strode straight out into the water's inky blackness. It was as if he had seen something I could not see, or heard something my old ears could no longer hear, for he did not hesitate one second, once he knew his course. Then, when I thought my lungs would surely burst, my breath escaped with a sigh of gratitude and relief, for out of the mist came Jesus, with a boat in tow. Not just any boat, but our boat, the boat with the disciples aboard.

What joy I felt!

I ran to the water to greet them as they leaped ashore and I helped them pull the boat the rest of the way onto the land. Everyone was laughing and crying at the same time. We hugged each other in gratitude and relief, for the cold, wet disciples (and I also) had feared that they were surely dead. Throughout this whole tumultuous affair, with all of us leaping and talking at the same time, Jesus stood back and simply smiled in the most calming and peaceful way, as if there had actually been nothing to fear at any time. Each man came in turn and thanked their saving Lord personally before Jesus sent them running off down the beach into the night toward the town, to garb themselves in dry clothes and assure the rest of the families of their safety.

When the last of them had left, my Master put his hand on my shoulder, then with a grin on his tired face and a note of weariness in his voice he slowly shook his head and said, "It's been quite a day, hasn't it, Asher ben Ammi?" It was then that I noticed his clothes were soaked up to his waist, and I urged him on to the town so that he too could change into a dry robe and warm himself by a fire.

Before leaving, however, he stopped me and turned me to face him. The storm had passed, taking with it the clouds that had hidden the full-risen moon. I noted that his hair, usually neatly pulled back and held by a leather thong, had fallen unruly and wet in front of the left side of his face. I could see too his calm, concerned face and those incredibly deep, clear blue-gray eyes shining in the light.

"Asher, tomorrow is going to be a very difficult day; there will be a falling away of many. I must speak the truth tomorrow, Asher, and it will cause much trouble among some of my followers. You will see, by tomorrow morning, this night will have become a miracle; and soon, if I don't stop it, that is all there will be to my being. That is all they are interested in now, and it must be stopped if we are to succeed. You have seen, Asher, you have seen what I am about. You have felt His touch. I need not explain it to you. Yet today, even you wanted me king."

His eyes bore into my own. The thought arched across my mind—how could he have noticed me among the multitude?

"I must stop it," he continued, "for if even you cannot see beyond the passing of His hand—not mine, Asher, not mine—what chance have those who have never seen my Father, nor felt His touch? It is for them that I have come. Do you understand? Through me, they will learn of the Father. I am the way, if they will but follow. I am but His servant who holds the lamp to light the path so that they will not lose their way—the path that each and every one of us must ultimately travel alone someday if we are truly to become One with Him."

He paused, and his face changed. Then he said, with a mischievous grin, "The truth is, Asher, I am freezing, and it is you who has kept me out here on this cold beach talking in the middle of the night, when I could have been warming myself by a nice fire in my own home by now." His arms waved back and forth in pretended exasperation.

"You are wrong, young Lord," I countered, picking up the rapid change in his mood. "It is the impetuousness of youth that has kept you jabbering in the cold night air, not I. For I, my dear Jesus, have grown wiser and more patient in my age, which is the only reason I have tolerated your madness for this long. Indeed, I judged you to be possessed and mad beyond saving long ago."

With this, we laughed together, the easy laughter of friends who can banter back and forth, comfortable in each other's respect and love. When the laughing stopped, however, Jesus sent a chill through me by saying, "Asher, you leave for Judea in two more days, and there is still much I must teach you before you go. Things will become very difficult for me soon in your land, and I do not know if I will have another chance to spend this much time with you again. Come to my home this night. We will talk till dawn." As he spoke I felt the hair on my neck stand on end, and as he finished, with his eyes speaking, as always, more vividly than his words, he said, "Asher, please stand by me tomorrow when the others leave. Please stand by me, if you can."

My God, what was he saying? I felt the sting of tears as they welled up in my eyes, and I felt a painful lump growing in the tightness of my throat. "Oh, Lord, you know I will. You know I will!" was all I could say, before he turned and headed down the beach to his home, with me pattering along behind, trying to keep up on my short old legs.

When we arrived at the home where Jesus stayed in Capernaum, we found that the fire had already been built, and dry clothing had been laid out for him. In this, the women who followed our Lord made sure that he was taken care of as if he had a wife. I knew him well enough to realize that, no matter how busy or how trying the day was to be on the morrow, he would find the woman responsible for this caring and touch her with his thanks. For the littlest things escaped him not, and the tenderness of the women touched him most. Much to the discomfort of many who followed him, Jesus gave women equal access to him, and for this the women loved him even more.

We settled onto a bench in front of the fire. The magic warmth of the dancing flames worked into our bones, and the deep shadows etched their fabric upon my mind for later days and easier times.

We stared at the fire without saying anything for a long time; the only sounds the crackle of the fire, the occasional gust of wind against the shuttered windows, the spatter of the last remnants of rain as the storm hurried on its way toward another land.

After he had sorted out his thoughts, Jesus said, "Asher, I need you to understand the nature of the miracles that are wrought in my name. For the things that happen are uncommon indeed, but they are not of my doing. My Father and I are One, and that does make me unique, but not exclusive. Asher, you have touched Him as well, and that makes you special. And some of those who follow me now will touch Him as well, and they will become One with Him. Then, there are some yet who follow later in our footsteps who will touch Him, and they will be unique and one with our Father as well.

Do you understand, old friend? Anyone who truly seeks Him with a humble and trusting heart can find Him. He is within, Asher, not without. He lies within each one of us. He is all about us. He is everywhere. This is what I have come to teach our people. He cannot be purchased with lambs or doves. He is not found in the laws of the Pharisees, nor is he found in the miracles that the people so demandingly seek. Why is this so hard for people to grasp?"

His question was rhetorical, we both knew.

He paused for quite a time, and silence dropped between us. Finally, after some time, I dared ask a question that had been bothering me since earlier that day. I was not immune to the excitement of the crowd, and I too had been carried away by the magic of feeding all the people with the most meager of supplies. And although I now heard his warning against pursuing miracles for their own sake, I didn't understand their harm. Even more, I didn't understand how he did them, how they came about. I had not seen him heal people with my own eyes, but I had heard the astonishing reports of those who had. In one case I had personally questioned a poor man in the Temple grounds who claimed to have been lame all his life until Jesus had cured him of his deformity at the pool, just to the north of the Temple grounds.

"Lord, if you will permit me to ask. What is a miracle, and how do you bring it about? And if I dare one further question, I would ask, if you heal one poor soul, why, Lord, do you not heal the rest? For there are so many who need your help." I didn't know if I was being too brazen with my questions, but in my own mind I needed an answer. I felt also that I was unworthy of his special presence and attention, when after being with him in God's radiance just three days prior, I could be so stupid as to try his patience again.

Yet, instead of showing annoyance at my foolish questions, he seemed to be warmly affected by my earnestness and more than happy to be afforded the opportunity to explain to me the mysterious happenings that surrounded him so much these days. It was as if this amazing human being found it rare indeed to be able to just sit and share with another soul who wanted nothing more than to genuinely learn. To be with someone who sought no gifts, healings, or favors, save his company alone—for he was besieged these days with people everywhere he went who wanted nothing more from him than the gifts I mention.

For a man who but a few hours ago wished nothing more than a meal and bed, I was now vitally alive with the anticipation of learning the most hidden secrets of my Lord.

"I will tell you, Asher, so that everyone you touch will also know the key to that which lies within me. I will tell you so that those who follow us will know that they, too, can touch our Father in the same way that I have, and that you did. I will tell you so that they will know that they too can be One with Him and know His special grace. For it is by His grace that any healing occurs, not by mine. I merely open myself to Him until I am overflowing, and then He can work through me to touch those in need.

"How many come to me each day, Asher, to be healed? How many?" It was a rhetorical question, of course, and needed no answer from me, so I waited. "Tens, hundreds, thousands? I do not know. I do know that if I had my way, I would heal them all. For I cannot look at any of their twisted bodies, their useless eyes, their mad stares, without wishing with all my heart to take their afflictions away. But it is not my way that brings Him pleasure. It is His way. And it is in doing His will that I have come. For it is in healing some and not others that His loving work of teaching the lessons we must learn is done. There is a universal law that governs everything, and no matter how we would wish to change it, it will stand forever and govern us all. To attune ourselves with it is what we must learn. As I have told my gallant men who fish these shores: we are the fish that swim in His ocean, and He is the one true fisherman. He bids us welcome to his boat. The hook is set, and whether we fight it to the death or swim to join Him is up to us.

"Our people are ignorant, Asher, not just those here in Galilee, but all our people. Our people's minds are full of evil spirits, demons, and curses that find no place in fact. Over half the people I have touched belong to this class. They are afraid, old friend, they are so very afraid. Life is a fearful mystery to them in all respects; so much so that if one comes who is strong and loving, one who cares for them, it helps—it takes away their pain. The secret is no secret at all, for this technique I learned from the Greeks and their physicians. Notice what I do. I must myself be calm, then I must get their total attention, which is not easy because of their fear and pain, but it must be done. Sometimes it can be done in a crowd, but at other times I must get them alone, isolated, perhaps in a small room, there to gain control. It isn't magic. It is knowledge of crowds, people, and how they are made. I take them apart to separate them from the fear of the crowd—which is very real. I hold them firm in my hands, which are strong; I speak to them in a calm, commanding voice, which they must believe; and lastly, I speak to them with my eyes, for with the eyes you cannot lie. If the problem is with evil spirits, or a perceived curse, they will be cured, for their problems were placed within them unwanted in their mind by an ignorant people and an ignorant time."

He paused and once again stared into the fire. I used the break to probe deeper.

"That covers some of the miracles of which I speak, Lord, but what of the rest? What of this day with fish and bread?"

"Ah, that, my beloved disciple, is a mystery of the greatest order and remains that way to me yet. For from the very beginning I have sought an answer, but none has come, save this. I have told you that if it were up to me, I would heal each and every one who comes to me, but that will never be recorded as happening. You must go within, and this is the one thing I try to continually teach those of you who will listen. You must go within and become One with our Father's will. In that way it is His will you seek in purity, not your own.

"This other half, the victims of diseases and twisted limbs, of blindness and parasites, they suffer the results of a thousand things of which medicine doesn't even know the name—not the least among them lust and greed and shame. Their afflictions are caused by disease and dirt and ignorance of the ways of health, birth, and accidents as well.

"It is for those too that I come. I walk among them and lay hands on many; some the Lord God heals because such healing has a purpose. God knows who needs to be healed. I can feel His light and power pouring through me at those times, and this thing we all can do. This is why you must go within, Asher. You must become One with His will. It is in this way He can walk with you and use you where there is need. And most importantly, you must understand, you must not judge, for the one He chooses might be the least in your eyes, but in His, the greatest. Sometimes you can feel sympathy for the one He chooses, and sometimes you cannot. It must be His will and not yours—and thus the greatest healer is often judged by his peers to be the least among men.

"Walk among our people, Asher. Reach out and touch the least of them, if you are to learn the secret of His will. See what goodness is in them, open yourself to the Father, and miracles will abound!"

This was a heavy load he had handed me—so much to understand—and yet he was by no means through.

"After I fed them today, I tried to tell them what I tell you now, but that is not what they came to hear. They came for the spectacle, for the sport, and it is this insincerity that I will not tolerate. I will go not to the place where I taught yesterday, for they seek only a show, and this I will not give them. I will tell you what more will happen on the morrow, if you wish, if you have need to know." Now Jesus was becoming more expressive, once more falling into his habit of talking also with his hands. As I watched him, his eyes had become distant, as if he were actually watching what was happening on the morrow—not like me, in the here and now.

"When I left you to be alone, I knew there would be no peace in the area of Tiberias where we had been, so I left to reason the happenings of the day and what very deep changes must be made. I walked north to Magdala, where I found a boat that would take me back to Capernaum. I have been teaching here for over a year now, Asher, more than one whole year, and although there are now many times hundreds, often even thousands, who gather (as you saw today), they are not interested in the words that I give them. Neither are they interested in the ways that will bring them everlasting peace. With each day that passes, they have become increasingly less interested in the ways of our Father and more and more demanding of the ways of the earth.

"The old covenant with our people is dead. They must understand this: I come not to take the land by force, I come not as a man of miracles, I come as a light shining in the darkness, leading them on a path that will take them to their Father's land. His kingdom is here and now. Imagine that! They can have it all, if they would but open themselves to Him. In His place, they will find everlasting light, total peace, and they will drown in His all-encompassing love. This simple beauty is bitter medicine for us Jews, but it is what my Father has shown me, and it is true. It is what I must teach to them until they can understand.

"There will be a great shaking out tomorrow, but those who stay will be those who have felt His touch within themselves and can do no less than follow the path to the end, no matter where it goes. For it is for those few among many that I have come, and it is for those few that my lamp shines brightest to lighten their way. Truly, no one can come to me unless my Father, who sent me, draws him close enough for me to whisper in his ear. Now is the time that I must go among the fields to hoe the weeds free of the stalks. Thus, the grain that is left shall sink its roots deep into the earth to drink freely of the living spring and turn its face to the sun to be guided by the spirit, and therein, its spirit shall grow strong."

Oh, my friends, I loved this man, Jesus, so much. If I could but tell you what it was like in those days to sit next to this man who had such incredible power within him that sitting next to him was like being in an electric storm. Yet peace also emanated from him at the same time, and this I cannot adequately explain. I was like a trusting child when with him. I guess that is the feeling I am trying to express. I was like the most innocent, trusting child. And I was also like a sponge in his presence, absorbing his radiance into me like the warmest, most wonderful dream.

Yet that still does not convey the meaning, for it was more than that. It was like being with your most intimate lover, whom you have grown to completely trust over the long and hard times you have had together. It is as if you were with him or her on a very special night, when everything was right, and you felt safe enough to finally open up your most closely guarded parts and lay yourself totally bare—you trusted that much. That's what it was like that night, alone with my Lord. He had such an amazing capacity to love those who came to him with simple and open hearts. Yet he knew that if his mission on earth were to succeed, he could not be all things to all people at all times. The events of the next day proved to be the exception to his softness.

The next morning the storm had completely passed, leaving no trace save on the minds of men. It dawned crisp and clear and so exceedingly bright that you had to guard your eyes from the pain of it. The early-morning light reflected from a myriad of tiny drops hanging tenaciously from the tips of the barren twigs. They sparkled from a thousand hiding places amongst the rocks, only to drop into the rainbows of puddles and slippery mud through which we picked our way so as not to mire our sandals in their deep. The freshness of the air was draped with the rich, pungent fragrance of the wet earth below our feet as we walked the short distance to Peter's home to take our morning meal.

Capernaum was a busy place where taxes were gathered from travelers, both near and afar, and strangers and friends alike were hard to tell apart. I enjoyed it because the mix of people seemed to have struck an easy accommodation with each other's customs that was rare in our land. This town was at the far edge of Antipas' rule and close at hand to the land of Philip, the easiest of Herod's brood, which made it less difficult for our Lord to live and teach in the way that he did.

For myself, strange as it may seem, I felt more refreshed and alive than I had in years. I noted it because I couldn't understand it, what with the lack of sleep and all the physical and mental strain; it seemed absolutely wonderful to me. The other disciples too seemed in unusually good spirits as they gathered about Jesus to hear of the day.

Meanwhile, across the lake, the throng that had gathered to hear our Lord the day before had once again come together, expecting Jesus to be there. When neither he nor any of the disciples arrived, some hired boats from the small port just north of Tiberias to sail them across to Capernaum, where they were told that he would be found. When these people arrived, Jesus was sitting in the synagogue with perhaps twenty or thirty of us, among them the twelve, and more whom he had specially chosen. When those who had come from across the lake entered the synagogue, they asked straight away, with no courtesy at all, why

Jesus had not come back for them, to teach as he had the day before.

I held my breath, for I think that of Jesus' followers only I knew what was about to happen.

"Why do you ask for me?" he demanded in a loud voice. Heads turned. The room became deathly silent as the Master spoke.

I could tell by his hard tone that the ordeal was about to begin. The sharp edge to his voice, totally unexpected by the disciples gathered about him, caused them to look up in surprise. Others, chatting a short distance away, fell instantly silent as they too turned abruptly toward Jesus, questioningly, while yet others exchanged shrugs and hidden, wondering glances.

These truly simple folk, who had come from across the lake with their demands, knew not that this gentle teacher could turn uncompromisingly rock-hard when he felt his purpose was God-driven. Little, too, did they know that from the mind of this "simple carpenter" could come arguments that would turn the wisdom of the finest minds in all the land into sand slipping between their gold-bedecked fingers; so these self-styled miracle-seekers and king-makers were nothing in his hands. The battle had been joined.

"The truth of the matter is that you want to be with me because I fed you, not because you seek what I teach you, nor because you believe in me." There was stunned silence in the synagogue as he began to purport to them much of what he had warned me of the night before. He told them about himself in a humble yet forceful manner. For he could speak nothing but the truth, and the truth was that he was the One who had come as the prophets had foretold.

Instead of believing, though, they were aghast at his words and began to whisper amongst themselves, "Who does he think he is?" And the boldest among them spoke out against Jesus directly. Standing with his legs spread wide, his arms crossed over his chest, this large man bore in on Jesus, challenging him in a loud, belligerent voice, "If you want us to believe you are who you say you are, then show us more miracles!" His provocation was given in a cynical, mocking tone and was accompanied by snickering and laughter from the others in his crowd.

The ill-advised man was not, however, finished. He continued his challenge to Jesus by saying, "Give us free bread every day, as did our father Moses! Only after you do this will we believe."

Now, at last, I thought, Jesus will put an end to this affair, for I had never heard anyone speak to him this way, and I knew Jesus could lash out with vengeance when he was of a mind to do so. But instead, feeling still that there were among them a few who might be able to hear, he changed his voice to an almost pleading note and tried one more time to open himself to them, to teach them. He tried to explain that it was only through his teaching that they would find freedom from the Law and find Him whom they called their Father.

He continued with lessons such as they had never heard, knowing all along, I think, that the crowd which challenged him would reject the mysteries in his teaching, yet knowing also that the real recipients of the lessons this day were those who already called him Master.

Toward the end of his talk, to my surprise, even his own disciples began to question him to one another; so difficult were his teachings for them to understand. For he held nothing back this day but gave them wisdom that is beyond understanding, in hopes that they could feel this truth within themselves.

At times his teachings were incredibly subtle, but that was not the case this day. Even on a superficial level, he cut like a knife into their hearts. And, at the same time, I understood their problem in comprehending, because Jesus' teaching brought with it a whole new way of thinking for those of us raised in the Law of Abraham and Moses. Jesus taught us to find our faith within, not from without, and it was precisely that to which we were not accustomed. Our Laws had been handed down for over a thousand years and interpreted for every man on every occasion by the great rabbis who studied and knew them best. But now, Jesus brought with him freedom from the tyranny of the intermediary, the scribes, the doctors of the Law, the very priests themselves. Through him, we could find our Father within our own hearts. No priest need tell us right from wrong! We needed only to love our Lord God with all our hearts, and all our minds, and all our souls, and love our neighbors as ourselves, and in this one law, we would find His loving, gentle peace within our souls.

More than once during this day I found myself going back to my awakening and the feeling of complete Oneness with God that was its result. I knew what my Lord Jesus meant when he said that he and his Father were One, and I knew also that if any of these people would but trust him, he would take them on a journey they could never forget. They would be changed forever.

Once when the crowd grew very upset, he looked my way, and out of the corner of his eye I thought I found in its sparkling glint the barest hint of a smile. I smiled back at him in a way I had learned from him, and in so doing, I hoped I would reassure him when the crowd was turning against him. In truth, however, I think he knew all along who of us would understand and who would not. For I was to discover that he was about to choose from among those there, and he needed to find them out with absolute assurance before calling them to his needs.

Before this day was over, he would find several who loved more than most. He would also find those who would not, or could not, for at this point many of his followers turned away and deserted him completely.

Then the most startling thing of all happened. As the now confused and angry mob milled about and the level of arguing and loud talk rose, he turned to those whom he held most dear and asked us with an angry edge to his voice, "Are you going too?"

It was a most disquieting moment for us all, for no matter how I had pictured this day, I could not have imagined that he would have challenged the loyalty of one of us, and most especially one of the twelve. For a moment, confusion reigned among the chosen who were now looking from one to another, hoping someone—anyone—would speak and save them from his gaze.

It was left to Peter, the strongest leader among them, to answer our Lord. "Master, to whom shall we go? You alone have the words that give to us all the eternal life we seek. We believe in you."

With that, Jesus swung about and called forth from the crowd, in addition to the twelve, a number to equal about twenty-three in all. Leaving John, the son of Zebedee, with me, Jesus departed with those he had chosen, to teach them what they must know.

Jesus swept through the crowd toward the door as if riding a whirlwind. As I watched him go, his face appeared to be set in stone. His robes were flying out behind him as he hastily strode out the opening of the building with his shocked and worried disciples hurrying to remain in tow. For just an instant, as he stepped over the threshold of the synagogue, one foot on the ground outside, he stopped in his tracks and cocked his head. It was as if a momentary thought had crossed his mind or he had heard a pointed comment from the crowd and thought for an instant that he might pause and answer the unheard. In that moment, the sun caught his head, and it shone as if illuminated by some mysterious and wonderful source. As I stared in wonder, I thought him to be the most beautiful and radiant being in all the universe.

Whatever had happened, however, it passed in an instant, and he was gone, leaving John and me behind with the arguing and hostile mob. Looking at John, I motioned toward the door and he and I silently slipped out into the fresh, cool air of autumn. What lay ahead, I wondered, what lay ahead?

Chapter 12

John, Son of Zebedee

A little farther up the beach, he saw Zebedee's sons, James and John, in a boat mending their nets. He called them too, and immediately they left their father Zebedee in the boat with the hired men and went with him.

Mark 1:19-20

John and James, the sons of Zebedee, were fishermen like Peter, but by their nature they were of a completely different lot. As rough, open, and robust as Peter was, the sons of Zebedee were the opposite. So different were they, slight of body, quiet, reserved, and introspective by nature, that Jesus often made fun with them, pursuing them and trying to draw them out. He called them the "Sons of Thunder."

When Jesus asked his twelve disciples for an opinion or urged them to interpret a story or parable, Peter's voice could be heard first among them reverberating through the valleys and over the hills as he gave free vent to his unshackled spirit. This unbridled display of energy and devoted emotion delighted Jesus over and over. More than once I saw a twinkle in Jesus' eye as this mighty man, whom Jesus rightly called "The Rock," took it upon himself to give orders or expound in an exaggerated, unyielding way upon a "hidden wisdom," the meaning of which Peter felt only he could rightly judge or view. He never lacked for conviction. He would speak with fire in his eyes, his body as unmovable as a mountain. Standing like a giant boulder, hands on his hips, he was like an angry lion that few cared to challenge.

After giving Peter free play to his will for a while, Jesus would turn to John or James and say, "We have heard from quiet, gentle Peter. What say now the Voices of Thunder?" Of course, John and James would flush red and stumble for words, to the howls of laughter from the rest of those gathered. Jesus was never mean, but he loved to banter when there was easy time with his closest followers. I am sure he also wished to encourage these timorous apostles to stand forward and be heard—now—before the going became hard.

As Jesus' days began to dwindle, Peter too felt the sting of his Master's words from time to time, for Jesus knew that if his teachings were to survive, it would be upon this stone called Peter he would have to build his house. Yet the supple qualities of the enduring reed were also going to be needed if Peter were not to be crushed to dust under the might of Jerusalem and Rome. Thus Jesus pursued the others as well with great vigor, yet with tenderness and understanding.

I will speak of Peter's training at the hands of the gentle-one in a moment, but first let me tell you of the man who on this trip had become my constant companion; Jesus' young disciple, John, the son of Zebedee.

I found that, although I would not have chosen this young man to be my companion, I was grateful that Jesus paired us together, for John was exceedingly interesting, and he lent me a look inside one of those who was closest to Jesus, without really prying. For in the innocence of his youth he was totally open to me. I write of him here because he was so different from me, and I think his perspective might be exceedingly valuable and timely. Thus, I will try to encompass hours of quiet talking and feeling into a story of this young man's searching, fears, and pain.

I will try to speak to you of these conversations with all the deep, strong feelings with which they were related to me. For I believe that in his unburdening, we too will remember that at one time or another we have all felt the same yearnings, great insecurities, and deep needs. He was a delicately sensitive young man who loved his Master very much. I think in many ways Jesus was like a father to him.

Interestingly enough, I also learned that during much of the years John spent with Jesus he was absolutely petrified. It seemed that he was afraid of everything. He lacked the total faith that some of the disciples had, and being young and of a timid nature, his shortcomings were only accentuated.

Like many of us, he often struggled with Jesus' teachings, which seemed so foreign and arcane to him. To John's way of thinking, however, it appeared that he alone could not understand what his Lord wished him to see. Yet he stayed, month after month, year after year, walking hundreds of miles in the Master's steps. Jesus' voice, his captivating eyes, the chance to be special—one of the chosen—and the infinite love that poured from Jesus into this young man were more than enough to stay John from ever leaving.

The morning after Jesus spoke to the crowd in the synagogue I sat at the breakfast table after a wonderful night's rest. Peter's mother had served me bread and fruit. John was sitting across from me at a rough, hand-hewn table, his elbows squarely on the boards and his chin propped on his hands. Although it looked as though he was trying to let a beard grow, his baby-like face was ill suited to cooperate. I had guessed him to be somewhere between sixteen and eighteen years of age, but when I asked, he said somewhat defiantly, "I'm almost twenty! That's pretty old, isn't it? I've been a man now for a long time!"

I sensed from his reply that he was a trifle insecure, and I drifted away from any more intimate questions that I thought might embarrass him. "Tell me, John, how did you meet Jesus? What prompted you to follow him?"

I was genuinely interested in how this young man, who was one of the very first people Jesus called, had come to drop his work and his life on a moment's notice on the same day and in the same manner as Peter and Andrew had done. His answer was interesting and insightful, if a bit circuitous; I recorded it later in the evening to tell others who might also question. I leave this poor Galilean's language as it was, even though I cringe to reproduce it in this manner for you to read.

"You know what Jesus' brother James says?" young John answered in reply to my question. I wondered in passing why Jacob was now using a newly popular Greek transliteration of his Hebrew name.

"He said that Jesus changed when he went to see John. You know," he said, looking at me with intensity, "the one who baptized thousands in the River Jordan. Before that, Jesus didn't think he was anything. But something happened when Jesus went to John, but he didn't stay with John, he was just baptized by John. Something special happened, he said. Then he went away—nobody saw him for a long time—I don't know how long, and then he came back, and he was down by the sea watching the fish and the fishermen. And, you know what? He walked right up to the fishermen like he knew them..."

A cloud seemed to pass over John's face as he paused to remember the scene. Whispering half to himself, he mused, "Maybe he did know them. I never thought of that." Then, deciding that the apparent mystery would have to wait for later, his face cleared, along with his mind, and he continued brightly.

"He walked right up to the edge of the water and called them, and he said, 'Come with me!' He yelled it! Can you believe that? I mean, they were right out in the water, and they were pulling up their nets, but he told them to come in. And I thought, 'That's strange!' You know, I was just sitting there by my father and I saw that.

"Then they did what he said, they came in to shore and they talked to him a few minutes and started to walk away with him—but one of them didn't. I jumped up from the nets we were working on and ran down to the water's edge where he had been standing and talking to the other men. As I watched Jesus and the rest walk off down the shore I grabbed the one who didn't go and I said, 'Who was that?' He said, 'I don't know, but my brother's leaving with him. He must think he's somebody.' And I said, 'Do they know him?' And he said, 'I don't think so. I don't know who he is. He's strange, isn't he? Did you see those eyes?' And I said I hadn't, I wasn't close enough, but I followed him anyway. They didn't go far, they went down to the village and up the street, and the fisherman, Peter, took him into his house, and I hung around until he got out, and I looked at him. Oh, my! He looked at me, and you know what he did? He grabbed me by my head on both sides by my ears like this..." John reached across the table and grabbed my head at this point, quite hard, "and he looked right into my eyes, and he was older than I was. He looked right into my eyes and he said, 'Son of Zebedee, I have come for you!' And, it was incredible! I mean, what do you do, right? So I've been with him ever since. I left with him, that was all I could do."

By the time John had finished his story of meeting Jesus, I found that I was enthralled by the events in this man's life. Here was a young man, hardly out of youth, fascinated by the same characteristic as I—Jesus' eyes!

I rose from the table, walked around it and gave John a big hug, thanking him for being so open with me. I was soon to find that although John was quiet and reserved in groups, he could talk incessantly when alone with someone with whom he felt comfortable.

We gathered the food that had been prepared along with the wine and headed down to the shore where a boat was waiting to carry us to the other side of the inlet, to the lake where John assured me we would find Jesus.

We climbed into one of the creaky wooden boat's that was swaying gently from side to side, rubbing up against the wharf. As I clumsily tried to find a place to sit, John haggled over the price of the fare to the destination he had in mind. To me, the sum asked wasn't worth arguing about, but for John, the price was an insult, and he felt it his duty to come within shouting distance of the price he had in mind. Finally, when all the arrangements seemed to have been worked out, two men pushed us out and away from the rock wall into waist-deep water. Then at the last moment, they hopped aboard the little vessel. The breeze unfurled the sails and we were on our way.

John waddled back to my end of the boat with a practiced gate, barely affected by the now rocking and bobbing boat, all the while muttering under his breath, "That stinking fisherman! He charged us too much for his boat. We are too easy with them. Jesus won't let me drive too hard of a bargain, he says they need the money—but so do we." With that said, he sat down beside me in a pique. It was all I could do not to laugh at this funny young man who seemed more a boy.

He pointed almost straight ahead of us across the top of the lake to a barely discernible spot far across the hazy water. "He told us to meet him on the far side, there's pretty hills there. That's where we are going to meet him later."

"Later?" I wondered at the timing as the boat gently leaned off first to one side, then the other, as we slowly made our way across the lake. The only sounds were the water rushing against the side of the boat and creaking wood rubbing against itself in the pitch-sealed joints. The breeze blowing in my face made me feel refreshed, and I was anxious to reach my Lord. I took the opportunity to fill the silence by asking John how his parents felt about him leaving home to follow this unknown rabbi from Nazareth.

"They hadn't seen me for so long after I left that day. I've only been home once for more than a day since I started following him. He sent me home to see them and stay awhile. My parents were so glad. They were so worried, but they had heard where I was, and they made sure I was all right. I'm not a bad son," he added, looking at me with a worried expression on his face, as if I were a visiting relative come to test his sincerity. "What could I do? I've followed him," he paused and slowly shook his head back and forth, staring at the water sloshing across our sandaled feet, "but I don't always understand him. You know, I haven't been to school or anything."

I found that almost all Galileans sorely felt their lack of education, and although I had often made fun of them in the past, listening to this young man try to explain his ignorance made me ashamed. I was ashamed for not feeling another's pain, humiliation, and desire for the same things that had been handed to me without my lifting a finger.

"I know the Torah pretty well, but that's all," John went on. "We don't have a rabbi in our village. Sometimes one comes, and that's nice. We men get together for the Sabbath, but I don't really like it when the rabbi is not there because we're not very good, and nobody can really understand the Law very good. It's kind of dull."

Then, the thought of Jesus and his teaching came to his mind, and John's face lit up with the belief he had in this rare Galilean who made the scriptures come alive for him. You could sense the pride this man had for one of his own kind who could rival the knowledge of the best minds in all of Israel. "Jesus knows!" John started again excitedly, "You know, he can take any part. I mean, people come to him, you know, they'll say, what about this or that, or something in the Torah, and he knows the answers! He makes it so clear." He shook his head again at the wonder of his teacher. Little did he know, little did he suspect, how very special this teacher of his was.

We were both quiet now as the small boat started to turn toward the shore. As we watched, for some unknown reason, a little knot of people gathered up the hill from the village not far away. John turned to me with an anxious smile on his lips. "It takes so long when you want to see somebody you love, doesn't it?" Then he turned back again to watch the land slip by. How simple this man, yet how exquisitely elegant! Nothing complicated; he just loved his teacher.

Still facing away, he said, "You know what's strange?" It was a soft, quizzical, far-off voice. "I don't even know why I love him. I think... I think I'm going to be someone special." There was a pause, then, "Maybe not, I don't know, but some of the people, they say that he's going to take the Romans by storm. I don't think so. He never talks about, about war, but he is interested, you know that? He keeps some people around him that scare me to death. They've got knives. They tell him where the Romans are and Herod's soldiers too, and so we stay away from there. Really, we don't go near them. Maybe that's why he keeps them around, because, you know, they know everywhere the soldiers are. They know before we get there." John glanced nervously at our shipmates, and then leaned close to me with his hand spanning the gap between his mouth and my ear and whispered, "They have spies everywhere."

We were fast approaching land now, and John finished his story by saying, "Some of the Romans aren't that bad, but a lot of them are brutes, and they smell." What brought this up I will never know, but in listening to John that week, I learned he had a particularly keen sense of smell and a very small range of tolerance of what he considered acceptable. He continued, "What do they eat to make them smell like that? Most of them don't like us, and we don't like them. I only saw them once in our village—just once—others see them more often I guess, but we are kind of out of the way. I really don't know if they're good or bad, but everybody hates them."

With this he made a leap at the rocky shore and turned in time to catch the rope one of the fishermen tossed to him on the way. Then with the naturalness that comes from spending years on the water, he helped the others pull the boat safely onto the gravel. There they held it steady while I shakily, cautiously climbed out upon firm ground.

Hesitating only a second, John then began to push the boat back out into the deeper water where the fishermen could start their journey home. I must have been daydreaming for I didn't notice him striding back up the beach toward me until he started to speak: "This is the very spot where I was standing when I first saw him."

His voice jerked me away from my deep, wondering thoughts of the morning, and suddenly I realized that he was standing right in front of me. "I'm sorry, John," I apologized, "I didn't hear what you said."

"I said, this is the very spot where I met Jesus," he repeated.

"This is it?" I exclaimed, surprised, waking completely from my absent reflection.

I looked about me and noticed the small piles of old and torn netting, a few small stacks of rock weights, and stone circles with remains of fires past. I smelled deeply the wonderful pungent odor of the fresh, dew-drenched earth mixed with a faint, elusive stench of rotten fish. I stared out at the water as the small fishing boat slid away, and thanked

God for the glorious morning and my part in it. I stretched my old body from side to side as far as it would go to get the kinks out of my muscles. Suddenly, I became painfully aware (not being accustomed to traveling on the water) that I must have been holding myself tense and tight the whole morning through. As I arched my back to get the muscles working and relaxed, I felt my advanced age wash over me as inexorably as an incoming tide.

"What a wonderful way to be spending the day," I thought, as I looked around at the stunningly beautiful countryside and the Sea of Galilee that reached out to the horizon far beyond me. The water reflected the light, rippling blue of the late morning sky, and through the last of the distant haze rising from the choppy sea, I thought I could just make out the sparkling white ramparts of the city of Tiberias shining in the crystal clear air.

"Come, sit where my father used to sit," John said as he motioned me to a natural, water-etched seat among the gray and ebony rocks. "This is where we used to mend our nets together." He pointed around us and again I noticed the remnants of more than one fisherman who used this place to while away the day.

"Where are the fishermen now?" I asked.

He pointed south and said, "The fish run there at this time of year." Looking up at the sun with an experienced eye, he added, "They should be tied up somewhere near the mouth of the river now, waiting out the day. They'll be back at dark, after fishing the waters at dusk."

The thought of fish reminded John of food. He reached into the pouch he carried slung over his shoulder and handed me a dried fish and a small loaf of bread. He shook his head as he handed me the midday meal, grinning apologetically. "We sure eat a lot of fish, don't we? Wish we had more money so we could eat something else. I like it when we visit Jesus' rich friends like you because then we get good food." To this we both laughed. Then I realized this was the first time I had seen this young man laugh. After what had happened earlier in the synagogue, it felt good; the laughter, the food, the cheap wine and bread, all seemed to break the tension of the morning past that still hung over us like a cloud.

As I was wondering what Jesus was doing right now with his disciples and when we were going to join him, John burst in with thoughts of his own. John was still young, and the thought of food was not so easily dislodged from the forefront of his mind. He began to giggle as he leaned forward and whispered (so the rocks wouldn't hear, I suppose), "I ate pork once! It's good. I didn't die either, and Jesus still loves me!" This seemed like the most wonderful joke to him, and he laughed and giggled and laughed again until I thought he was going to choke on his food. I couldn't help myself either, for his good humor was infectious. I happily joined in the fun, slapping my thighs and wheezing with delight. Leaning forward, which my eyes wide for emphases, I gasped, "I have too." That sent us into peals of laughter all over again.

When we gained some semblance of order, he continued, wiping the tears from the corners of his eyes.

"He does strange things sometimes. Jesus, I mean. You know, I think he tries to make them mad at him or something, because he does things he just shouldn't do. On the Sabbath for instance..." He took a huge bite of bread and fish at the same time, and I marveled at how he could speak, eat, and breathe all at once. "He'll keep on doing what we do every other day, and it makes them furious!" "Who?" I asked. "You know, the priests, the Judeans, the people from Herod—almost everybody that counts.

"The people love it though because they're so sick of it—all the rules and all." By now I was marveling at John, for I just couldn't believe that this slight young fellow could eat so much. I wondered incredulously how he did it. Finally assuring myself he wasn't going to choke to death, I relaxed and whiled away the afternoon listening to him talk.

"The people love it because he just stands right there, and no matter what they ask or say, he has an answer. And the men who come to test him or catch him saying something he shouldn't, they go away furious. The people love it because they have all been humiliated by them because they are poor and have no learning and have no money. We have nothing, you know. Jesus doesn't take money. I mean, we're taken care of sometimes, but—and I know we must have money someplace because we have to buy bread and stuff—but there's very little."

He paused, then in his own manner of speech, suddenly changed the subject in mid-thought. "They all want the Messiah! You know what? He is the Messiah... I think. I think he is. He's strange. He doesn't come out and say anything, he just tells us stories. I understand some of them, but not all of them. He's so confusing to me. Timothy just, well, he just feels from his heart, he doesn't need to think. I wish I could do that a little more—just trust him—but I keep thinking, I keep wondering... We're such a motley little band, what could we ever do? We've got to get a lot of people. We've got to get a lot of the people and grow and grow everywhere because they are so strong."

I assumed that the vague "they" he referred to was the existing power structure, which, if he could think clearly about it, probably included me. The poor young man now began to actually tremble as he told me of an incident that had happened not too long before, perhaps during the last hot season, I would judge, from the freshness of its telling.

"He's so mysterious!" John exclaimed with finality. He sounded frustrated at not being able to understand this man who often spoke in parables. "Why doesn't he tell us where we are going? I remember once, we were heading for Caesarea; I knew that much because we were approaching the sea—but why? I didn't want to go to the coast. The Procurator was there because it was so hot everywhere else; and then we heard that Antipas was to be visiting there too." John now began to wring his hands in fear. How this young man stayed with Jesus I will never know, for Jesus never shrunk from a confrontation if he felt that it served a purpose.

"We were getting closer and closer to the city. It was so hot and dusty. I was covered with sweat and wished only to rest and cool myself under a tree. But Jesus kept up a horrid pace all that day and the one before. Then we saw them. It was just as we came over a rise; the city laid before us, and behind it the sea. Still there was no relief from the heat, no breeze to cool us this day, but worse—what I feared most—soldiers! I couldn't tell whose they were from this distance, but what did it matter, we were dead! Two of the disciples were carrying daggers (not me of course), but Judas and Simon. They are... Sicarii!"

The word Sicarii hissed from his mouth, as if saying it were in and of itself an evil, a word not to be mentioned in anyone's presence for fear of reprisal.

I knew the meaning of the name, of course. The very mention of the term, Sicarii, sent waves of dread through me as well as John, for I too feared that I could one day fall victim to this party of killers drawn from the Zealots of our land. They were bent on the destruction of everything we had built. This secret group of Jews from all parts of our land kept daggers beneath their robes and, when mingling in a crowd, silently, cowardly, slipped their poisonous deeds between the ribs of an unsuspecting Roman, Greek, or highly placed Jew like me. They wanted the Eagle of Rome out of our land, and one's race meant nothing to these despicable men if it served their needs. I myself had great cause to fear and loathe these evil jackals.

I knew that Judas and Simon were Zealots, but I didn't know Jesus counted Sicarii among his disciples, and I must admit that the thought disturbed me if it were true.

John actually had tears in his eyes as he continued with the story; so incredibly frightened was he that Judas and Simon would be uncovered. It was almost as if he were pleading with me to understand how frightening it is to travel in the company of some of those closest to our Lord.

He started again. "As we got closer I... I could tell that the soldiers had seen us. We were going to be stopped. I thought, oh God, why would twelve men be traveling together at this time of year if they were not up to no good? If they search us, they will find the knives. We are dead. We are dead!" he moaned.

There was a long pause as John once again gained control. He then apologized, quite embarrassed for breaking down like he did. I assured him that I was just as afraid as he was of the dreaded Sicarii, and this seemed to make him feel quite a bit better; in fact, it seemed to cement our relationship even more closely in his mind than before. I asked him if he could finish his story, and he nodded his head.

"Actually," he said, "there's very little else to tell. I believe it was a miracle as surely as many of the healings I have seen. Jesus spotted the soldiers long before I, and as we approached, he began to speed his walk, so as to reach them before the rest of us got too close. Immediately upon reaching the dreaded men, he began an animated conversation. To this day I don't know what he said, but to be sure, it was one of the best stories he ever told.

"I suspected that the story was meant for the soldier's ears only, and judging from the manner and extent of their laughing and gesturing at us, I would guess the story to have been of a vulgar nature—and we undoubtedly were the brunt of the joke. I fairly wet myself with fear as we silently passed them by. We were so close that I could smell their foul breath, and even more, their foul bodies. They wore armor, and in the hot weather, they smelled like the pigs they ate. I held my breath and glanced at Jesus, who was walking in the lead as if he had not a care to his name.

"I don't understand him, Asher. I try, but I just don't understand. Why we even made the journey I do not know to this day, for when we reached the city he went straight to a most specific house, knocked, and we were immediately let in. Once inside the court, Jesus further disappeared inside the house and was gone from our sight for the rest of the day. The servants brought us water and wine, figs, grapes, and food of every kind; but he never told us why we went there."

It seemed that John was in no hurry to join Jesus as yet, I was sure by instruction, so to ease his agitation from the emotion in his story (and the locking once again of my stiff joints), I urged John to join me in a walk along the shore. This we did for a while. Then, as I had seen him do on several occasions, John glanced toward the now falling sun and said, "Come, it is time to go."

I was curious. "Where do we go, John?" I asked, trying to keep up his pace.

"Jesus asked me to bring you to him late in the afternoon. He bade us join him at suppertime. Come, your needs have already been seen to, you will stay the night in the open with us." With that proclamation, we headed north, following the river that emanates from the cliffs of Pan. It was not a difficult journey, for John, deferring to my age, slowed the pace as the afternoon wore on; thus, the trip became no more than an easy stroll, even though we seemed to be continually climbing. As we walked, I quizzed my host for more stories of his years with our Lord. He seemed as anxious to tell someone about Jesus as I was to listen, for I think few among the most intimate paid John much due.

"What do you wish to hear?" asked this slight, bearded man with a darkly tanned face, already showing wear and tear from his years on the water and in the sun.

I replied, "Tell me, as you travel about the country, he surely doesn't have followers in every town and village. How do you eat? Where do you all stay?"

"That's easy," he replied with a twinkle in his eye, "it's his charm with the women!" A big grin of dubious origin slid mischievously over his face. I didn't know at the time, but I was soon to find out that John held women in a somewhat different light than did Jesus, and this was reflected in the manner in which he told his stories. In fact, that same night I was to hear Jesus deliver a lesson in this regard, much to John's discomfort.

Wary of the look on his face, I asked, "What do you mean?" Whereupon John contentedly continued, aware now that he was teaching this wealthy Judean, and he was beginning to enjoy his new and prestigious role.

"Let me ask you a question," he said, his voice deepening and his hand raised in gesture, as I am sure he had seen Jesus do on many occasions. "If you arrived in town, perhaps in the afternoon, and you wanted to let the people know that you were there, where would you go, who would you tell without standing on a rooftop and yelling 'I am here'?" I had to admit, I did not know. "You go to the well!" he exclaimed with an exaggerated flourish and lordly flash of eye, communicating to me that he felt himself the purveyor of a delectably obvious truth. "Jesus' first stop when we arrive in town is the well. And who is at the well?" I shrugged. "You don't know?" he said with a mocking exaggeration and a shocked look on his face. "I will tell you then. Servant girls! The servant girls for the wealthy come in the late afternoon to fill their jugs at the well—and swap stories about their mistresses and their families, of course."

This caused John to chuckle awhile as we continued to climb the winding trail. I know not of what he thought, nor why it was so funny. Moreover, I must admit that I was becoming tired and a bit annoyed. A few moments later he continued.

"Jesus comes up to one of them and asks if they would kindly let us drink from the jug of cool water they have just drawn. He has such an easy, warm manner about him that I have never seen him refused. Then as we are washing away the thirst from the dust of the day, Jesus begins to speak to them. You know, Jesus can look into someone and right on the spot tell everything you guard as most secret and dear. By the time we have finished quenching our thirst and have begun to look for the welcoming shade of a tree, the women are already scurrying off to tell their mistresses of the wonderful stranger they met, with the most amazing deep blue-gray eyes. And, oh yes, he just happens to mention that his followers have need of a place to eat and rest for the evening."

I knew the story from there, for I myself have seen many times how Jesus can come into a home of a complete stranger and within a few precious moments capture not only the women of the house but everyone in it. An ordinary dinner becomes a feast if he is your guest. Within an instant he knows the hearts of those present, their needs, their hurts, their most secret desires and wants. Then, like no one I have ever met, he can weave a story like a flower with a thousand petals, the outermost of which fall at the table as he speaks, but the youngest and most tightly wound to the tender bud fall later, in a quiet time of reflection. Sometimes, days and weeks later, these petals of wisdom suddenly fall before the person's eyes and reveal their moral with an intuitive flash back to the special night with my Lord, and an awakening response takes place within the people's hearts as if Jesus himself were right there with them.

It was late in the day when we reached a shady spot to rest. John said that we would stay here and repose until sundown, then head up the hill a bit farther, where Jesus and the others would be waiting. I nuzzled up to a fallen tree and wearily eased my tired bones down, closed my eyes, and listened to the peaceful stream at my feet.

I wasn't the only one feeling the effects of the long climb, however, for John, lying flat on the grass and looking up at the mellowing sky, commented, "I love this time at the last of the day, because the sun's low, and it's never so hot. My feet are sore!" That was the last I remember, for when next I opened my eyes, the sun had fallen another notch from the sky and wrapped itself around the gnarled tree on the distant hill. As I rose and stretched, the sky was alive with streaks of gold and a passionate red that was deepening to wine.

John was perhaps fifty paces ahead on the crest of the nearby hill, looking intently at something at which these old eyes could only guess. When he saw that I was awake and about, he waved at me to join him up the path that wound its way to the top of the hill. When I finally joined him, it was obvious that I had not as yet gained my second wind. As I bent over and tried to catch my breath, I suddenly felt every one of my sixty-plus years complaining as if it were their last gasp before they all let go of my feeble frame.

It was a good thing we did not have too much farther to climb for I was totally exhausted when we came upon the group Jesus had taken that morning from the synagogue. He was sitting, as usual, a little above them on a log atop a small rise, so that they could all see him and hear him equally well. Two of the disciples were off to one side working on the evening meal over a spit and fire, and they were shoving something in the coals. Jesus was talking quietly as we approached, so we merely picked a spot and sat down to listen with the rest.

We were at the rear of the group, and I found it difficult to hear. My quizzical look at John set him off, and from then on he felt duty bound to keep up a running commentary on what Jesus was saying, whether I could hear him or not.

"He's talking about someone they met today. You wanted to hear about girls, huh? Well, here it is, he's talking about a girl again." I glanced sideways at John, wondering what on earth he was talking about. What little I heard of what Jesus was saying had little bearing on the interpretation John was giving me in my ear. "You know, I don't understand that." he decried, "They don't count; women, I mean. He seems to think they're just the same as we are. Listen to him."

I was trying!

"'She's so sweet.' I've heard that so many times. 'Did you see her eyes?' I've heard that so many times too!"

John's voice was mocking Jesus, and I found that my temper was beginning to rise a bit despite myself. I remember that a rather crude explanation presented itself to my mind as to the cause of John's discomfort with women; however, it best remains only my hidden thought.

Jesus started speaking once again, and John (much to my despair) started up his commentary again. "I think that they love him so much because he likes them. I wonder if I'm jealous? Maybe I am jealous. Wouldn't that be awful? What's got into me? I must be tired."

He continued to give me a running commentary. I continued to try to ignore him.

"Did you hear that, Asher? He said that he saw her in the crowd, and he saw that her heart was pure and sweet. He must have called her out of the group; I think that's what he must have done. He's asking if the others saw her eyes." John was now leaning over next to me, whispering in my ear, to my great discomfort.

"He's telling about her. He's saying that she'll probably be in heaven before most of us will because we don't understand, and the girl understood. See—he keeps saying that! He said the girl understood him, and we don't!" John was becoming quite agitated, and several others were looking around at him and giving him looks that clearly meant for him to quiet himself—all to no avail.

"What does he want from us? We're with him every day! In fact, I've been with him almost every day for almost two years now. I don't understand. You know I'd do anything he asked. What does that girl do that makes her so special? After all I..." He was now quite loud as his agitation grew. He took no notice that everything had turned silent, everyone had heard his last declaration ("What does that girl do that makes her so special?"), and everyone was looking at us.

At that point Jesus too looked John's way and stared at him for a moment without saying a word. John began to moan, "Oh, it's so difficult to understand." Nervously he began to look around as he saw everyone staring at him. Mercifully, Jesus turned his attention elsewhere, and the rest followed.

"Oh, its getting dark, and I'm afraid again," he hissed in a low whisper. "I know it, I just know we are going to get caught someday. Arrested! I'm so glad we've got a large fire going." With that, he clutched his arms around his drawn-up legs and began to rock back and forth and moan inconsolably. He reminded me of when I was a child; when the events of my little world became too much for me, I would grab my dog, hold him close, and rock to and fro. Somehow, it seemed to help.

Jesus was done speaking for now, and the group was breaking up, most of them heading happily toward the warmth of the fire and food. I began to look about to see if anyone could help me with John. All of a sudden Peter was at my side, and Jesus at John's. Jesus gently lifted John to his feet, put his huge arms around him, and held him—just held him ever so tightly. Tears were streaming down John's face as Jesus handed him some food and gently led him to a seat by the warm, friendly fire. Before Jesus left, he held John's face in his hands and John knew that he was loved and safe. And in that instant, I knew why John followed him. It was the same reason any of us followed him: it was his unconditional love.

No matter what our heads told us was right or wrong, no matter what we had been taught, no matter how many called us fools, when Jesus silently stood before you and looked into your eyes, nothing else mattered, nothing, save to do his will. Yet we all knew he was but a man, and it was not his will that he sought to accomplish, but his Father's. He wanted each and every one of us to grow in the ways that he showed us, closer to our God. He urged us with every tool at his command to use all the strength that we could muster in our search for Him who gave us life and reason to live. He taught that we were just as he, and that those things he did, we could do too, with grace and humility. And, on wondrous nights like this, I believed in my uniqueness—and his—with all my heart and soul.

Peter, sensing my inner thoughts and sharing my adoration for our Lord, smiled warmly at me, and together we walked over to the fire where we were handed plates loaded to overflowing with food. Peter motioned me over to a large rock by the coals, and silently we began to eat together. The sun had long set, and only the faintest trace of cobalt blue held back the coming cold black of night. The first star could be seen near the horizon. The quiet of the hillside was broken only by the muted voices of the men who had gathered here to be with their Messiah.

I was feeling the welcome warmth of the fire when Peter, a piece of bread in hand, pointed at John and quietly said, "I remember another time when I saw Jesus do that." I looked at him questioningly. "Hug a man like that, I mean," he clarified. "He was a cripple named Timothy."

I watched him in the flickering firelight. Peter's cracked and weathered face took on the look of the ancient earth itself. I could see the valleys and ravines, the upturned furrows of new beginnings, all etched there for anyone who cared to see.

I also understood now why, after Jesus, Peter was the leader of this diverse band of men; for even speaking as quietly as he could as we sat by the fire together, his voice was like the low rumble of an earthquake before the ground begins to tremble and shake. His face, lacking the inner peace reflected in Jesus' visage, had instead a hard look, which, accompanied by his massive voice and outgoing personality, made him a natural leader of men.

"We were walking along the road one day," Peter started softly, a far-off look in his eyes, "when suddenly we came upon a man who was crippled. The poor man dragged along a lifeless leg, which made a furrow in the dirt as he slowly hobbled his helpless way along the hot, dusty path toward some distant town. As our band of maybe eight or ten came upon him, he moved to the side of the road so as not to hinder us. I still remember his face; it shone like an angel. There was no fear nor hate nor resentment there. He had found a gentle peace in his affliction, which was a marvel to see.

"When Jesus came close, he looked into the poor man's face and his heart went out to him. Jesus, fascinated by this person's apparent inner joy, turned to us and said, 'This man's suffering has ended! No more has he a need to carry this leg about; his lessons have been well learned.' With that, Jesus' overwhelming love poured into the man. He put his arms around the astonished cripple and held him tight, so tight that the man screamed out in pain, but Jesus would not let go. Then, when Jesus had worked his way, he let him free, and the traveler was crippled no more!"

I don't know why this story touched me so, but I suddenly felt the sting of tears welling up in my eyes, for I knew what the healing must have meant to that poor soul. Now the man would be useful, he could be employed. No more would he be an outcast, a burden: neither to himself nor to his friends nor his family. He would be whole.

Peter, seeing the wetness of tears glistening in the firelight, looked at me and smiled knowingly, saying, "The man is there." He pointed across the fire to a figure sitting opposite me, who had been listening silently all the while to Peter's story. The man looked at me, and the most radiant smile came across his face.

I looked back at Peter in astonishment. "Yes, Asher ben Ammi," Peter quietly said, "it is he. I want you to meet Timothy."

Chapter 13

First Hint

No one lights a lamp and hides it! Instead, he puts it on a lampstand to give light to all who enter the room. Your eyes light up your inward being. A pure eye lets sunshine into your soul.

. . . If you are filled with light within, with no dark corners, then your face will be radiant too, as though a floodlight is beamed upon you.

Luke 11:33-34 & 36

The next morning dawned crisp, clear, and bright. This was to be the day that I would take my leave from Galilee and from the man who made my life sing. I approached it with mixed emotions. So many memories crammed into such a few short days—experiences that will remain with me forever.

Jesus touched me on the shoulder shortly before sunrise and motioned for me to follow him past the eastern rise. Several of the others were beginning to stir as we quietly crept out of camp and headed for the hill. Once out of sight of the rest, Jesus put his arms around me, as he had with John the night before, and held me awhile. I felt a strange sense of sadness as he held me on that lonely mountaintop, yet at the same time I could also feel the hidden power of his indomitable spirit flowing into me and making me whole.

He stepped back and looked at me with a small grin, saying, "You look ten years younger than when you came. This outdoor life must agree with you." I held up my hands in protest, for although I may have looked ten years younger (which I doubt), my bones felt ten years older after having slept on the hard ground all night. He clasped his arm around my shoulder, and together we climbed to the top of the rise. Once there, we sat next to each other, wrapped our robes tightly around us to keep out the early-morning chill, and fell within that sacred part of our souls where only God dwells. There, on a deserted hill, I sat with him and felt the warm sun sweep my face, then drench my body with its vitality and warmth, and my soul sang.

I opened my eyes to capture one of the most wonderful and poignant pictures I ever experienced, one that lives in my memory as clear today as it was that morning on the Galilean hill. I opened my eyes in time to see the deep yellow rays of the sun illuminate Jesus' bearded face, and there for me alone to see was a man of consummate peace, lost in the highest realms of ecstasy. In that rare glimpse of my Master, I saw the heights to which we all aspire. I saw him in a state of rhapsody.

He must have felt me watching him in adoration, for slowly his eyelids lifted, and a strange smile of knowing crept over his face. Then suddenly, without warning, a shock went through my whole body! My face turned ashen white and I shook violently for a second, not knowing the cause. It was as if the icy grip of death had passed through me as swiftly as a gust of wind.

"Yes, Asher, you feel it too," Jesus said, his eyes locked onto mine. "Our time rapidly approaches, my dear friend, for too soon both of us will be at death's door. Remember, there is a sweetness in passing, and now that you have tasted heaven, you know there is nothing to fear on the other side of the veil." These words sent more tremors through me, and I pleaded for him to stay away from Judea, where his healings and teachings had drawn such hatred from the priests. "Don't worry, Asher," he said, "I will not come south until the Feast of Tabernacles next, and then I will come in secret. I will get word to you somehow." Those were the last words we had alone together until he returned to Jerusalem, preceded by a messenger, the following autumn.

Silently then, we rose and walked the distance back into the camp of his disciples. There I was surprised to find my servant waiting with our horses and our baggage to begin our long journey home. When I saw the horses prancing in the morning air, pawing at the ground in anticipation, I shot a glance at Jesus and saw him smiling as he turned away to tend to his little flock.

Late one evening over half a year later, a knock sounded at my door, and a man entered and asked for me. I alone from among my household would have recognized him, for it was a man who once was a crippled beggar until my Master passed his way. It was Timothy. "Come in, my dear friend, you have walked a mighty way. Please, my home is yours. I want you to meet my family. What a wonderful surprise for all of us here." I had told everyone about our meeting that night with Peter around the campfire, and they all wanted to question Timothy at the same time, and on the very night that he arrived. I insisted that everyone leave him alone until he had been fed and was able to catch up on his sleep, then I left it up to Timothy to fend for himself.

He stayed two weeks with us waiting for Jesus to arrive, as he had been told to do. Then, one day, without warning, Jesus showed up alone at our door. As requested, I swore my son, John, to secrecy and sent him on his way to alert those who were to know that on the morrow he would arrive. The following morning, after a good night's sleep, I escorted Jesus and Timothy as far as Lazarus' house—and that too was an experience to behold.

Friends since their youth, Jesus and Lazarus were inseparable whenever it was possible for them to be near, and so it was with a great deal of anticipation that each awaited the arrival of the other whenever their paths came close enough to cross.

Lazarus' home is in Bethany, just a short distance from Jerusalem, and it didn't take us long to walk. As we circled around the hill of the Mount of Olives, we saw a man running toward us waving his arms excitedly. It was Lazarus! As he approached, Jesus said, "What brings you here?" and laughed uproariously as they embraced. "I was waiting for you, Yeshu," Lazarus said, bending over with his hands on his knees, trying to catch his breath from running. "And what of your sisters?" Jesus continued. "They wait for you too, Lord. We heard from Asher and Timothy that you were coming. I'm so happy—so happy, Lord! We were so joyous when we heard of your coming. I ran all the way out here to be with you just a few moments sooner. We're so delighted that you're coming to grace our home again."

He turned to Timothy and me then, waving his arms to include us as well, saying, "You're all welcome. The women are making bread and baking for you. And the wine merchant, I've told him to bring wine. It's a happy day, Lord, now that you've come to visit once again. I even bought this new robe to honor you. Isn't it beautiful!" Jesus, Timothy, and I were all laughing heartily now as Lazarus spun around and around in the dust, showing off his new clothes in childlike glee. He was totally unaware of the spectacle he was making in the road, much to the equal delight of the passers-by, for honest, lighthearted joy is truly infectious and makes everyone happy to be a part of it.

We couldn't have calmed Lazarus even if we had wanted to; he continued to happily babble as we headed up the well-traveled road toward his home. "It's been so long, Lord, months, and we haven't heard from you. Come, make your steps light, we welcome you all."

Lazarus turned and walked backwards a few steps, to better see his boyhood friend. Jesus started to turn red at the ears with all the unusual attention. Timothy and I looked at each other, smiling, and exchanged a wink of delight. "Where have you been, what have you been doing?" Lazarus asked. "We hear that there are many more with you now, Lord; where do they come from?" Jesus was about to say something in answer when Lazarus held up his hands and said, "No, wait. Save it for Martha and Mary, they want to hear too, they don't want to miss anything." Then, leaning close to Jesus, he said in a conspiratorial tone, "However, you can tell me just a few things, can't you? Things they wouldn't understand, just man to man, eh? After all, they don't have to know everything!" I think this was a private joke, with a meaning just for the two of them, for they both began to laugh merrily.

"Lazarus, my friend, it has been good, and it is good to see you. My dear brother, your eyes do sparkle so. It's good to see you so happy. Now, tell me of your sisters." With that query, Lazarus leaned close to Jesus' again and whispered in his ear. What he said, I do not know, but it brought peals of laughter from them both. Then Jesus groaned and said, "She shouldn't wait for me. I love her, but if she waits for me, she'll wait forever!"

"I've told her that a thousand times, Yeshu, but she doesn't believe me, does she?" Lazarus shook his head and shrugged his shoulders in resignation.

"Oh, well," Jesus continued, "it's all right, I'll talk to her again tonight. I'll make her understand somehow, but you're right, it's nearly impossible, isn't it?" With that, Jesus changed the subject away from the personal, became more serious, and went back to the way we are used to knowing him—teaching.

"Yes, my friend, you have heard right, we have gathered more about us. Oh, Lazarus, my brother, if only I could..." For a moment he paused in his walk and looked at his friend as if he were about to tell him something of monumental importance. Then, shaking his head, he said, "No, there is no way I can share this with you, no matter what I wish." No one knew what Jesus was speaking of, least of all Lazarus, yet we were all immediately concerned, for our Lord's seriousness lately frightened us all more than any of us cared to admit.

I stepped up to Jesus and silently put my hand lightly on his arm to see if he was all right. He turned to me. Our eyes locked, and I found a sorrow there I didn't know existed. He patted my arm, and in a strange voice he said, "It is a wonderful thing. Our Father's work, I mean." His words seemed as much for himself as for us. "Just think," he went on, "all those years growing up, all these years preparing, and now the moment is at hand." Jesus seemed to be carrying a frightful burden; you could see it in his eyes. "All these souls..." He paused, still holding my eyes transfixed in his, "All these souls. Some nights they weigh so heavily on me. So many souls, so many that I cannot touch them all! My time is so near, I just can't touch them all!" The hair on my neck stood up just as it had on that last morning in Galilee when death swept through me in that icy blast.

Then, I believe, sensing that this was neither the time nor the place, Jesus caught himself, took a deep breath, shook as if ridding himself of a deep chill, and changed the mood as rapidly as it had come. He turned away from me. He was again light and bantering.

"Wonderful, Lazarus, everything is wonderful." He slapped Lazarus on the back, and together they started off again on the road to Bethany. He glanced back over his shoulder at me still standing transfixed in the middle of the road, and his look told me, "Later, later I will explain."

Turning back to his friend, he picked up the happiness of the day once again, saying joyfully, "They flock to us more and more, brother, in greater numbers every day. You'll have to come and spend a week or two. You can take the time. You will have to come and see for yourself and let me introduce you to many of them.

"But, for now, it will be good just to be in your home, dear brother, and to relax. Can you make arrangements for my followers as they come? Food, lodging, and so on?" Lazarus said that it would be his delight. "But please, find them lodging in a place other than in your home, for I need the rest. I can tell you that, brother, I do need the rest."

With that, Jesus stopped, for we had rounded the last hill, and there, higher up the path leading from the road, were Mary and Martha, waiting and waving. Seeing them, Jesus pointed and exclaimed happily, "There are your dear sisters! Ah, it's going to be good to see them and to forget everything for awhile." Jesus rushed forward to throw his arms around them. The greeting was tumultuous and wonderful to share.

Later, as I stood to the side of all the activity, leaning against the back wall of the living room in this simple, two-room home, watching the happy homecoming, I thought about what had happened on the road. For the first time, it occurred to me that no one, not one of us, worried about him—Jesus—we worried only about ourselves. I thought, "Here we have a man who gives of himself totally, each and every day, and yet when have we ever heard one word of complaint? When does he rest?" The thought had never even occurred to me before. "When he has walked all day, and he takes his rest in a friendly home, when his disciples take their ease with food and drink, without a care in the world, what is Jesus doing? He is teaching, teaching, teaching. He can never allow himself to stop, for continually in his ear he hears: 'Help me, Jesus,' 'Tell me, Lord,' 'Why me, Jesus?' 'Teach us, rabbi,' from early morning until late at night. It never stops."

Thinking back, even when he had been at our home, could he rest from the constant questions, even there? The answer was, unforgivably, no. For even there, my son, or his wife, or my wife, or I were always occupying his time with questions. No wonder he could not stay with us when, as now, he needed to get away from the crowds, the questions, and the pleadings. I felt again the pang of shame.

As I stood there in the home of Lazarus, in the back corner of the room, watching, I remembered back to just before we arrived, while we were still on the road, how Jesus' heart gladdened when he saw the women. He had grabbed Lazarus and said, "What would I do without you? Oh, sweet brother of mine, you have always treated me just the same. Since our boyhood in Egypt, always my friend!" Laughingly, he admonished, "Tell me, is your sister going to get emotional again tonight?" Lazarus responded, "You have to deal with her tonight, Lord, not me."

"I suppose I do, I suppose I do at that, you're right. All right, but no stories late at night, understood? You tell her that. I'll be here for a few days, and there will be plenty of time to talk. I need rest tonight."

Mary loved Jesus with all her heart, and I wager she would have given her life to have been allowed to take this man as her husband, but that was not Jesus' lot in this life. He came not to grace but one; instead, he came to give everything he had for us all.

Mary's love touched me though and reminded me of my dear Miriamme. Once in the living room and seated on cushions spread about, Mary came to Jesus, bowed before him, sunk to her knees, bent over, grasped Jesus' feet in her hands, and began to sob. Once again I struggled to hold back my emotions as I watched this woman, who loved this man so dearly, try to wash his feet with her tears.

The room fell silent as each of us watched this heart-wrenching scene.

"No, Mary, no, Please don't." He spoke softly to her and tried to lift her gently to her feet, but she was determined in her love. "Don't, Mary, not with your tears, Mary, please," Jesus pleaded. "I know they are tears of joy, but you mustn't." Mary continued to worship her Lord in the only way she knew—totally. Jesus' eyes were filling with tears now too, as he tried again to dissuade her. "No, Mary, dear one, I understand, but please, enough." Then, bending forward, he touched her still-bowed head and said, "Dear one, I love you with all my heart. No one has ever loved me so much as you, and I will repay you this love shortly." He shut his eyes very tightly and murmured, "Oh, God, if she only knew how soon it will be, if she only knew." There was that far-away look in his eyes again. I moved deeper into the shadows of foreboding and wondered at his words.

He released her bowed head from his gentle hands, and Mary started to back away from him, to go help with the preparations for the evening meal. Jesus lay back against the pillows with a sigh and said, "Let me lie here for a moment, just one moment, please. Don't leave me, Mary. Sit by my side. Your sister works well enough for two; please, just let me rest a moment. My poor body grows heavy and feels the walks more acutely each day. The days seem to get longer, and the path shorter all the time. It's all rushing so fast, so fast now, Father, so fast." His voice began to trail as my precious teacher slowly sank into an exhausted sleep. You could barely hear him intone, "The words... the memories... Abba, Abba, I love you. Guide me, Lord. Make me strong. They all drain me so, Father. Abbaaa..."

With a heartfelt sigh, his breathing deepened, and he dropped into sleep. Mary was curled at his feet as I silently slipped away and headed for the loneliness of the hills beyond the town.

Chapter 14

The Turmoil Begins

Jesus was moved with pity for them and touched their eyes. And instantly they could see, and follow him.

Matthew 20:30 & 34

Then Jesus placed his hands over the man's eyes again and as the man stared intently, his sight was completely restored... Jesus sent him home to his family.

Mark 8:25

As he was walking along, he saw a man blind from birth... Then he spat on the ground and made mud from the spittle and smoothed the mud over the blind man's eyes, and told him, "Go and wash in the Pool of Siloam."

Matthew 20:30 & 34

Now begins a period of months of anguish for me that ended in the death of my Lord, which I could do nothing to forestall. I know now that it was ordained by our Father and carried out by His son with a degree of timing and a sense of eloquence incomprehensible to any of us at that time.

Soon after I returned from my trip to Galilee, Jesus set about to prepare for the culmination of his teaching, and we, along with him, were mere players in this drama of life, death, and then life again. For, sure to his word to me on the hilltop, he did venture south into Judea to Jerusalem to celebrate the Feast of Tabernacles. Then, from the period of the Feast of Tabernacles (that autumn) through the Feast of Dedication (in early winter) unto Passover (in the spring of the following year), Jesus taught in the Temple and throughout the surrounding area of Judea without returning to his native Galilee.

As he taught, he healed; and the more he healed, the more he became the focus of the people of Israel; and the more he became the hero, the miracle worker, the prophet, the Messiah, the more the priests and rulers wanted him out of the way. Within a week of his arrival, a very agitated Nicodemus visited me at my home. My old friend was beside himself with grief, worry, and rage. I had no more than got him settled down and had asked Miriamme to pour wine when he spurted out the happenings at the Temple that day.

"As you know, the rumors have been rampant that Jesus was somewhere here in Jerusalem, and I among them wondered too. Well, I was in the Temple today, as is my custom, when to my surprise there began a commotion in the outer court which grew to such an intensity that we all left the buildings to find the cause. To my astonishment, there before me was Jesus!

"People were running from everywhere as word spread that the miracle worker from Galilee had arrived. Most of my colleagues pushed their way close to hear what this fellow they had heard so much about—who was rumored greater than the Baptist—had to say. I tell you, Asher, he made no hiding of it; in fact he fairly shouted it out. You could not hear his words without knowing that he was declaring himself to be heaven-sent and special—yes, maybe even the Messiah himself. Yet so clever was he in his words and deeds that any who heard would be hard pressed to stone him for blasphemy. But, so close did he come, and so aroused did the crowd become, that the Temple guards were sent to stop him and bring him to Caiaphas for questioning.

"As Jesus spoke, we were all watching the fortress nervously for signs of what the Romans were about. With the Temple full to capacity during these holidays, a confrontation had to be avoided at all costs (lest we forget our lesson at the hands of Archelaus). But, arrest him, this I could not stand! So, when the Temple officers returned empty-handed, I gave a silent sigh of relief. He had escaped them, Asher, and I was glad."

With this, Nicodemus most uncharacteristically downed an entire goblet of wine placed there by my wife as refreshment; and he did this in one swallow. "Oh, Asher, then I did a most terrible thing," he continued.

By now I had lost all semblance of patience. My worry was escalating throughout Nicodemus' never-ending story. "What, Nicodemus, what did you do?" I asked with exasperation.

Miriamme tugged at my sleeve, urging forbearance.

"I'm getting to that, Asher, patience, please." I sank into the chair and thought, "He will never tell me—never!"

"Old Annas was there," Nicodemus finally continued, "full of righteous indignation, and said mockingly, 'Is there a single Sadducee or Pharisee among us who truly believes that this carpenter king from Galilee is the Messiah?' No one uttered a sound as Annas looked from one to another. 'The stupid crowd will believe anyone who will heal an ache or a pain. I spit on them!' Then he bid the officer of the guards to go again and arrest 'this man called Jesus.' I could see old Annas' son-in-law, the High Priest Caiaphas, lick his lips with delight. I was so incensed, Asher, that I did something I can't believe as yet—I stood and challenged Annas. Can you believe I would challenge the High Priest past, and the entire house of Caiaphas?"

"What did you say to him, Nicodemus?" I said, gritting my teeth. Miriamme refilled the wine goblet.

"As the officer started to walk away to do the high priest's bidding, I stepped in front of him and said, 'You shall go nowhere to arrest anyone this day!' The officer stopped in his tracks, looked at me in surprise, then turned to see what his orders would be. While there was a stunned silence, I grabbed the moment and asked, 'Is it legal to convict a man before he is even officially accused?'

"Annas screamed, 'Are you a Galilean too, Nicodemus? Search the Scriptures and see for yourself—no prophets will come from Galilee!' Still incensed, I continued undaunted, 'He was born in Judea, like you, Annas, and from the house of David—not in Galilee!' This so upset the group gathered around us that they all began to argue among themselves.

"Annas realized he had lost the moment of decisive decision. Thus, with a quick glance at Caiaphas for his approval, he angrily dismissed the guard and ordered everyone out."

"You did very well, my friend," I told Nicodemus. (I really was quite impressed and surprised.) "Very well indeed. Why do you appear so worried now, though?"

"Because, Asher ben Ammi, that was only the beginning, just a skirmish. They will kill him, Asher, believe me, they will kill him. And now that I am counted along with him I have lost the element of surprise; I will be counted as one with their enemies. No longer will I be privy to what they hatch behind their people's backs. Please, Asher, find him and warn him that the priests will not tolerate too much more."

With this warning ringing in my head, I saw poor Nicodemus to the door and bid my manservant to see him safely home, which was not far away, while Miriamme called for John. Together we sent him heading for Lazarus' house in an attempt to find Jesus. As for me, I headed to the Temple, glad that I had remained a hidden disciple, or at least not an open one here in Judea, for I planned to listen to what I could behind the closed doors of the Temple gates. But my plans fell by the wayside as I inadvertently picked up my Lord's trail in quite an accidental way.

I came to the aqueduct, which I had to go under before reaching the bridge over the valley leading into the Temple grounds. There, at the intersection close to the market, stood a mixed crowd listening intently to a man, a poor man by the looks of him. I pulled my cloak about me and started to hurry on my way, when I was halted in my tracks by the name "Jesus."

I swung on my heels, suddenly interested in this man wrapped in rags, an Arabian I guessed from his looks, but certainly not a Jew. I could hear enough from the edge of the crowd to learn he had been blind in one eye all his life, could see but poorly out of the other, but now he was on his way home, healed in both eyes, because of a man named Jesus.

From the periphery of the crowd I found one of the shopkeepers who worked for my son, John, pulled him aside, and paid him to fetch the poor man and bring him to my house. "Tell him that a follower of the man who healed him wishes only to see him fed, bathed, and sent on his way home after a good night's sleep in a clean bed and with clean clothes." Then I anxiously covered the short distance left to the Temple and knocked on the massive doors for admittance.

The Temple was closed at this hour of the day, save to those of us who had paid our way well through the years. Thus, I was admitted into the Temple where I spent the better part of an hour trying to ascertain from the priests, and those I could still find there at that hour, exactly what had transpired that day. From what I learned, it appeared that Nicodemus had not exaggerated. He had made a few enemies that day but won some admirers as well (for few there are who will stand up against the fury of the high priest—or his father-in-law). Upon leaving, I had pretty well assured myself that there was as yet no coordinated effort to bring Jesus up on official charges. I felt relieved, at least for the moment, and headed home, wondering what luck John had in Bethany and whom my strange guest would prove to be.

Upon returning home, I met John just coming through the stable gates with news that he had seen Jesus and that Jesus had given him his assurance that everything would be alright, that we should rest easy. He had told John that his time was not yet come, and that although there would be much furor over his preaching, there would be nothing done that would bring him harm during this holiday.

Much relieved, I clasped my son around the shoulders and explained what I had learned while he was gone. Together we entered our courtyard to find the stranger just coming out of the guest quarters, where my manservant had garbed him in one of John's finest robes. I saw my son's startled look, followed by the blood of anger rising to his face. With mock gravity, I looked at him with concern and said, "John, I am surprised at you. Have you forgotten so soon what Jesus has taught you, that it is more blessed to give than to receive?"

I caught him more by surprise than I thought, for now his brightened skin was from embarrassment. He apologized to me and strode ahead to meet our guest with open arms. Our guest's name turned out to be Maston. He had little or no education, but I was right about his heritage; he was an Arabian of mixed but very handsome blood. In fact, quite to my discomfort, I noticed Miriamme's eyes more than once that night glancing toward this good-looking stranger. But, ignoring that, what a story he told, one that I could hardly believe!

I think, if I had not seen the multiplication of the loaves and fishes with my own eyes and heard of the healing of Timothy's dead leg in his own presence, I would have dismissed this man's testimony as being too far-fetched to be true. Yet I will let you judge for yourself, as you must anyway.

"Please understand," he started, "I have been blind in my right eye since birth. I have never seen out of it. Although at one time I could see with my other eye as well as you, about a year ago it started to go bad as well. I saw so poorly that it was of little use plying a trade or making a living at anything at all. I came to Jerusalem, the Holy City, to find a cure, to find some hope for me. I came from the desert, where my home lies, and that is where my family awaits my return.

"For almost a year I sought a cure for my eyes. I went from one doctor to another, but I searched in vain. I was out of money and had no way to earn enough even to return to my home again. I was reduced to lying by the healing pool, waiting my turn to get close enough so that when the water boiled, I might be healed. Have you been there? Have you seen what it is like?" I had to admit that I hadn't. I tried to stay away from places like that, which served only to depress me greatly.

"It is a filthy place. The small pool is maybe forty or fifty paces across and suffers the refuge and waste of hundreds of people each day. It is more a wallow than a pool now, and the water is the same color as the mud around it—brown. The ground around rises up to about the height of a man on three of the sides—the fourth provides the outlet and is covered with bushes of several kinds—and from there it levels away. Any ground cover around the pool has long since been worn away or trampled into dust by the teeming mobs that come each day to be cured or saved. It is said that when a miracle is about to happen, the water begins to boil.

Maston continued, "From my position atop the ridge, I could hear and vaguely see people of every ailment and infirmity—except lepers—lining the dirt, awaiting the movement of the holy water below. I had seen it happen only once. 'Experienced it' is a more accurate description, for at that time, the stampede of people became so intense that the healings (if there were any) were far outweighed by the trampled bodies that were left behind to be hauled away. Yet, even as I say this, I feel little remorse, for it was only by someone's death that any of us could move our allotted place any closer to the water. So it was that when the miracle made the water boil, we willingly threw our bodies into the water, no matter what the risk. So miserable had our lives become that death was preferable to this living hell within which we lived."

My stomach reeled as my imagination filled in any gaps it found in this poor creature's story. In my wealth, I could not, no matter how I tried, imagine what it must be like to live as this man had.

We urged him to continue.

"As we sat there day after day, our lot became worse through lack of food and care. Once in a while people would come as an act of charity and bring us food, but that was rare. As for myself, I stayed alive by walking each evening to the village and begging. I also picked up scraps of food that had been thrown out from behind the homes. Meanwhile, at the pool, each of us had our spot, you know. We would have fought and killed if someone tried to take it, thus everyone knew his place. I had no idea how long it would take to find my way to the bottom of the hill to a spot that might allow me to throw myself into the water should it begin to rise. For up to then, I had been too far away to get to the water, or and even try.

"Once in a while someone wealthy would come with their retainers, and sometimes soldiers would come with their men. They would simply wade in and clear a path. They would just throw us away! It was easy because most of the people were so emaciated; they couldn't have weighed more than a small bag of salt. The soldiers just threw us away, as if we were less than animals lying in their path.

"I remember one poor man who was the only exception to the rule of position. A group of men brought him there. They picked him up by his rags and threw him down the hill, caring not a twit upon whom he fell in the human refuse pile. His legs didn't work. Nothing worked at all. He just lay there for the longest while, face down in the dirt. It was hard to tell whether or not he was alive. His legs were just bones; there was no meat on them at all. But slowly, ever so slowly, he lifted his head, then stretched out his arms; then, with the strength only of his will, he dragged his body inch by inch, with his fingers clawing at the earth, down the hill. Closer and closer to the water's edge he went. His legs I remember so clearly—they were the thinnest things I had ever seen. Each and every one of us, no matter how terrible we felt, began to hold our breath as he worked his way agonizingly closer to the water's edge with singular intensity.

He dragged himself across the ground and bodies, too, which lay in his way. As he would pull himself over a poor wretch, he'd look neither left nor right but with glazed eyes stared straight at his goal, hearing not his dead legs thud and crack as they bumped and bounced over rocks and bodies alike. Nor did he feel the blows delivered by some of those whom he crossed. I am sure he had made up his mind that he would be healed or would go to the bottom of the pond. It mattered little to him how it ended, just so that it did.

"As he got to the edge of the pool, he couldn't throw himself in. He had only one way to move, and so, slowly, deliberately, excruciatingly, he began to drag his torn and mutilated body into the water, head first, the only way he could. Then he took a breath and dropped beneath the surface. Thank God, some poor wretch like himself took pity on him then, for he would surely have drowned before his legs flopped in. A man with crippled arms and back gave a mighty growl and kicked the rest of him in.

"At last, I thought, the agony has ended. It became deadly quiet. Everyone's eyes were riveted on the unmoving water. Then, when everyone thought the drama had run its course, we suddenly saw his head begin to emerge from the pool! Then slowly, steadily, he started to rise. He started to stand! It was like a lost continent, ponderously beginning its rise from the depths of some great, murky sea. He didn't say a word. First his head, then his shoulders, then, as he still stared straight ahead his waist broke free. We thought a demon was holding him up, and many in his way began to shake and back away in terror and fear.

"He walked out of the pool on his own two feet, which, although bloody and bruised and still thin as a sliver of wood, were working and strong. He walked over the top of the rise and left. We never saw him again. There wasn't anything said for the longest time. We were so shocked. Then... it was awful!"

The poor man in front of us began to break down and cry as he finished telling of this grim scene. "It was just awful!" he cried again. "They came by the tens, by the hundreds, all rushing and clamoring to get into the water while the magic lasted. The stronger fought over the weaker, and the weaker died. That's when the man kicked me. That's when he kicked me in the eye! Water gushed out of the socket, and, oh God, it hurt so terribly. He kicked my blind eye, and he didn't even care! I never got to the water. I simply lay there, staring into the flaming pain."

We were all sobbing as we listened but hardly comprehended this poor man's story of abuse and terror beyond anything we could understand. Miriamme became sick and had to rush from the room, but Maston kept right on with his story, seemingly unaffected by our loss of composure.

"I lived that way for a month and a day, existing on scraps people gave me to keep me alive—though I barely cared. In fact, today was like all the rest. I didn't even notice the man when he came. I lay on my back and looked up at the sky with what was left of my one ill-seeing eye. It was a hazy morning, and I remember that the sky was a light, egg-shell blue. I just lay there and watched the one fuzzy, wispy cloud off near the horizon as it changed into a hundred different shapes before disappearing into nothingness. The sun was bright and the air warm. Nothing else entered into my consciousness, nothing; it was empty. For the past few days I had been lying like that, staring into nothingness, caring little when the end came. Until somewhere an urging inside told me that something was amiss.

"All of a sudden, I knew what was wrong: the noise, the arguing, the chatter, the moaning, and the wailing of the people had stopped. I propped myself up to see what was happening. It took a minute for my one eye to adjust, for the ground was dark in comparison to the livid sky, and the sight from my one marginally working eye was hazy at best. In front of me, there was the man—the man I learned they call Jesus.

"He was wearing just his loincloth, that's all. Someone off to the side was holding his robe for him, but now he was up to his thighs in the water. He stood there, right in front of me, but I couldn't figure out what made all the people quiet, for although I could see the man looming up in front of me from this short distance, I couldn't understand what brought about the unnatural hush that had fallen all about.

"Then I noticed. He stood there in an easy manner, his arms were limp at his sides, but he was looking straight at me! I mean, there were hundreds of people there, but he was looking straight at me. There was not a sound to be heard, except the roaring in my head as I realized that for some reason I had been singled out of the crowd. Then he held up one hand in my direction, as if he expected me to come and take hold of it—and still he stared. Then he held two hands toward me.

"I had to get up. There was nothing else I could do. I thought I was going to be killed. I thought, 'They will stone me; they know I am not a Jew. That is why he has singled me out, he has come to have me killed.' I started to walk, if you could call it that. I stumbled and slid down the rest of the hill because my legs were so weak from hunger. I fell and got up again, and fell again, then reluctantly entered the water. Slowly I walked toward him, trembling as I went, tears streaming down my mud-caked cheeks.

"I saw his robes being held by his men, and I knew that he was a Jew. I was panic-stricken; I wanted to run, but there was no place to go. I pleaded, 'No, Lord, I'm not of your race. Please, you're a Jew; they'll stone me, they'll stone me for sure!' Inside I was wailing, 'Doesn't he know he's killing me? You might as well drown me, I'm a dead man when they get hold of me.' I stepped into the water. The pool was hot! And, the deeper I went, the hotter it became. I struggled to keep my balance on my tottering legs. They were burning so bad that I cried in pain. Then my agony was over, for I was in front of him, and now I knew I was surely to die. I remember I was up to my waist and he up to his thighs, so I knew he was taller than me.

"He put his hand on my head, over my face and my eyes, and I could feel that he was slowly forcing open my bad eye. 'Don't!' I shrieked, 'Don't, I'm blind! Please don't, oh please, it hurts so. Don't open my eye!' I screamed for the last time, in a mixture of terror and agony, trying to clench my eye tightly shut against his prying. At the same time, he was slowly pressing me down into the water. I knew I had finally met my end. I could not have resisted him if I had tried, but I did try, with all my strength. 'OPEN IT!' the man shouted in my ear. 'OPEN YOUR EYE!' I was whimpering and gasping for air, but he wouldn't let up. 'OPEN YOUR EYE, MASTON!'

"Slowly I sank beneath the agitated waves as the sound of my name rang in my head. 'How did he know my name, how?' The water was over my head. I couldn't breathe, yet longer than I could hold my breath he held me there without letting me up. I let my breath out with a gasp and started to sink into oblivion; then all of a sudden I was standing again, facing him, but this time... I could see!

"'Who are you?' I gasped. 'You can't be a Jew, or you wouldn't have done what you have done to me, a nonbeliever. Who are you, Lord? Who is your god? Tell me so that I may worship him. My god could never do this. I will follow your god anywhere. Just tell me who you are, and who he is, so that I may follow him.'

"Then for the first time this man of miracles spoke quietly to me. 'Maston, your god and mine are one.'

"'But, who is your god, Lord?'

"'Maston, your god and mine are one; neither is better. I say again, they are ONE!'

"Suddenly I was afraid for this man who had brought me back my sight. 'No, Lord, don't say that. You'll be killed along with me for saying that!'

"'Maston, was your eye blind?'

"'Yes, Lord, you know that.'

"'Maston, do you now see?'

"'Yes, Lord, you know that, too.'

"'Maston, your god and mine are one. When you go away from here, you will know there is only one Lord God.'

"'Master,' I said, 'I will proclaim that—but they will kill you for it!' He suddenly put his hands on either side of my head. Instantly I saw a brilliant light. Speaking very slowly he said, 'Maston, can you now see?'

"'Yes, Lord, they are One, Lord.'

"'Yes, Maston.'

"'Then they will kill you, Lord.'

"'Yes, Maston, they will kill me.'

"'Then not from my mouth will they hear this.'

"'Maston, you won't have to watch long.'

"'Watch?'

"'And when I am gone, then you can tell.'

"'How long will I watch you, Lord?'

"'Maston, have I not given you eyes to see? Go now to your home, tell your wife, your family.'

"'You won't ever see me again, Lord?'

"'Maston, have I led you this far only to lead you astray? Watch after me, Maston, and when I am gone, come to my people and tell them what you see.'

"I started to sob uncontrollably. 'Yes, Lord. Thank you, Lord. I will tell them that I can see. I can see!'

"I am still confused, noble Asher ben Ammi," Maston confessed. "He left me then, just walked away without saying another word. The people paid me no mind, for they were screaming for him to heal them, too. And those who could still walk followed him as I stood looking after him. I didn't know what to do, so I started walking to the edge of the pool and out. Then I found my way into the city on my way home, and that was when you found me."

A cold fear ran through me, a fear that I had felt once in Galilee, then again the previous week in Bethany. It was a fear that I could not quite isolate but which struck me as an emptiness in the pit of my stomach, a void so immensely deep that I felt it could never again be filled.

I forced my thoughts back to the frail, handsome, middle-aged man in front of me. What a change from the dirty street beggar I had seen just a few hours before. How many more could we welcome into our homes without question if only someone cared enough to help?

Maston was speaking to me. "Did I do right in telling you as I did?" He was more pleading than asking.

"Hmm? Oh, yes. I'm sorry, Maston, my mind was somewhere else," I apologized. "Yes, you did right. But I will ask you to fulfill your promise to him as he asked. Cling to this man's teaching, my friend, and I think in time you will understand his message to you. Yes, I am afraid you will understand it all too soon.

"Come, Miriamme, dinner is waiting, and our guest has not had a decent meal for a very long time." I took my wife's hand and led her into the next room where the evening meal was being served. On the way out the door, I could not help myself from saying to our guest (just loud enough for John to hear), "My, that robe does look good on you. It was an ill fit on its previous owner anyway. I swear, if you keep dressing like that, Maston, we will make you Jewish yet." Everyone laughed, save my son, who shot me a dirty look in return and, I might add, plotted his little revenge.

The next morning, after I came down from the rooftop where I customarily meet the new day, writing and meditating, my guest was waiting for me in the court. "If I may be so bold, sir," Maston started, "what do you do so early on the roof of your house?"

"My friend, you have a bright and curious mind. When once you greet your family and friends and have a proper time to settle your affairs, why don't you return? Bring your wife and children too, if you have any, and return to Jerusalem to join my household and serve me in any capacity you might choose. There is much to teach you, if you have a desire to learn. Then I will tell you of my Master whom you met yesterday at the pool. I think you will find that your stay will be most rewarding in many ways, and I think you might be most happy here too."

"You are very kind. I accept your offer only too willingly. Thank you. You will see. Someday I will return." With that, we joined John, his wife, and Miriamme for a light morning meal. Then, giving Maston food and enough money for his journey home, we set about to give him a horse to send him on his way. I bade him farewell from the courtyard, entrusted him into my son's hands, then climbed the stairs to the roof to watch and wave goodbye from there.

I couldn't believe my eyes. Was I seeing right? As Maston flew from our stable yard, he was riding my own black gelding, not the horse I had selected for him the previous day. I vaulted down the stairs, yelling at the top of my lungs, and when I hit the bottom stair, I started running across the stones toward the courtyard door. "He's got the wrong horse!" I screamed as John started closing the double stable doors.

Pushing him out of the way, I turned back toward the interior to get another horse to chase him down. "You let him have my horse! I just can't believe it!" I fumed as I turned the corner, going out the back way to find another steed.

Five steps did I take before the last of John's soft words sunk home. "I think the horse goes well with the new robe, don't you?"

Chapter 15

The Lessons Continue

I am the true Vine, and my Father is the Gardener. He lops off every branch that doesn't produce. And he prunes those branches that bear fruit for even larger crops. He has already tended you by pruning you back for greater strength and usefulness by means of the commands I gave you. Take care to live in me, and let me live in you. For a branch can't produce fruit when severed from the vine. Nor can you be fruitful apart from me.

John. 15:1-4

I don't have much more time to talk to you, for the prince of this world approaches. He has no power over me, but I will freely do what the Father requires of me so that the world will know that I love the Father. Come, let's be going.

John 14:30-31

The story of the healing of Maston's blindness and his ominous warning to Jesus set me on edge. Thus began a week of foreboding, alarm, and torment for me. Each day found me at the Temple early to wait for Jesus to arrive, and each day found Jesus preaching to the people, whose numbers grew proportionately with the days that went by. Nicodemus and I could only shake our heads, for Jesus spoke out mightily against the leaders among us. Not one was spared the lash of his wit and sharp tongue, and we (all of us who followed him) were desolate that we would ever be able to save him once the time came for the high priest to seize him. For in the end, we knew that it would not be the rabble that would build him a power base, but rather we who were at the source—or so I thought.

When word of the blind man's healing reached the crowds, with those who had seen the miracle witnessing to all those who would hear, the crowds that sought Jesus became almost unbearable. And as the story grew, as is natural, so did his "followers."

They were not his true followers, I well knew, for as soon as the holy days were finished, they would vanish with the wind; back to their homes, their towns, their villages, and their tents—then where would Jesus stand? I was very bitter and discouraged during this time, for the man I saw was not the gentle man of Galilee, with whom so short a time ago I had spent the happiest moments of my life.

I was sick with what I saw happening, and powerless to stop it. The problem was not with the people, for truth and hope are hard to fault, and the people were more than happy to follow anyone who would lead. In their desperate need, they saw in him the promised power, wealth, freedom, and fame that had escaped them in their own ruler's greed. So they encouraged him and cheered him in this futile aim.

If it had not been for these very masses, which everyone feared could easily be whipped into religious fervor (bringing the Roman might into sway), and the Zealots (the Sicarii among them), who now surrounded Jesus wherever he went, he would surely have been stoned for blasphemy, much to the priests' delight. As it was, almost nightly those of the inner council met to plan his death. They waited only for the right moment: just one miscalculated deed and they would do with Jesus as they had with other messiahs, and even with the baptizer, John, before him—they would have his head.

As the holy days ended and the people began to disperse, Jesus disappeared. He just vanished. I, as well as others, sought in vain for word of his whereabouts. Neither he nor his disciples could be found.

I sought an answer, and so it was that I inquired after Placidus, to see what he had heard. Had Jesus yet attracted undue attention in the Roman camp? I knew that the Tribune Placidus would have heard. Desperate times call for calculated risks, and so I ventured to the Baths to find this Roman who, although as yet would admit it to no other, I believed that he had become a secret follower (or at least an ardent admirer) of my Lord. Anyway, I had to take that chance; and if need dictated, I felt that Placidus would be discreet in his questioning of the proper authorities and would answer me honestly if the news was bad.

Yet, being the Jew that I was, I could never have expected the tidings that he brought.

I found him in the Frigidarium, the coldest of the baths. I never could fathom these Romans who put so much stock in the appearance of their bodies. Upon gaining his attention (which wasn't hard, for I was the only Jew about) and motioning him to come my way, he agreeably swam over to where I was leaning at the edge. "Please, Placidus, I need a word with you in private, if I might." He nodded and said he would meet me in the garden as soon as he could get dressed.

I was pacing nervously back and forth when, true to his word, he approached me alone across the green of the garden. "Placidus, my friend," I started hesitantly, "my heart is troubled, and I know not where else to turn. There has been trouble in the Temple, and I fear for Jesus' life. The high priest Caiaphas would see him dead, if he has half a chance." I caught myself pacing again and wringing my hands, which I stopped as soon as I noticed, and with great difficulty held my calm as best I could. Just being put into this situation of confiding in a Roman made bumps stand out on my skin. "To make matters worse, he has disappeared with his closest followers, and we know not where he is."

Placidus could not conceal his surprise. "Why, Asher, I am amazed, for I saw him just last night, at a dinner party thrown by Lacayus. He seemed fit and well and provided the most wonderful entertainment I could imagine."

His shock at my question was more than equaled by my own at this stunning turn of events. Had my Master lost his mind? If the priests heard this news, it would surely seal his fate, for no Jew would defile himself by going to a drunken dinner party at the home of our unclean, heathen masters. The thought was too excruciatingly painful to contemplate. I turned ashen as the blood drained from my face, and Placidus, fearing I was about to stroke (and being ignorant of our deep-seated social and religious prejudices against dining with the Romans), sought only to seat me more comfortably upon a bench before I passed out.

Thinking he was cheering me up with this new and wonderful news of my Lord, which I had not as yet heard, he was only too happy to begin telling me everything that went on at the dinner, in the minutest detail. I tried to conceal my feelings, but the thought of Jesus at a Roman party, of all things, was most difficult for me to understand.

I tell you of this event now because it is only now that he is gone, and I have had time to take within me the impact and the detail of Jesus' planning, that I see those things I could not see as they took place. Only now, after speaking to Peter, am I able to fill in the last gaps to the mystery of these last months of Jesus' life. But this must wait for you to see for yourself. Be it enough for now that I tell you of the events that took place that night. Jesus, indeed, had friends and alliances I knew nothing about.

Jesus had been invited to this gathering of wealthy patrons of the Roman Lacayus. He came to the home with two of his disciples (Peter and Judas—the reason for which I will try to make clear). He found before him both men and women of great means, each at ease, lounging on couches and taking their meal. Most had eaten and drunk too much already, and Jesus knew that Lacayus had invited him more for sport than for any lessons he might give.

The dimly lit chamber was heavy with shadows and noisy with alcoholic laughter as Jesus looked about the room. Jesus' eyes stopped when he spied a young Greek diplomat named Theodore, whose eyes were beginning to glaze with drink and whose mind was full of lascivious thoughts. Theodore, for his part, stared through blurry eyes and tried to focus on the man who had just entered the room. Jesus was glad to find the Greek. He would purposely address his comments to him, for compared to the Romans (whose minds usually missed the subtleties of his teachings), the Greeks were possessed with insight and intellect.

The Romans, thick of mind, envied and imitated the Greeks; and Jesus knew that if he drew young Theodore into the conversation, then the interests of the Roman guests would soon follow. A keen judge of people and events, Jesus could size up a complex and difficult situation such as this in an instant and accomplish what no other could.

The Roman Lacayus thought that this Jew, who was rumored to be an intellectual of the highest order—and no friend of the high and mighty priests—might prove to be a wonderful surprise for his guests. If Jesus were as witty as Lacayus had heard, then it would provide interesting entertainment, indeed, for Jews were honored for nothing, except their ridiculous stiff-necked religious tendencies. If, on the other hand, Jesus made any slips at all, Lacayus knew his young Greek guest would lick the spittle from his arrogant lips and devour Jesus alive with his own words. This is why Lacayus had made sure this young, arrogant, sharp-witted, and equally sharp-tongued guest, had been invited.

Theodore, however, had only one thing in mind for the evening: he had accepted the invitation to the Roman's home because he had been advised that the lovely (and unbedded) Diana was to be there. Never shy of his skill at winning favors from women, Theodore saw the slight, young, delicious Diana as a challenge he could not pass up.

The wine of the evening was already beginning to rise to his head as the proud young Counsel to Judea first noticed his host welcoming in three of the dirty, smelly, unkempt Jews he so detested. What nonsense had this idiot Roman planned for the evening? He thought, "If he spoils my evening with this beautiful girl, now that she is within my grasp, I will have his head."

But the crafty, if not overly bright, Roman had read his guest perfectly. He greeted the rabbi and bid him to sit on the couch next to his. He glanced at his guest who was swinging his lean, well-manicured body into a listening position, with obvious enjoyment beginning to show in the tenseness of his manner.

Lacayus' attention was snapped forcibly back from his social scheming, as he heard Jesus address him in a soft, yet forceful voice, "Where are you from?"

Slightly annoyed with the unquestionably ridiculous query from this Jew, he answered with little thought and a pride that was impossible for any Roman to hide (which served them both well, and ill, in their conquered lands). "I am from Rome!" he proudly exclaimed, with an arrogant obviousness that delighted Theodore no end, as the Greek sensed, by intuition more than word, a trap being set by this unknown rabbi for the simple-minded Lacayus.

Theodore's quick mind was leaping ahead now as he relished the game and sought out an opening in the conversation to join the fray. Already he was positioning the pieces well ahead of the present moves being made by the Jew. There was a flash in Jesus' eye, and Theodore thought for just a second that the rabbi had glanced his way as he spoke, aiming his words and barbs directly at him—could that be? Was it just his imagination? Could this simple Jew truly be setting a trap? And, if so, was it for him or the idiot Roman? He would soon find out.

Jesus remained silent and looked at the Roman, studying his face as if he were still waiting for him to answer. Becoming uncomfortable when Jesus didn't respond to his simple declaration of origin, thinking him perhaps dull of wit, Lacayus repeated, "I am a Roman, I am from Rome!" Then, more out of duty as a host than anything else, he added, "Where are you from, rabbi?"

Jesus answered softly, "I am from my Father."

Suddenly annoyed by the ridiculous direction the conversation had taken, the Roman barked with an irritated air of finality, "We all come from our fathers, what kind of an answer is that?"

Jesus answered so quietly that every eye and ear was now tensely straining to hear him as he said, "But, you do not claim my Father as yours, why is that?"

The silence was deafening as Jesus held his host's eyes with his own, as only Jesus could, saying not a word. The quiet in the room lasted forever for poor Lacayus. He had no idea what to say. None of this made any sense to him. The sweat began to pour from under his arms, and his proud forehead beaded with moisture as he sensed every eye on him now, demanding an answer.

"Because he is not the same father!" he yelled far too loudly, which annoyed him even further as he heard his voice echoing through the hall. He noticed with great discomfort that even the eyes of the guards, trained to ignore everything, turned as he startled them with his outburst. In over his head now, he wondered how he could ever have been so ill advised as to have invited this filthy Galilean to his home. "I am a Roman, and you are a Jew!" he blurted out, trying to control the volume and anger in his voice.

Jesus, a master of people and of the moment, paused for the barest second to gain the attention of everyone present, then said with gentling eyes, "Our fathers are not the same, as you point out, yet our Father is One. How can this be, Lacayus—if we are not brothers?"

The guests (including my friend Placidus) greeted the obvious skill with which the riddle and the lesson had been delivered with great delight. Approving sounds spread throughout the room (not shared, of course, by our poor host, whose head was now splitting with the throbbing pain of humiliation).

Sensing that he had better grab the moment away from Lacayus before the buffoon (seething in embarrassed rage) had his guards do something impetuous, Theodore stood up. With the practiced ease of an experienced orator, he clasped his hands behind his back, feigned a look of deep concentration, and slowly began to pace the center of the room. Once he was sure he had everyone's attention he turned to Jesus and said mockingly, "Tell us more, rabbi. Everyone's attentive to your words, teach us, please."

Jesus smiled warmly at Theodore, then said, "I have no father, no mother, yet with my Father I am One."

Without pausing, Theodore responded, with derision in his voice and barely pretended respect, "Sir, this father you speak of, could he be Zeus?"

"No," Jesus said softly, knowing very well the pattern this conversation would take.

"No? Ah, then would it be Mars, the god of war in whom the Romans believe?"

Jesus again spoke, but so softly that every ear was again straining to hear. "You toy with me, sir; ask your questions that have meaning."

"Ah, then you understand me, sir. I have been told that you Jews believe in but one god. If this is true then tell me, why does your god blind some and allow others see? Why are some poor and some wealthy? Why does he make some dumb as an ox and others as bright as a star? Tell me the answer to that if you will, rabbi." Theodore turned to his delighted audience and was grinning broadly now, very proud of himself.

"I will answer you in a different way, with questions of my own," Jesus said, pausing. "Why are there a thousand flowers on the road? Why do some flowers have fragrance and others rare beauty? Why are some homely, yet they attract bees, and others as beautiful as a crystal, yet attract nothing with their scent? Why are some plain of color and yet others emanate beauty from every pore? Tell me, my dear Theodore, why are there so many flowers? Is one more precious than another?"

Theodore knew at once that the rabbi had had his way, and he could respect him for that. He answered forthrightly; "Why, no, they are all beautiful in their own way."

"Ah, then you do see, my wise Greek," Jesus said, a widening smile now coming over his face, his eyes sparkling in the reflected firelight of a hundred torches. "And so it is with our Father."

Placidus congratulated himself on his judgment of character, knowing now that he had not judged this strange man wrong when first he met him on the hill, shortly after he arrived in Israel. He was indeed an unusual man.

"Well done, Master. Well done!" Theodore graciously bowed his head in respect as the dinner guests clapped and roared their approval. Walking up to where Jesus was sitting, Theodore invited him to sit with him and share his table. Lacayus was more than glad to turn this unpredictable guest over to the Greek, and although he had no idea what pleased his guests so much about the dirty Jew, he relished in the praise that now came his way for having invited such an entertaining guest.

Placidus overheard Lacayus tell the couple next to him that he was just toying with Jesus all along. Placidus' next comment on Lacayus' parentage is best left unsaid.

"What a party this turned out to be," Theodore mused, as he shepherded Jesus over to his couch. "First I have Diana, now I have you.

"You speak well, rabbi, you have learning."

"And you speak well, too, noble Greek, you have learning," Jesus chided as they sat down laughing and began to take their food together.

"Fair enough, rabbi, let us drop the testing and enjoy each other's company." With that they settled into an easy conversation that lasted well into the night.

Thus ended the story from Placidus. He told me everything he knew, he had taken it as far as he could go. I had to wait in agony for nearly a month before, without warning, Peter showed up one night at my door. Jesus had sent him to fetch me to Jericho, to the house of Lazarus' sister, Ruth, at whose house I had first met my Lord face-to-face and in whose house I had first broken bread with him. Jesus left Peter with instructions to start the journey back to him that very night (for Jesus was still in hiding and wanted no one to see us set on our way).

We had a moon, though not full, yet light enough to make travel along the well-worn road safe enough for those who knew their way. Peter had walked to Jerusalem that day, but now rode somewhat tiredly and uncomfortably beside me on the way down the Judean mountainside. By the time we had gone a short way out of the city, it became clear to me that Peter was far more used to the bob and sail of his small wooden boat than the jarring ride on the back of a horse. So, to ease his discomfort, I slowed our gait to an easy walk and engaged him in a conversation that took him back to the night of Lacayus' party.

Peter, relieved that we had slowed to ease his painful and jostled insides, seemed more than willing (as he usually was) to openly tell me of an experience with Jesus.

According to Peter, all during the dinner he and Judas remained in the entrance shadows, silently standing, neither talking to anyone there nor taking any of the defiled food that the Romans proffered. As long as they had been following Jesus, they still were unable to understand why he periodically associated with people who were unclean, whether it was a prostitute or a Roman or a Jewish collaborator—it made little difference to them. It was certainly not done to gain popularity among the followers he must win. And, to Judas, who had sworn an oath to rid his country of the hated enemy, even unto his death, joining Jesus this night in the camp of the enemy was particularly galling. Earlier, when they realized that Jesus was actually going to take them with him—out of hiding—here into the house of a Roman, they tried their best to dissuade him from this folly, but he would hear nothing of it.

Now, after standing all evening waiting, their nervous and sweating hands never far from the daggers hidden beneath their cloaks, they saw that Jesus had finally finished his meal and was heading toward the door looking for them.

Seeing one of the guests making ready to leave, one of Lacayus' servants started for the door to open it for Jesus and his disciples. Suddenly, Jesus put a hand on the servant's arm, stopping him in midstride. "Hush," Jesus warned, "there's someone outside the door. We wait until they are gone." The servant looked quizzically at the other two, hoping for some explanation, but receiving only impassive stares, he waited patiently with them until, at last, Jesus said it was safe—then out the door they went.

Jesus was in upper Jerusalem, in the wealthiest section of the city. The richest and most powerful Jews in all of Judea surrounded this Roman house, and he did not want to be discovered associating with Lacayus and his kind as yet. He had dropped out of sight of the priests and Pharisees (in whose neighborhood he was now dining) in precaution of his life, and this was not the time to be seen, even by a stray servant running an errand in the streets at night. The time to draw the fullest attention to himself was not yet come. And, with the relatively quiet, wide-paved streets here, it did not pay to have three poorly dressed Jews found out alone, especially in this part of town at night, for that in itself could lead to arrest. And if the daggers were found, it could mean arrest for sedition... and death.

When he felt that the street was again empty, Jesus hurriedly led Peter and Judas out of the house. Speaking softly and with some urgency, he said, "Now, let's walk. Draw your cloaks about you. Come, don't tarry." Then they hastened past my own home, down the steps of upper Jerusalem, along the southern wall, then through the poor section where the common tradesmen and workers lived.

The last sounds and smells of the day were comforting as the moon first showed itself over the houses above the narrow streets ahead. These men of Galilee, used to the open country of the north, could never totally relax within the confines of any city's walls. They turned south for a moment at the bottom of the gully of Tyropoean, past the Pool of Siloam and out the gate on the road to Bethany and Jericho. Here, the slow cool breezes coming up the open Kidron Valley refreshed them for the long walk ahead. No one said a word, but as they passed above the olive press of Gethsemane, Jesus began to speak, and speak he did, with a tone as hard and cold as ice. Time was becoming so very precious and lessons had to be learned—and they had to be learned now. The time was soon coming when he would be gone; then there would be none to offer up what had to be done.

"Now, you see, my 'dark ones,' all the while we were in that room tonight, you kept your hoods on and laid your hands upon your hilts. It wasn't necessary.

"Do you see?

"Do you understand?

"You can be the master of the situation. I take you along to show you these things. Do you see? They invited us to make sport; and do you understand yet that you can even teach the Greeks? Do you see that? Keep your wits about you, know that your Father will help you—he is always with you!

"When I send you out to do His bidding, do you think you can carve your way through every situation? Do you think you can carve your way with your daggers into men's hearts? Do you see, my dark ones, standing in the corner with your hoods on, all night in the shadows? Do you see that every guard you sized up was also sizing you? Do you see that you wouldn't have lasted two steps before being cut down, and me along with you?

"Do you not see that I can walk among any of them? I can be with them, and never be touched by them—in any way—until I choose. Learn this lesson this one time. I have no time to repeat it! I walk among them, among your enemies, to teach you that you can walk there too."

Judas, wanting to speak, to tell of his anger, grasped the hilt of his dagger.

"Judas, when will you ever learn? The sword is not why I come! You can carve out a nick with your sword, but the animal will devour you; or you can give our people a living spring—with your tongue and your heart. When will you throw away your sword? It will destroy you!"

Peter said that his ears began to burn, as Jesus now turned his attention to him.

"And, Peter, you big animal! With your great strength, you could have broken two or three men before they took you. Don't you see either? I don't want you to. Don't you see you have a golden tongue? Don't you see that it is with your soul that you carve your way into men's hearts? You big, dumb fisherman, use your eyes, and your heart, and you will capture the world!

"Now, go before me, I want to be alone with my Father."

Peter began to protest. He felt that he had been unjustly accused, and he wanted to defend himself in his Master's eyes; and he was also uneasy about leaving his Master alone in a now hostile land.

"No, do not argue, Peter, I'll be fine. Our Father is with me. I need nothing else. He is with you, too, Peter, if you would just open yourself to him and see."

This time it was Judas who protested as he reached for Jesus' arm to urge him on with them. Trying a tentative grin in the growing silver light of a rising thin moon, Judas started to speak. Still stinging from the rebuke he had received he sought to change Jesus' menacing mood. He didn't understand Jesus when he was like this. Judas liked the Roman pigs even less than Peter did, but now was not the time to argue—he would leave that for tomorrow. He felt wronged, hurt, and upset, but that too would have to wait. His only desire now was to be gone from this place, with Jesus safely in tow.

Jesus' look, without a word, was enough to freeze Judas' hand in midair as Jesus hissed, "Go! You make me angry. You still don't see. Think on your blindness today. I will find you on the morrow. Go!"

While Peter felt hurt, upset and misjudged, Judas was enraged by his Master's harsh words; and thus was planted the seed of evil in Judas' heart, a seed that was to fall upon fertile soil, and in the next few weeks become an all-consuming monster in Judas' heart.

Both Peter and I fell silent after his telling of the story of the party and the harsh words between our Master and two of his disciples. We continued, each in our own deep thoughts, along the long road down through the hills with our plodding mounts toward our goal, Jericho.

Chapter 16

My Awakening

I am leaving you with a gift—peace of mind and heart! And the peace I give isn't fragile like the peace the world gives. So don't be troubled or afraid. Remember what I told you. I am going away, but I will come back to you again. If you really love me, you will be very happy for me, for now I can go to the Father, who is greater that I am. I have told you these things before they happen so that when they do, you will believe in me.

John 14:27-29

Peter and I rode all night, reaching Jericho just before the sun broke above the hills beyond the Jordan. Before us, the lightening sky silhouetted the mountain steeps into great pools of mysterious blackness, broken only here and there by torches lit earlier to start the work of the day for those who plied their living from this dry but fertile land.

The smell of the desert air rising to the nostrils in the early morning is something I have always cherished. It is as impossible to describe it as is the total and absolute unbroken silence that can also be found only in this place called "the wilderness" by people who have come here for centuries to hide—and called "hell" by those who have come here to die.

My excitement grew as we neared the house that gave me such fond memories of my last visit here. As soon as we reined the animals to a stop at the gate, two men followed us into the stable area next to the house. There they took our tired and dusty steeds to brush, water, and feed. Meanwhile, Peter and I were led, each of us in turn, to bathe and change before taking a light meal of fruits, honey, and bread.

Looking around, I could stand the suspense no longer and inquired about our hosts and Jesus, of course. Peter said that our hosts had been with Jesus, but had left on an extended trip earlier this week, leaving their home and servants at our service to use as we saw fit. I was very anxious to see Jesus again, especially since, upon this occasion, he was the one to send for me. In addition, with all the trouble of late, my mind was in a foreboding state most of the time anyway.

"We must wait," Peter volunteered in his usual unintended, authoritative fashion.

"But, for how long?" I asked, with shortness brought on by a long ride and no rest at all for the past twenty-four hours.

"Until he sends for us," was all that he said. So, with my body still aching in every joint but relaxed from the bath and food, I accepted the bedroom proffered by one of Ruth's handmaidens, and like a child, I fell instantly asleep.

I slept most of that day, and a good part of the next, still without a word from Jesus. During my waking hours, I paced nervously back and forth through the house, in the garden, to the stables to check on the horses, and back again. I didn't dare leave the confines of the grounds for fear that the minute I did, a messenger would come, and I wouldn't be there. All during this time Peter seemed totally unconcerned and at ease. I noticed that there were always people coming to the house, one or two at a time, and Peter seemed always willing to sit with them and talk with them.

On the second day, I begin to watch Peter very carefully. At first I didn't know why, but suddenly it hit me—this man had changed. This was not the same man I had seen just a few months ago in Galilee. Yes, he still had his blustery ways, but there was something different about him now that I had not seen before. I watched him with both poor and rich alike, who came to seek his strength and advice, and I noticed that his voice and demeanor had mellowed in some way. There too was a new gentleness about him that I saw reflected in his eyes.

As people came to him, he would take them into the garden, apart from everyone else (as I had seen Jesus do before him), and listen to them with a new earnestness and caring, both for them and for their needs. I listened to him encourage them in the most eloquent of ways; cajole them, with a pleading in his voice; and inspire them in the ways of our Lord. In so doing, he elicited a response that I had only seen in our Master before him.

I thought back on the conversation Peter and I had two nights earlier as we rode together to Jericho from Jerusalem, and I reflected on the way that Jesus had chastised him for not learning his lessons well enough. With these things in mind, I began to look at Peter with new eyes and with a new respect born in my heart. For this had been a rough and ready fisherman, and now he was a wise and gentle soul. How far Jesus had brought him in the last two short years. I also wondered if I, too, had been changed in ways as yet unnoticed by me.

As I thus pondered within the depths of my soul and sought answers to questions untold, the waiting ended. It ended as quickly as it had the night Peter had come to my door. Without warning, there was John, son of Zebedee, standing in the entranceway holding out his hand. It startled me, and I gasped as he said, "Come, Asher ben Ammi, give me your things, I will carry them for you." That was all he said as I hurriedly gathered up my few belongings to go. Peter was already waiting for us at the courtyard gate. Following John, we silently left on foot, heading away from the gathering shadows soon to chase us across the desert floor. We were heading for the village of Bethabara when John said, "That is where Jesus is quietly seeing people, teaching, and healing." How appropriate, I thought, for this is where Jesus first met John (beheaded in his prime) and was baptized. This is where Jesus found his beloved Abba before retreating to the mountaintop where he and his Father became totally and irrevocably One.

We walked at a good pace for about two hours, then slipped into the village unnoticed, except for a mangy dog that came snarling out of the darkness and into the middle of our group before any of us could react to stop him. He went right for me, and tried to take my old leg for his evening meal. A whack from John's staff sent the cur whimpering and yelping away, but not before he had done considerable damage. It's a good thing we were close to our destination, for I had to be helped as I limped the rest of the way to the house in which we were to stay.

They sat me in the courtyard, and the mistress of the house went to fetch water, ointments, and rags to wash and bind my wound. I was inspecting my torn and bruised leg under the light of the lamp when suddenly I became aware of a robe and sandaled feet before me.

Slowly, I raised my head to find in the flickering lamplight, my Master standing in front of me with the gentlest of smiles etched upon his face. I tried to rise but was restrained by his powerful hand upon my shoulder. Then, as I sat there, my heart coming to my throat with the pain and exertion of the trip, and all the worry, frustration, and sickness of the month gone by, he slowly bent down to look at my wound. With a grimace, he bent down on one knee and reached out with his hands and gently touched my torn leg. He didn't have to say anything; he didn't have to hold the bruised and battered flesh of my weary old limb; just being in his presence again was more than my emotions could bear. I tried to hold back the tears that were rushing to my stinging eyes, but it was useless. They broke as if from a dam, down my worn and dusty cheeks. "Oh, Lord. Oh, Lord," was all I could say, as two dear friends held each other in the sheer joy of just knowing each other and knowing that the other was still alive.

Finally, my sobbing ceased, and a new and wonderful calmness descended upon me, as if I had been anointed with a balm. My Lord then knelt down in front of me once again, and looking into my eyes, placed his hands on both sides of my face. We were alone, with only a flickering lamp, the muffled sounds from the house, and silent desert darkness all about. "Asher," he started, "I need your help." There were now wrinkles and deep furrows in his sun-baked brow, and for the first time since I had known him, there was a sense of urgency and pleading in his eyes.

Here was my beloved Master, whom I would have followed anywhere, my teacher who opened the heavens unto me and gave me everlasting life, now bent at my feet asking me for help. I answered the best way I knew. "My dear Jesus, you have been like a son and father to me at the same time—no—you have been so much more. Master, you have been my teacher and given me life. Without you I would die. Will I help you? Lord, but say the word, and I will give you everything that I have."

"I know you will, dear friend, and that is why I have called you to me this night. Tomorrow I want you to come with me to a place east of here. It is a humble farming home, but filled with love. Here the crowds will not find us, and I will tell you what you have sought from me... and so very much more."

With that, Jesus rose to his feet, and I rose to mine. We embraced each other again, sharing a love that to this day I cannot describe. And in so doing, it happened again, as if by magic: he held me, gave me his love, and no fear, no anger, no doubts in him could I find. He was my teacher, and as I watched him retreat into the flickering light of the house beyond, I knew I would live as long as he would—and that, like him, my days grew short.

When the woman returned to bathe my leg, I was already gathering my things to retire for the night. It was only when she insisted on seeing my wound that I sat again, pulling up my robe for her to inspect.

"Where is the wound, sir? Perhaps it is the other leg." I looked down. She was right; there was no trace of a wound. Although I knew it was my left leg that had been mauled, I couldn't help looking at my other leg just to be sure. It was fine, as I suspected. The leg had been healed. Quietly, lovingly, without special notice or request for any thanks, he had healed my leg. He had completely healed my leg!

The tears glistened in my eyes as I rose from my seat and headed to the room set aside for me to sleep. I tried, but I couldn't talk, nor could I even thank the kind woman at my feet; my emotions were too strong and too deep. I just picked up my things and silently padded to my room and fell asleep.

Sleep was indeed an easy blessing that night, for which I was thankful. Knowing my Master's habits, I judged waking would come well before dawn so that we could be on our way without notice. My prediction proved right. Before the first hour of the morning there was a tiny tap on the door. I was ready, and silently my Lord and I slipped out the door. We headed east, out of the town, toward the mountains. Our destination was not too distant from the town of Abila, which lay directly east of us in the foothills along the road north to Philadelphia, and Syria further still.

Abila, like Bethabara in the valley below, depended for a great deal of its existence on travelers who constantly came and went. Abila lay as the last village before starting the long climb up the hills of the Perea and furnished forgotten items, such as refreshments, various sundry provisions, and necessary water from their wells. As the first village upon coming out of the hills, the town also had its share of travelers staying the night before crossing the desert that lay spread out before them to the west and Jerusalem beyond. Our destination was the home of a disciple who had the most lovely date farm I had ever seen, slightly above and just south of the town.

The edge of the orchard looked over a magnificent view of the desert plain below. From this vantage point, one could see the land dip and roll its way down from the high hills on both sides of the river, which coiled itself down the valley as it meandered its way to the sea. The River Jordan gushed from the mouth of Pan north of the lush and beautiful Galilee in the north, down the steamy Valley of Aulon, and ended in the waste of the long Dead Sea, which, memory records, covered the evil cities of Sodom and Gomorrah to the south.

We arrived at our destination in the afternoon and later found ourselves sitting on the wall surrounding the grove of trees looking across the valley. From this vantage point I could envision so much of my people's history. Looking back on our trail, I could see the white walls and rooftops of the few houses that made up the village Bethabara, now looking as if it were afire in the last rays of the afternoon sun. Bethabara lay close-in to the patch of green that marked the ford across the River Jordan where our people first entered into the promised land and where twelve hundred years later Jesus had found the harbinger John, been baptized, and been spiritually born.

Looking across to the other side of the valley, I could just see Jericho in the gathering shadows of the wilderness hills. It is said that Jericho is the oldest living city in the world. For thousands of years it has seen every king and would-be king that has come its way. Its irrigated trees and gardens are famous far beyond our lands, and the balsam plantations produce the rarest essence in all the world. The palm and date trees produce abundant crops and shade. Banks of flowers and beautiful gardens adorn this favorite city of our now dead tyrant king, Herod, who used the people's money to build himself a lovely palace, theater, amphitheater, and circus, all with the finest of imported marbles and tiles, all from the sweat of our people's brow.

To the south, the barren hills rise steeply on both sides from the Dead Sea far below. Nothing grows in this sun-baked earth, nor in the water that lies below, but in the mellow colors of the dying sun, sinking low beyond the hills, everything seemed to be at peace and rightly in its place.

I turned to look at Jesus, whose face was now a golden brown in the late afternoon sun. He, too, had been looking out across the valley with a far-off look of an eternal dream deep in his soft blue-gray eyes. He didn't turn to me immediately but continued to stare out across the ages, past or future I was not sure, and spoke in a voice that was at the same time sad, and yet filled with resolve and hope.

"Asher, I think you know my time is coming to a close. Only a few months remain before they hammer me to a cross, and there is so much that still remains to be done. Our Father has set the stage, my beloved disciple, and now, at long last he beckons me home."

He said this while he still stared out across the void. His voice was not grieved. Perhaps there was a note of resignation or finality, but not grief. He spoke as if he had carried a terrible load for many years, and at long last, the end was in sight. People hounded this beloved soul day and night. I worried so at times that he was being pushed beyond all human endurance, and so one part of me could understand the need for the eternal rest. Because of this, I cannot say I had not expected that the end was coming near, but just the hearing of the words, made a great, empty sadness appear in my heart—a kind of hoary dread.

"I have given my people all that I can give," Jesus said, "and they have absorbed all that they will. Now it is time to complete the act. Someday, dear Asher, my people will have grown, and then it will be time for them to know much that will be lost through the ages or never told. Listen very carefully to what I tell you, for in my words now, I will give you the kernel of truth that you must give to all who come to discover the truth.

"My kingdom is not of this earth, Asher. I think you have lived long enough in years to also realize this, long enough to know of what I speak. It hurts my heart, though, to sometimes see those closest to me still clinging to this thought, of kingdoms and courts, and princes and generals, and armies and who knows what, for ultimately they all will fall. For all of what man builds, I tell you, must surely come to an end.

"Of all my disciples, Asher, you are the only one I was able to take beyond these earthly bonds into the world of our Father. After you, only Peter was able to see a part of me, and thus it is to him that I turn over my reins. It will be to him that I will invest my trust in the future that my Father has foretold. And for two millennia it will be his first halting steps that will endure and grow. Then that, too, will pass from this earth, as the religion of our forefathers has during our lifetime come to its pinnacle and past. For I bring the new covenant of our Father's hope, a covenant that some will be able to accept and others will not. I tell you also that, in time, even this Law of our Father will have become so twisted as to be lost to the people, and then the time will come to pass when my spirit must walk upon this earth again.

"I ask you to seal all these things in your heart so that when the time is ripe I may call upon you to give my love to those who wait. Tell my people that wherever they find cruelty or hate, wherever they find sadness and hurt, anguish or fright, wherever they find a soul in search—that is where I ask them to be. I am not different, Asher. I am no different than you, or your son, or that woman whore you once saw me save at the Temple door. I am in each of them; I am One with them. And if you wish to follow me, you must be One with them, too. For the people of this world are my Father's creation, as surely as am I, and He lives and dreams and suffers in the lowest of them, too.

"I become so furious at the priests who prescribe a rule for every imagined sin or social ill. Tell my people that if they could truly see within their brothers and sisters, they would know that each one is doing the very best he or she knows. There are evil ones around, but they have only a longer road to travel before they, too, come around. Even the hated Herod suffered more than you realize. I pity the hell that man must suffer before he finally comes to know that there is only one true Law in the universe, and that Law pervades all that we know, and that is the almighty Law of His unending love.

"Wrap yourself in the light, Asher, the light you saw upon that mountaintop. Wrap it about you, and make it you, in all you say or do. Someday it will become you, and in that instant you will know without question what I am saying when I tell you that my Father and I are One.

"Perhaps it will be a million years before our souls find perfection; I don't know, but surely we will try over and over and over again, for it is in our nature that we all shall grow. I only lead the way, as others have before me, and as others will who follow. I show you that to gain everything in this world, you must also give everything you have or know. For those who give everything, unto them my Father bestows the most. One day, of this I give my solemn word, they will awaken and find themselves at last in the arms of our beloved God, and no more shall they be made to go out.

"When I picked my disciples, Asher, you chose me as much as I you. For each of you were required for a specific task, and each of you vowed your life to me long, long ago. Whether I found you as merchant or as priest, as tax collector, rebel, fisherman, Roman, or saint, I knew you from the past, and you knew me, and willingly you took up your appointed task. I say this to you so that you will know too that when the time comes, even poor Judas will fall to his fate, as surely as the last leaf falls in the bitterness of the winter-coming wind.

"And now, with mention of the one who will betray me, I will tell you of what is to come and what services I need of you, my dear, beloved friend, to ensure my Father's plan unto fruition."

I pause, even now, as I write, for the impact of what my Lord Jesus gave me was more than I could then (or can even now) imbibe. My head was whirling until I felt as if I would faint. My mouth had long ago dropped open and shut again without a sound. Within me, I was beginning to feel a funny, strange kind of lightness, almost as if I was about to lose my senses, almost as if I was about to float silently out of my mortal body. I was changing. Something inside of me knew of what he spoke, and with that part of me, I knew I had to unite.

Suddenly, I grabbed him, to steady my balance and keep from falling off the wall. As my senses struggled and my vision blurred, I thought, "Indeed, this is death!" I felt myself slumping against his shoulder and arm. I knew he grabbed me; I know it now, intellectually, but then it was different, for I was lifting away and into a light that was brighter than the day. And the light and I merged, and I heard a voice, and I saw the Path; and finally, within me, I knew with the knowledge of self that I had truly merged with our Father. His love flooded me until I could hold no more, and then, in peace, I gratefully slept the silent sleep of ages past and ages yet to come.

Of the experience I had that afternoon, I can speak no further. Not that it is not my wish, nor am I unwilling, but I simply cannot. The memory of this time is beyond words to express and any attempt I might make would only defile something that belongs between my God and me in sacredness. It will never leave me, and yet, strangely enough, it is also beyond my understanding. I tell you, though, that no one can come back from an experience like that without his life being inexorably changed. As Jesus said before me, and as now I finally understood, my Father, my Master, our people, and I were finally and truly One!

I opened my eyes. I could hear the tiny, twittering birds outside the window as the first rays of sun streamed through the opening in the far wall in one brilliant beam.

The morning was cool, and I could smell fresh-turned earth somewhere close as I moved my head to orient myself to where I was. How had I gotten into this room? The last I remembered was sitting outside with Jesus, but now I was in a small room; all the walls were immaculately white and clean. The floor was of an earthen tile, the door of dark, worn wood. Along the wall by the door I saw a plain, undecorated cabinet for storing one's clothes, and upon the top stood a pottery vase, holding water, I guessed. The bed upon which I lay was simple enough, made of scraped tree limbs with rope supports between them, and over me was a thin, down-filled coverlet. The vision of the night before had left, and in its place there was a beautiful peace. I felt wonderful! I reached up and stretched as far as I could while filling my lungs to bursting with the crisp, cool, dry desert air.

My robe hung on one of three pegs on the back of the door, and my sandals were neatly placed at the foot of the bed. What a beautiful way to wake, I thought, as I poured the water into a bowl and washed my face. Hurriedly, I dressed and mused over what had happened the night before, sitting there on the garden wall with my Lord. Then, opening the door, I strode down the covered walk toward the heart of the home—the kitchen. I entered the open door to find Jesus sitting comfortably at the table talking to the woman of the house, Deborah by name, who, like the rest of us, loved this man named Jesus with all her heart. Having Jesus alone without the crowds was indeed a delight for her husband (long out in his fields that morning) and for her as well.

Jesus had his hands around a steaming drink made from barley and herbs, and the aroma was wonderfully enticing. The smell had awakened the hunger within me, and I suddenly remembered that I had not eaten last evening. I was famished. Actually, my stomach was first to notify the others and me by growling in anticipatory delight. It was so loud that both Jesus and Deborah stopped their conversation and turned to face the source of the strange gurgling sound. Upon seeing me standing at the door, Jesus threw up his hands in mock surprise and simulated fear, saying, "Asher, you're alive!"

Deborah couldn't maintain her composure and, holding her apron up to her face, turned away and began to laugh. I played along with the happiness of this bright morning by feigning a look of horror. I started feeling all about my body to see if I was really there. Then, shouting with glee, I whooped, "Your greatest miracle, Lord! You raised me from the dead."

I thought I saw a strange tremor sweep over Jesus as I said those words—just a flicker of surprise—then something of a glazed look came over his eyes. It lasted only the barest fraction of a second, and then it was gone. He gave a little shudder and shook his head as if to clear a thought that wanted to hold him. Then his face changed as the dreadful mood passed, and he was happy again.

A grin caught him midstream; he winked at Deborah, then grabbed his sides and doubled over with glee, as did Deborah. I added to the merriment by continuing my charade, but inside I catalogued the startled look upon Jesus' face and the fraction of an instant when I saw him shudder, and the distant look upon his face when I joked that he had raised me from the dead.

When Deborah finally regained her composure, she set before me bread and drink, which I ate ravenously. Talk was light during the meal. Deborah wanted to know the latest from Jerusalem, of people and events, and most importantly about my Miriamme and other friends she had met who were followers of Jesus. Eventually Jesus took the bundle of fruit, goat cheese, and a sealed jar of local wine that Deborah had already prepared, shoved back his stool and looking at me with a wink, said, "Well, young man, do you think you are ready for a walk?" Not waiting for the unneeded reply, he approached Deborah and gave her a friendly hug, and grateful thanks for the meal she had prepared that morning and for the food he carried for us to eat later in the day.

The climb was often steep, and Jesus had to wait several times for me to catch up as we made our way up the barren mountainside. We said little to each other, which was all the better for me, for I needed all the strength I had to make the climb up the well-traveled trail of the holy mountain called Nebo. It was on the desolate plateau atop this mountain, more than a thousand years ago, that Moses stood and looked out upon the Promised Land of our people before he gave up his staff to Joshua and finally let his massive burden slide. And it was here that Jesus was taking me, for what, I could only guess.

The location Jesus had in mind was well short of the top, and at a point that could be discerned only by his senses, not mine, he left the trail and headed down a little incline that showed no sign of any prior human passing that I could see. The slope turned around the face of the hill several times before ending on a flat outcrop of rock where Jesus now indicated that we were to take our rest. After setting the food upon a stone, he turned and motioned me to climb upon the rock and make myself at ease. He held out his hand to help me up the waist-high rock. Once safely balanced, I dropped to the hard surface, grateful for an end to this difficult climb. From there I surveyed the view; the lofty perch suddenly made me feel a bit giddy. Looking out for miles, I had the strange feeling that somehow it was all mine.

The silence of the spot was broken only by the breeze rising up the hill as it rustled through the dry, golden grasses, caressed its way across our faces, then cascaded into the sky, where a hawk screeched its defiance high over our heads. The graceful hunter rode the endless rising currents of air higher and higher, gliding noiselessly out over the great active fault in the earth toward the Dead Sea valley far below.

I followed Jesus' look and his outstretched hand, pointing to the west. There, in the dry afternoon sun, I could just see the white jewel of Jerusalem, a mere speck in the Judean hills, sparkling and shimmering in the waves of heat rising from the barren desert floor.

"It was here that Moses died, Asher. He died with contentment in his heart as he saw this view of 'The Promised Land.' His God, and the God of our fathers, was a harsh God, Asher, for a harsh time and an unruly people. But now it is different, everything has changed. It is a different time, and we are different people. We are all one people in Him, and now that we have conquered ourselves, we must dare to help all peoples know Him, too."

I looked at him in surprise, for I had not heard him speak in such a way before, and, in fact, he assiduously kept his disciples away from the Gentiles, of whom I assumed he now spoke. He read me clearly and continued. "Yes, Asher, even the Gentiles. For you believe that there is but one God, do you not?"

"Yes, Lord, but..."

"Yes, and so it is," he interrupted. "We have always believed that we were his chosen, haven't we? And indeed we were, for He needed a people to show the way, to remain faithful, to die for Him if need be—to be an example to all nations of the One living God. But now is the time for the new covenant, a covenant for all people and all lands. He loves them not less because they were born outside his 'chosen.' He loves them more. For, just as I have come, not so much for those who already know Him but more for those who do not, so too our Father has determined that now is the time for His light to flood the world, so that all may see. If you look within you, Asher, you will know that they are His children, too. It is time for humanity to take an unfathomed leap outside our narrow land, and it is in so doing that I am about to die.

"There is only one way this can be accomplished, Asher, and it is a bitter cup indeed that is forced upon my lips, but one that I willingly take. In so doing, all His people will have an opportunity to find Him, not just the elect, not just the few."

"You speak of your death, Lord, but why? Why must it be? Isn't there any other way?" The fears were rising again. I could feel them wind themselves around me as if a terrible, poisonous snake was slowly encircling me. Yet as I now looked at Jesus with searching eyes, I could see no fear, no pain, no questioning at all. He looked at me with his gentling eyes, and the peace I had known the night before once again settled about my being, and fright took its leave. His smile spread to my lips too as I reached within to a Source, a great quiescent pool that I had not known existed before the events of the previous day. In the calm, I also knew that his death was a joy, not a thing of dread.

Jesus handed me cheese and bread and passed the sealed jar filled with wine as he continued to explain why it was that he had taken me apart. I put the food and drink down upon the stone and continued to listen.

"Asher, I am not looking forward to my death, for I have found more love here among our people in the past few years than I could have ever imagined. But now you, too, have felt His calling, and you know that all life is in Him anyway—it matters little whether I am here of this earth or beyond. For this life on earth is but a passing dream, reenacted time after time, and it is only in finally knowing from within that we are special that we are truly born again.

"And now that you have experienced death, Asher, in its truest sense and know yourself from within that there is no such thing, but in its stead, eternal life, you alone among my people know for certain that I can go to a Roman cross in absolute peace. My beloved one, there will come a time for you to help His people just as I have done, by giving freely of what I have taught you, sharing the knowledge that all peace lies within. For this is where our Father resides, and it is here within you that all mystery lies.

"You do not need me, only what I teach you; and you do not need the priests to intercede for you, for peace will come only when you take responsibility for yourself. His grace can take you only to the edge of His kingdom, but there is more. You must make the effort if you are to see, as you have seen. To find Him and merge with Him in bliss, you must work very hard.

"For those who tell you that I will save them with no effort at all on their parts, tell them what I required of those who were closest to me. From them I have required much more than they will ever know. Yet it was not difficult for them, and that is really the highest mystery of all. For when you truly give all you have to give, without any reservation, you will find that you have had the secret peace within your grasp all along. And this, all of mankind must ultimately find—all by themselves.

"I have called you apart to see, Asher, and now that you have seen, I need your help. I need your help desperately, because you are a man of power in the court, and your money finds answers where there were none before. Everything is coming to a fixed point now, Asher, and there is no room for error; every action I now take, every word from my mouth must be calculated to find its mark. If you see or hear something that would ordinarily cause you to wonder or bring you to doubt or pain, ignore it, and follow precisely the plan we will lay out together. I tell you that the time has come for a preciseness of action that will allow no error, a plan that will bring me to the culmination of my life on an exact day, and even at an exact hour! There is no room for an uncalculated delay; once we set the play in motion it must be without error. Asher ben Ammi, will you help me to die?"

"My God! Will I help him die?" The very sound of the word made me turn cold and tremble involuntarily.

Then, strangely, for it seemed but a moment later, the feeling passed. In its place a strange peace fell about me, and I knew that it was God's plan for Jesus to hang upon a cross and that I could do nothing less than help him when he needed me most. He was waiting for my answer, his attention held closely upon my face. He saw the moment's hesitation; then watched his blissful peace seep into me, a small smile forming at the corner of his lips. I needed to say nothing more, for in my eyes he saw the answer—yes.

Have you ever been at a place in time when a moment of monumental decision has come upon you, when a choice has to be made? You are not sure what to do, but you can no longer delay the inevitable. The time leading up to that moment is fraught with anxiety and unbearable tension; then, when the decision is finally made, for better or worse, it is over. You sigh, and it feels as though a tremendous weight has just lifted from you. Well, that was what it was like. Once he saw in my face and in my nod that I had agreed, he changed. He seemed to soften and release the tension that must have gripped his body, too. It was as if there was at last a friend he knew he could trust implicitly, and now he could relax and know that everything would come to pass as he had seen.

Suddenly he took the goblet that was sitting next to me, broke the seal on the clay jar, and slowly filled the goblet until it overflowed symbolically upon the stone beneath. Then, slowly again, he picked up the cup, closed his eyes, offered it up to the Father, then brought it to his chest as he recited from the Psalms. "Thou preparest a table before me in the presence of mine enemies; thou hast anointed my head with oil; my cup runneth over."

Then, with his eyes still held shut, he lifted the cup to his lips and seemed to be quoting an ancient source of which I knew not. His last words spoke of the mystery "revealed to us while we are in the cave." He took the small cup and drank from it until it was but half full.

I cannot explain the radiance that seemed to surround him as I watched in awe. Then, as I sat in reverie, the strange floating sensation started within me again, but this time I seemed to be able to control it and remain in full awareness, while somehow my senses became heightened to a wondrous degree. All of a sudden, I was watching that mysterious light I had seen around Jesus in Galilee, and not only in him, but also in the cup; I now saw it shimmering with a radiance all its own. This ordinary wine had somehow been transformed into the living waters of which the mysteries spoke—and it was beautiful beyond understanding.

After taking the cup from his lips, he opened his eyes, and I saw the God within him, all in a moment's time. As I took the cup now offered to me and in my turn held it up to drink, Jesus said with a softness that took my breath away, "This cup I give to you surrounded by a brilliant golden light; this light of love of every Master past and every Master soon to be. Take and drink, feel the light in you, of you, around you, and with you, in God's own peace."

I tipped the cup and drank it to its end, while he asked me to, "Give this overflowing love you have been given to a thousand others in turn, for there is no end to His love, His peace, His bliss."

Chapter 17

The Pieces of the Puzzle Begin to Fit Into Place

As Jesus and the disciples approached Jerusalem, and were near the town of Bethphage on the Mount of Olives, Jesus sent two of them into the village ahead.

"Just as you enter," he said, "you will see a donkey tied there, with its colt beside it. Untie them and bring them here. If anyone asks you what you are doing, just say, 'The Master needs them.' And there will be no trouble."

Matthew 21:1-3

As the two of us sat together on this lonely mountainside, neither of us said a word, for words would have invaded the sanctity of the moment. So we sat silently and partook of the meal that had been prepared for us.

I ate absentmindedly, for I had little appetite now. My mind continued to go over and over the events of the last few days and my last trip to Galilee. Almost an hour passed before I noticed the gathering clouds coming toward us from across the valley. It was a beautiful sight to see as we sat high on the mountainside and watched the gray-black shower of water sweep from under the ominous clouds. Slowly the clouds worked their way across the clear blue sky, inching closer and closer to our side of the valley. Then I noticed something that can be seen only in a place such as this. By watching very carefully, I could see that the water, which fell in torrents from the clouds above, never touched the ground below. The rain evaporated and disappeared into the hot, dry air as if consumed by an invisible source.

The rolling and boiling clouds rushed north toward Galilee, and the now rapidly moving wind smelled wonderfully of the wetness of rain.

Our side of the valley remained in the bright sun, accompanied only by God's own sign, His brilliant, multicolored arch across the world—His promise—His rainbow. I was divinely full, in both body and spirit. In staggering amazement I watched God's beautiful play being acted out in all its majesty in front of my eyes. It made my spirit light and happy. I looked over to Jesus, whose eyes were twinkling with delight.

"What are you thinking, Asher?" he asked, with a grin crossing his face.

"I was remembering a story about you, Lord, that John, the son of Zebedee, told me as I whiled away an afternoon with him waiting for you on the shores of the Sea of Galilee."

"Tell me the story, Asher," Jesus urged. "From the smile on your face, it must have delighted you."

"It did, Lord, it did." I proceeded to tell him the story as John told it to me.

"As he told the story, Lord, it seemed that you and several of your disciples had gotten a late start one morning and had walked all the rest of the day with little or no rest at all. He said that you pushed them hard to reach your destination before dark. However, at the close of the evening it was clear that you were not going to reach any village or town in time to spend the night. You would just have to make do with what you had—which was precisely nothing.

"'There were no miracles that evening,' John told me. You all wrapped your robes around you and tried not to think of food as you drifted off to sleep. That was a night John was not to forget, I guess, for he was cold, tired, hungry, and, most of all, mad—at you!

"John did make an admission though, for he said, 'Of course, I didn't think of anyone else there that night. As usual, I was only thinking of my own miserable self.' He just couldn't understand how you could have allowed them to have fallen short of the goal and gotten into such terrible straits." I related all this to Jesus, who seemed to be enjoying the story.

"Apparently midway through the night, John was awakened by the rumbling sound of thunder in the distance. As usual, fear gripped his loins, for as he lay there, wide-awake, he could hear the roar coming closer and closer. Suddenly there was a clap of thunder right over his head, he said, and a bolt of lightning shot out of the dark, silhouetting an unearthly black-and-white landscape. The staccato effect of the flash turned the rest of you into unmoving, lifeless things, which nearly scared him to death!" Jesus and I both started chuckling as I continued with the story.

"Then it started; huge drops, first one, then another—splat, splat—rain! John lay quietly and heard the popping and sizzling sounds as the rain began to descend in an ever more serious way. It put out what was left of the fire and soon drenched all of you. There was nothing he could do but lie awake, cold and wet to the bone, and stare into the pitch-black, endless night as the rain turned into an unending torrent. All he could hear was the noise of the rain, now coming in a deluge. The once firm ground soon became a quagmire of ooze and slime as John lay in the mud and contemplated his pathetic state of affairs."

The more of the story I told, the more I could see that Jesus was enjoying it. By the time I reached this point in the tale, he was laughing uproariously, wiping the tears from his eyes.

"Stop, Asher, for heaven's sake, stop! I can't take anymore." I don't know why I continued, but I did; I couldn't help myself. Perhaps it had been the heaviness of the trip, or perhaps it had been so long since I had heard him laugh from the depths of his being that I wanted it to continue, to lighten his load just a little for the smallest moment of time. I don't know, perhaps it was just the evil one in me. I do know that the more he laughed, the more animated I became in the telling and the more I exaggerated poor John's manner of speech.

"'Ever see drowned rats?'" I mimicked John's telling as I stood up, pretending to scrape the mud from my face, arms, and hands, as John had shown me the men had done in the morning gloom. He told me that his wet clothes were clogged with layers of muck from tossing and turning all night in the mud. "He must have been quite a sight, Lord, for then John turned to me and said, 'Jesus was sitting there in the slop, just sitting there looking at us—and grinning! Yep. That sure was fun! You tell them that it wasn't all sunshine... you tell them that!'" Really worked up by this time in the story, John had been gesticulating all over the place—which, of course, I dutifully mimicked.

By now, I was afraid Jesus was going to fall off the rock; he was doubled over with laughter, begging me to stop. I finally did pause long enough for Jesus to wheeze, "Asher, you can't imagine it. John pointed his finger at me that morning and said, 'You promised this, did you? You didn't tell us about this! Said all sunshine, all light... Well, where is the light? This is a mess, you know that?' He fumed and ranted with rage, his face turning such a brilliant purple I thought he would stroke for sure."

Jesus continued, "Judas said, 'I saw you rolling around in it last night, John. You looked so comfortable, I thought for sure you must have once been a pig.' Then one of the others said, 'Just tuck it up, John, it will be all right.' That was all poor John could take." Jesus smiled with delight in remembering the scene.

"He headed out for the next town without us. We didn't see him all day. When we met up with him later, he had washed and cleaned himself, and he pretended (with an air of haughtiness) that nothing had ever happened. Poor, poor John, I will have to try to spend more time with him before it is time to go."

The mention of his going brought back the reality of this world: my own precious teacher's coming end and sobering thoughts for me to contemplate from within. Not Jesus, however, for he continued to chuckle every now and again as the thought of the muddy scene drifted repeatedly in and out of his mind.

As Jesus started to gather up the things that were left, I stood to move and stretch my weary legs. Then we started the long trek back down the hill. We hurried, for the sky was getting darker and more ominous by the moment as the lead edge of the storm hurtled north across the sky, and as it did, the follow-on mass spilled over the lip of the mountains to the east, which usually meant that the rain would soon be coming down in sheets. My feet were killing me as we reached the short path to the house, for we had kept up a mean gait down the steep hill, and my toes had been forced down into my closed-toe sandals until they crumpled and complained of unbearable pain.

I silently thanked our Father for holding back the rain until we were but a few short running steps away from the warmth of Deborah's kitchen. She had seen us coming and had the door standing ajar as we burst into the heaven-sent sights and smells of her culinary delights.

We stayed in the kitchen well after the evening meal since the warm and friendly oven was kept well stoked, and much to everyone's delight, Jesus told stories until it was far past time to go to bed.

It rained off and on most of the following day, so Jesus put off our return and used the time to brief me on what was expected of me and what he felt was about to happen. I could see that my role was going to be pivotal if everything he had laid out was to succeed. Three powerful forces had to be played against each other—Herod Antipas, the Romans, and the Temple priests (especially the power of the High Priest Caiaphas)—if we were to see Jesus through to Passover. Jesus told me that commanding events were unfolding that would show the world in a very real way the powers that are available to anyone who would follow his way. He said that it would quicken the end, but at that time I had no idea it was already starting in Bethany as we spoke.

A thousand thoughts seemed to be going through my head as we left early the next morning to walk back to Bethabara, where the disciples waited. My quiet mood agreed with Jesus, for he too seemed to be preoccupied, and we walked most of the way in silence.

As soon as we entered the courtyard of the home in which we were staying, all the disciples greeted us at once. Each had something to say, and none of them could be understood. Jesus held up his hand for quiet, and gradually the turmoil died down. "There is a guest among us. Please let him be properly greeted and let him speak his mind." With that, the stranger stepped forward, saying that he was a messenger sent by Lazarus' sisters, to tell Jesus that Lazarus was very sick. The sisters needed Jesus and asked if he would come without delay to save their brother. Jesus nodded his head yes and bade the messenger return immediately to tell Martha and Mary that he would be along presently.

The messenger left at once to prepare for his immediate return with the message that Jesus was sure to come. The man was no more out of the courtyard when bedlam broke out. Again, everyone was speaking at once. Jesus sat down quietly upon the bench where he had healed my leg and again held up his hand for silence. Peter stepped forward to speak what was on all their minds. "Sir, it was only a few weeks ago that we barely escaped from the Temple alive. The High Priest will surely kill you if you return!" There was general agreement with what was said. Jesus, with his head down, waited until they quieted again.

"I go not only for the obvious reason that my dear friend Lazarus lies sick unto death but also because in his rest, I will be brought one step closer to the glory of my Father. The authorities will not dare to take me in the daylight hours, for the people whom they fear will not allow that—nor will you. Therefore, we need watch only during the hours of darkness, that our position is not revealed." Then Jesus looked up at me standing in the crowd and asked, "What do you think, Asher? Do you feel that it is still safe so close to Jerusalem?"

I chanced an answer, although I was not at all as sure of myself as I sounded. "Yes, Master, I think if care is taken by those who love you, you will still be safe."

"See!" Jesus said, slapping his leg with finality.

As the men stared at him, he looked from man to man for any objections. Finding none, he gave a shrug of finality, rose, and, leaving the men standing where they were, went inside.

Even though they would not challenge Jesus to his face, I don't think many of the disciples were yet convinced of his safety (or their own, for that matter). For, as Jesus left, Thomas said, "Come, let us get ready to go too, all of us, and die with him if that is what is needed of us."

I left the group still in the midst of a heated debate as to the wisdom of the trip so near to those who would have him and bade my Lord good-bye. There was much for me to do, and I was useless here in this little out-of-the-way village near the bottom of the world. My place was back in the council halls where my Father's plan needed to be set in motion.

My leaving was made easy, for my things were yet unpacked, so I left Jesus and the other disciples within the hour and headed west in the company of the messenger. It was a fortunate turn of events, for both the messenger and me, as I had no desire to travel these roads unaccompanied, and the messenger, having come on foot, could certainly use a ride to ease and speed his journey back. During my journey here with Peter a few days earlier, I had left two horses in Jericho, which would now serve us both well on the journey back up the steep road that led to Bethany. Once I dropped the messenger off I would lead the extra horse back the short distance to Jerusalem.

I wondered at Jesus' farewell words to me as I walked along through the desert toward the cool springs of Jericho. He told me to have my son, John, meet him in Bethany in three days, there to report to him of my activities, and John in return would report back to me of the coming "miracle." Of what he spoke, at that time, I could not have known. I thought perhaps he spoke of healing his friend Lazarus; but to bring a body back from the grave, that I could not have guessed. My quizzical look to Jesus when he mentioned the "miracle" was met with no reply.

He just held me closer, and with a look of peace on his face, he bid me farewell. Of course, now I know, save his own reported rising, this was to be the culmination of his ministry here and was to set the stage that would cause the wheels of darkness to begin their move toward the final blow—the taking of his life.

What happened next, I am sure you have heard for the word of it spread rapidly everywhere.

Jesus came to Bethany after tarrying two more days, and there in front of many witnesses he raised his friend from the grip of death itself. When word got to me that night from my son that Jesus had raised a body from a rock-hewn grave, I remembered the words spoken to me by the Master almost a year ago, when I had asked him about death and dying. He had looked at me, then hesitated for a second, measuring me, I think, to see how much he could trust with me, how much I could understand. Then he had responded with a great softness, using gentle words that seemed to caress me with their touch.

"My beloved one, no matter what I or anyone else tells you of the mystery of death, the simple fact is that the truth lies within. No religion, neither the Greek, Roman, Hindu, nor even our own, can tell you differently; for there is no religion higher than truth—and that truth you can find for yourself by merging in Him.

"I have shown you how to go within, to touch the ultimate truth, to become One with your Father, to know with certainty that you do not die. Life is a continuum; it does not end for any of us in the brief span of forty or fifty years. Open your eyes, Asher! Your Father gave you eyes to see. Can you make any sense out of the injustice of this world if there are but forty or fifty years to spend? You have lived sixty years and two, Asher; have you seen justice prevail? Have you yourself found perfection in those things you do? Do you have perfect love for your brother as yet? How about your beloved wife, Miriamme? Do you have perfect love for her? How about me, do you even have perfect love for me?

"In truth, we both know that you do not—neither do I—and that is not a sin! The sin we commit upon ourselves is the sin of not trying, for it is in trying that we learn and grow. And it is in experiencing and growing that we are most dear to Him. He does not fault us for trying to find Him and failing. He loves us all the more for it. For it is in the trying that ultimately we will succeed! We are all His sons and daughters, Asher, and if we open our eyes, we all see the same Light. That Light calls both Jew and Gentile alike.

"Why am I here, dear brother, tell me that? I am no different from you. I am trying—and yes, failing too, sometimes in a big way—but I will never give up my efforts to come just one step closer to Him. For it is in Him that our ultimate happiness lies. It is as easy, and as hard, as totally letting go. Give up unto Him totally, Asher, and your life shall be everlasting more."

He said these things not just to me but to others too, but usually with the crowd he spoke more carefully and simply, using simple, well-chosen examples and parables that helped them understand. All of this, the priests, through their spies, surely knew. But on this day there was to be no hiding. On this day when he apparently conquered death for them all to see, he struck the final blow that no one could deny, nor could he hide. A fact I'm sure that he knew, and probably orchestrated as well.

I cannot tell you what turmoil this caused among my peers. A special session of the Sanhedrim was called within the Temple to deal with just this situation—this Jesus of Galilee—for the High Priest and other leaders among the Sadducees and Pharisees knew Jesus' timing couldn't have been worse for them.

The word of this miracle came just six weeks before the highest of all the holy days, just time enough for all of Israel to hear of it and come to see this man of miracles—and perhaps demand of him to declare himself king!

This dangerous man had to be dealt with—and soon—otherwise the crowd could get out of the control of the High Priest and his followers, and into the hands of the Romans the matter would surely go. And if it were determined by the hated Pilate that Caiaphas could no longer govern and control the people, then unto another would go the dubious honor (and the incredible wealth attached thereto), for Rome gave Caiaphas the title and Rome could take it away.

My first concern was for Jesus' immediate safety, for his ending time, as he shared it with me, called for Passover, which was yet well over a month away. The priests meant to hear him scream well before then if they could. Thus, that very night, under cover of darkness, I sent my trusted servant to warn Jesus of the situation as it was developing. Thus, because he had been forewarned, he and his followers disappeared into the darkness well before dawn, to the village of Ephraim at the edge of the wilderness, where he stayed with his disciples and taught no one until he knew his time had come. Spies sent out by Caiaphas searched high and low, but they found him not and the High Priest fumed.

A week before Passover, word came to me secretly that Jesus was on his way to Jerusalem again and that I should make ready. To be sure, the next night found him in Bethany with Lazarus, where he planned to stay until the end. For in this village he was surrounded by friends and those who knew him to be the Messiah, and here he felt safe, even though he was but a short walk from the city itself. From here, too, the road to Jerusalem could be watched by night, to ensure he would not be taken by stealth, and here in the village where Lazarus was raised, they didn't dare take him by day. And so it was here that a dinner was prepared by Lazarus for Jesus and his disciples, for no greater love was there for him than that held by Lazarus and his sisters. I stayed completely away from Jesus at this time, for if I were to serve him well I had to appear to have nothing to do with him now.

Word of Jesus' arrival spread from Bethany to Jerusalem like a wildfire before the raging desert wind. From all parts of the city, people by the thousands flocked to the road as it entered the city gates to the east when word came that he was on his way.

That morning before dawn, as Jesus had asked, I sent two of my servants from my stable to the village of Bethphage, near the Mount of Olives, with a donkey, her colt dutifully following as close as possible in its mother's footsteps. There my servants were to wait with the animals until one of Jesus' disciples identified himself as needing them for our Master, then they were to give them willingly to him.

Up way before dawn, I made sure that the donkey was on its way, and then I proceeded to the Temple, telling my family only that I was going to the morning service, which began shortly after dawn each day. It was a beautiful service to watch, especially during the holidays, when even the morning service was crowded beyond the inner Temple courts. The service began with the proclamation by one of the priests atop the Temple walls, "Priests to their service, Levites to their stand, and Israelites to their post." The priests entered the court in two groups, each carrying a burning torch. One group went around the covered porch to the east, and one to the west, meeting back at the entry gate, declaring that all was in order. Then the priests removed the ashes from the altar and arranged it again for the new day. From this point, the priests, who were now sanctified, waited for the announcement that the horizon had become light, even unto Hebron.

Then the trumpets sounded as the gates opened to the sanctuary. All activity everywhere on the mount stopped for the service, for now the lamb was slaughtered and its limbs were offered upon the altar. As many people as could crowded into the Chamber of Hewn Stone and, with the priests, read the Ten Commandments and part of the Shema. Then they left the Chamber, once again to offer up prayers, as the priests entered the sanctuary to prostrate themselves following the offering of the incense. At this time of year the curtain that normally blocked the view into the sanctuary itself was rolled up so that all who assembled could see the Holy of Holies: the ceiling joists of cedar, the hanging crowns, the walls, the service vessels, all of pure gold. The crowds were so numerous, however, that few could actually enter the Court of the Israelites or the Court of the Women and see. Yet they all joined in the morning prayers with the priests with a dedication found nowhere else in the world.

When the priests finished their prostrations within the sanctuary, they stood outside, raised their arms, and pronounced the sacred name of God, whereupon all the people fell to their faces. After the benediction, the priests offered up the animal limbs for sacrifice on the altar, then they offered up the meal. The trumpets sounded, then the cymbals, and then the Levites began to sing. Because of the holidays, young boys were added to the choir to increase the melody. Then the wine was poured upon the altar, and the service was complete.

For those who had never seen the ceremony, it was an incredible sight. For a moment that morning, I stood transfixed, thinking of how all this must have looked to a young boy of twelve, here for the first time from a little town in Galilee so many years before. I reflected on how this beautiful service, dedicated to the Lord our God, would now, in its most human form, kill the most holy son our nation had ever produced.

I left the service with tears running down my face as I realized with clear brutality what was about to take place.

I proceeded out of the Court of the Israelites, through the Court of the Women, out through the Beautiful Gates that had meant so much to our people, and then on past the lattice fence that separated Temple Mount from the Court of the Gentiles one level below. I crossed the courtyard, then climbed the stairs that led to the Royal Portico at the south end of the Temple's outer court. Once there, I could see over the Valley of the Kidron to the east and the Mount of Olives, where I should first see him come toward the city walls.

Jesus had planned his entry to the city well. He had allowed just enough time for those who had attended the morning service to finish their obligations before they heard the crier who had been sent ahead to announce that he was on his way along the road from Bethany. I had not heard the crier, but the excitement spread through the courts like a wave. "He is coming! He is coming! Come see!" People began running for the gates and high places to get a better view of this Jesus who could raise the dead.

I marveled at his planning and knowledge of the psyche of our people. His timing was absolutely perfect. The city in general was now teeming in preparation for Passover, and the largest concentration of pilgrims, by far, was in the open area just north of the Temple by the Pool of Bethesda. Here, in the ramshackle congregation of tents and shelters of the poor, he would find those who cared least for the pomp and high-handed authority wielded with scorn by the priestly Judean castes since the time Herod the Great first came to power. These were the very ones who would support him now when he needed numbers most. Here, too, he would find the largest grouping of his own people from Galilee, who would find pride in one of their own kind and erupt with rage if a Judean laid a hand on him.

Through the middle of this mass of people he now would walk. He had chosen this, the only entry to the city that passed not only through the city of tents (the same place he had himself slept with his mother and father when as a child he first trod these stones) but also right under the noses of the Romans in the fortress Antonia. Pilate was always present in Jerusalem during the holidays to ensure against rebellion, and this year was no exception.

Yes, he had thought out his plans with infinite care. I had felt they would work when he first laid them before me in the desert, but now that I saw them becoming a reality, I knew that they were nothing less than brilliant.

Thus with thousands gathering to welcome him into the city, he chose the one entry to the city that would most arouse the ire of those with the powers to decide his fate. There was no doubt in my mind that this man could have been king, if that is what he had set out to be. But this king was of a different sort, and that was so hard for the people to understand. Even Judas, who should have understood, gave him up as a "pretender king" when he came this day on the back of an ass instead of a mighty steed. For Judas, within the Zealot's cause, had pleaded with Jesus to declare himself King of the Jews when his brethren attacked the Romans earlier in the week. Romans and Jews alike had died in what Jesus thought was a ridiculously futile attempt to conquer a militarily unconquerable foe. Judas was outraged that Jesus would hear nothing of the plan and had lifted not one finger to help. He had told his brothers of stealth that with Jesus, the people would rally, and the Holy City would be theirs. Jesus had berated Judas and sent him away with his plan of death. Thus, blamed by his co-conspirators for having failed them, he grew desperate to force Jesus into the open. This too was in preparation for the end.

The people met Jesus on the far side of the Kidron valley, on top of the hill where the sacrifice of the red heifer is held. They came in numbers hard to believe! Having heard he had raised Lazarus from the tomb, they came to welcome Jesus and see him for themselves. I could not pick him out from among the crowd at this distance, but I could mark his progress from the swelling of the human tide down the side of the hill. His path was strewn with palm branches and the very cloaks off people's backs. They sang his welcome and praises so loudly that their songs could be heard clear across the valley. Those who had known him not were soon staring in wonder at this man who had gathered this tumultuous crowd; and they too added themselves to the growing throng.

As he neared the entrance to the Temple, the roar of greeting drowned out all else that was going on within. I could see the Romans atop their ramparts coming from all parts of the wall to see what the gathering commotion was all about. They were very watchful of trouble that might spill unchecked into the streets and be directed against them, especially after the earlier events of the week. And I was sure (as I had confided in a message sent the night before to Jesus in Bethany) that any entry such as he had planned would be met with action, if not by the Romans, then by the Temple powers, to assure that the Romans did not think that the priests had become involved in anything such as this.

Unlike Jesus, the crowd surged into the Temple courts without ever stopping to observe the proper cleansing rites. But so many were they, and in such a frenzied state, that the Levites, whose job it was to ensure that the ritually impure were not allowed entry, ran in fear of their lives. From my place above the court, I watched those gathered within the court splinter and run as, like a maddened bull, Jesus strode right through them with a raging gait and fire flashing in his eyes. He headed straight for the place below me where the moneychangers and merchants held court. He never saw me; he disappeared out of sight under the floor below my feet. I stepped to the stairs in time to see my gentle Master throw over tables and people alike as he rampaged the length of the colonnaded court. The startled merchants and moneychangers went scurrying to recover their animals and upturned wares, to the exalted cheers of those who watched and the excited joy of the poor who rushed for the coins scattering about in profusion upon the floor. The animal cages tumbled to the ground, many crashing open and spilling their contents. Birds and lambs set off squawking and bleating, rushing hither and thither in a tumultuous frenzy of fear and noise with beating wings and clattering hoofs. The sound and flurry of man and beast alike was quite a sight to see!

This had to stop! The poor Temple guards didn't know who or what had come amongst them, nor what to do. A military assault they could understand, but this? This was beyond their ken. I watched as this strong, gentle soul, who taught only love, began his quest for the end that he now sought. His Father had set the timing and the stage; now it was up to him to play the part that would ensure his teaching throughout all eternity. The stakes were no higher than the minds and souls of men. And the master of the playing board was in front of me, railing at the very men whom he had courted such a short time ago.

Even Jesus could not know how at that very moment the pieces of this terrible puzzle were one-by-one falling into place. As he stood now in the Temple court far below me, I watched him lecturing the crowds and showing them the evil ways of the Temple castes. All the while, Pontius Pilate, with cropped hair and cardinal striped tunic, was pacing back and forth in a fury on one of the rooftop patios of the Antonia. His young assistant took the brunt of this cruel man's anger as my informer, Placidus, sat quietly on the edge of the rooftop balustrade outside and watched the man with the strange eyes, whom he had met in Galilee, excite the ragged mob below. He told me later in the Baths that the scene had an unreality about it that troubled him a great deal. Not knowing why, he felt that for some strange reason he was watching history being made as he sat there in opulence high above the Temple grounds, watching the effect of Jesus' words on the crowd far below.

Jesus' entry into the city had not been missed by the ever-watchful Romans. Pilate had been summoned to the fortress walls as the teeming, noisy mob approached. Watching the mob stream past at his very feet and hearing cries of "Savior... Messiah... King!" directed to a man he called a "dirty beggar on an ass," Pilate decided these demonstrations were going to be stopped "by any means necessary!"

"I will not tolerate another demonstration like this one today!" Pilate screamed, purple with rage. "I want to make an example out of someone. I want an example now, before the start of the Passover. That will dampen their fervor. These Jews must be taught another lesson in humility. We are the masters here! I want a leader whom they all know. I want someone who will make them quake until their bowels turn to water. Find someone, and hang him with the rabble we took this week. That will quiet them down."

With that, Placidus told us, Pilate stormed from the sun-bright patio, through the darkness of his office, and out of the room, knocking over a wine pitcher on his way, sending it crashing and clanking across the marble floor. An uneasy silence followed as the more experienced Placidus quietly waited for Pilate's junior to react. He didn't have to wait long, for the young man came quickly up to the unmoving Placidus, wringing his hands in indecision and talking all the while.

Placidus' face wrinkled with disgust as he related the incident to me. He considered the young man offensive and weak, yet typical of so many sons of rich and powerful men who now inhabited the senate and secured positions of power for their progeny. Placidus, unlike many, was not of wealthy stock but had been chosen for his honesty and bravery to represent the common man in this august assemblage, and as such, he despised the wealthy inept he found throughout the empire.

"The young man's thoughts were rambling," Placidus told me, "but deadly in the conclusion that they reached. 'Placidus, I don't know quite how to go about this. How do I find a leader, a rebel at that? If we had one, he would already be hung. How do I find some poor devil?'

"He looked at me, expecting me to answer. Can you believe that?" Placidus said. "Then the idiot lit up like a lamp. 'I have it!' he cried. 'I'll let the priestly peacocks do the dirty work for me. I'll call for the High Priest, Caiaphas; it's time he earned his keep. I'll tell him what the Procurator wants; just maybe we can work this out together. That's it, I'll let them find one of their own; they know their people better than I. It's perfect! They want no trouble, and they don't want us to choose from among them either, so this task they will perform to my satisfaction with glee. They disdain their own people as much as we do.'"

The last statement, given with no offense by Placidus, hurt me from within. For I, too, had judged my people for so many years, and to see this Roman point the finger of justice my way was more than I cared to bear. But I couldn't afford the luxury of letting my mind wander because I needed to hear everything Placidus had to say.

I picked up on the conversation as he was quoting Pilate's assistant again. "'...stupid habits. You can't just invite them to supper with you because they won't come. I would much prefer to do business like this over a fine meal and wine—but not with the Jews. They say we can't keep our food clean, whatever that means. Oh well, it would probably drive our cooks crazy anyway.'"

One thing we Jews had in common with the Romans was that we talked as much with our hands as with our mouths. Placidus was mimicking all the gestures of this young man who paced back and forth like his master Pilate, from whom he had learned. The statements about my race didn't bother me; I had become numb to them through contact with Romans throughout the years. Now the conversation got back to the points I needed to hear—how this man would be chosen.

Pilate continued, "The young man stated, 'It's very easy now. I'll send for the High Priest's emissary. Caiaphas is too haughty to talk to me personally. I'm not clean, he says! I will tell them the predicament I am in. I will tell them that if they do not pick one, then we will go among them and pick our own. Instead of this, I will say, why not work together? Surely there is one among you whom you would rather see out of the way. Just give me someone you want to get rid of.'

"'The plan is perfect in its simplicity,'" the young man continued. "'The priests can choose whom they like, the people won't know anything about it until it's too late, and the man will be crucified just on the approach of Passover eve. Seeing their people on the crosses will surely sober any hopes they might have had for a savior on this holiday. Most importantly, however, Pilate will get off my back, and the people will be quieted for another six months, at least. That will take care of all the politics, and this mess can be neatly wrapped up. They will all have just what they want.'

"'Just two more of these horrid holidays to go, then my tour is over and I can go back to Rome,' he added exuberantly. 'I'm not suited for this work anyway, eh, Placidus?'"

I will delete Placidus' unprintable response to the young official's remarks. I cared little for the remainder of his story anyway, for it spoke only of the man's connections and wealthy ties in a Roman city I could never bring myself to care about nor even comprehend.

Thus, as I watched Jesus leave from the Temple that fateful night, with cheering throngs following him around the Temple wall prostrating themselves thirteen times, as was the custom when leaving, his fate had already been sealed in the wax of a Procurator's order—an order that Pilate himself would never see. The decision of a minor functionary had sealed my Master's fate, a fate that was but three days away.

Chapter 18

Jesus Answered Simply, "I Am"

And he replied, "As soon as you enter Jerusalem, you will see a man walking along carrying a pitcher of water. Follow him into the house he enters, and say to the man who lives there, 'Our Teacher says for you to show us the guest room where he can eat the Passover meal with his disciples.' He will take you upstairs to a large room all ready for us. That is the place. Go ahead and prepare the meal there."

Luke 22:10-13

Jesus came each day into the city to teach in the Temple. Each day his manner of speech became more caustic for those in power to hear; yet, each day, his teaching to the common and poor became more loving and sure. Each day those in power sought new ways to trap him and show him up as a traitor, a blasphemer, or a fool in front of the crowd, but nothing worked. Each day those cocky and arrogant ones who went into the courts to try their hand at tripping him up came back empty of hand and red of face. And as a consequence of the presence of this man, the members of the Sanhedrim informally gathered each day in the Court of the Israelites, in the Chamber of the Hewn Stone that was located at the southern end of the court. Jesus was the sole topic of conversation.

There were many supporters now within the council who in private conversations honored him with beautiful words and praises, but in public, few there were who spoke openly for fear of the wrath of Caiaphas. Caiaphas' position was clear, for he had the most to lose if indeed this was the Messiah—and if he truly were the Messiah, what then? The conversation and arguments went on and on.

In actual fact, it mattered not at all what happened in the council that met within the Chamber of Stone, for as has always been the case with governments, it is the holder of the throne alone who makes the real decisions, and the rest is all for show. As a result, while those who were yet foolish enough to think that they had a hand in Jesus' fate endlessly argued and debated, the fact was that the agreement had already been struck. Caiaphas had his man to sacrifice to meet both his and Rome's needs.

My job was clear. I had to know what was going on, and of this I had to be sure, for as Jesus told me, "The history of the world will turn on what just a handful of men do this week, Asher. Let us all make sure we do our parts flawlessly."

It is interesting to learn exactly how much guards can see and hear when they are paid enough. During that week, I guarantee they made a year's worth of salary by having eyes and ears for me. There was not one moment of the day that I did not know exactly what occurred behind the closed doors of Caiaphas' private chambers, as well as at his residence and that of his father-in-law, Annas, the High Priest before him.

And so it was that through the eyes of the unblinking watchmen, Jesus observed his disciple Judas deliver him up for silver to the merciless Caiaphas. Little did they know that for all their planning, they were but puppets and pawns in a force whose time had come.

This was a difficult time for me, for I knew of the horrible end that awaited my beloved teacher. Crucifixion was a far more cruel way to die than I could contemplate. For a man who gave so much, it seemed more than I could endure to know beforehand the suffering that he would soon have to bear. If it had not been for that time alone with him in the desert, I would not have been able to carry out my task successfully; and I am sure that is exactly why he devoted over two precious days alone with me so close to the end. He told me that our Father had need of me, and in that I would not fail him. But even as I carried out my appointed tasks, I knew, as Jesus himself had alluded, that my life, too, was soon to end.

Because it was of vital importance that I remain completely away from him during this week, I watched him only from afar. I entrusted the carrying of messages by stealth each eve to a man who owed Jesus his life and thus was more than willing to give it again, if need be, for the man who gave him sight. I entrusted the messages to Maston, who had, sure to his word, returned with his family to serve me (and, as an embarrassing aside, had returned my fine black steed).

Jesus did make one promise to me. Knowing that I yearned to be with him just one more time before the end, he agreed to eat his last meal at my home. He asked for me to make a room available to him and his closest disciples.

He looked at me with total love as we remembered all the wonderful times we had shared together in front of the fire, talking and telling stories far into the night. Those were beautiful, easier times.

Then he gave me the following instructions: "Go on the day before Passover eve, at the exact time you hear the trumpets from the Temple walls sound the sacrifice over the city. Have your manservant dip his water jar into the well by the lower pool; Peter and John will be there and will follow him home. Make sure that whoever you send is not known to Peter or John, for I do not want them to know in whose house it is that we will eat, in case they are intercepted. Also, make sure that your man does not go directly to your house, for the faces of Peter and John are well known, and they may be followed closely. I will set the time of my arrest, not the Temple whores, and having the last meal with my twelve is more important to my Father than any of those at the table will know."

That day and the next are etched in my memory like no others. At the morning service, I watched carefully for signs of nervousness in the High Priest or in any of those closest to him, and there were plenty to see. They knew that their time was running out, for Passover eve was but one night away, and they had as yet failed to deliver up their "scapegoat" to the Romans, who grew more impatient as each day passed. I took pleasure in their anxiety, yet I knew that, as far as they were concerned, they would still have their "victory"; and unbeknownst to them, it lay only hours away.

I too was nervous as I waited for the start of the Temple day. Maston was well on his way by now to the well that lay at the lowest end of the city in the Tyropoean Valley, which in turn led into the Kidron Valley and the road to Bethany beyond. Although both Peter and John had seen the raggedly dressed Maston when he had been healed long before, I knew they would not recognize this handsome, wealthily dressed man as the same beggar Jesus had healed almost half a year before. As it turns out, I was right, and the three of them made it to the house quite easily, apparently, at least to their knowledge, without being followed.

Even to this detail, Jesus had thought of everything. For up to now, he and his disciples had entered the city each day by the road north of the Heifer Causeway that spanned the Kidron Valley from the Mount of Olives to the City; not once did they enter from the south. Therefore, there was no reason for the authorities, which now had spies everywhere to ensnare Jesus by any possible means, including stealth, to suspect this entrance through the southern gate.

Maston had been easy to find, as Jesus had undoubtedly known, for I would bet that at no time had a Jew ever seen a man carry a water jar anywhere—especially dressed as Maston was. That is strictly a woman's job, and certainly not one for a man of means. When Maston had Peter and John in tow, he set aside the jug and walked with them up through the poorer part of town, where streets and houses are tightly packed, to the marketplace, swollen enormously by the influx of the holiday crowd. It was there, we thought, that any who followed would soon be lost. From there, Maston and the disciples followed the aqueduct back to the upper part of the city, then through broadened streets and well-kept homes to their destination.

By the time they reached my house, I had also returned home, having received the report I had awaited during the prayers of the morning service. I did not see Jesus because of the tremendous crowd, but I knew he was there to worship for the last time in the house of his Father.

When Maston flung the door open, Peter and John knew, of course, whose house they were at, and Peter threw his big arms about me and gave me a death-threatening hug. "I am glad to see you too, Peter," I wheezed, "but please, leave enough for Miriamme, or she will never forgive you." We all laughed, and Miriamme, Peter, and John left to inspect our large upper room and then the kitchen, to ensure all would be in readiness for the evening meal. As they cheerfully left, I slumped against the courtyard wall and grieved, "Poor Peter and John, they have no idea. They will be so all alone... so will I."

The guard had told me that Judas did not yet know where they were to gather for supper, but Judas had told the High Priest he was sure that the disciples and Jesus would eat together. Judas told Caiaphas' men that once he knew where Jesus would be and when he would be most vulnerable, he would slip away and tell them; and Jesus' arrest could follow. Little did Judas know at that time that he would be eating his last meal with Jesus at my house and that the house of Annas was but a short walk from my door.

As the day passed, I paced like a caged animal. I couldn't stay in the house and wait, nor did I want to return to the Temple to see Caiaphas in his golden robes defile that shrine I held so holy. So I did the only other thing that I enjoyed—I went to the Baths to wile away the day. Although I stayed until the afternoon and made small talk with several there, my heart found no peace in it, and I sought to stay alone.

At the ninth hour, I returned home to find everything in readiness. Now we missed only our Master and the remaining ten disciples, who wouldn't be coming until their path was covered by darkness. "For heaven's sake, come into the other room and sit down. You have been standing by the door all evening. He will be here soon," Miriamme chided me as she put her arm around my waist and prepared to guide me to the living area of the house. I had given in and was starting to follow her when the knock came in three hurried raps. I turned and ran to the door as Jesus and the rest of his disciples walked in. Jesus greeted Miriamme, John, and John's wife warmly as they all converged on the door. Jesus shot a glance my way, and I nodded to let him know that I had news. Jesus was starting to walk my way when Miriamme took his hand and pulled him to the bench along the wall to the side of the door. There, Miriamme bowed down upon her knees and, taking the bowl of water and clean towels brought to her by her maid, carefully removed Jesus' sandals and washed his feet. As she washed, Jesus looked up at me, his eyes glistening wet in the lamplight. Bending low, he held her head to his lap for the longest time, and then kissed my sweet Miriamme good-bye.

In the excitement of the holiday mood, the meaning of the moment was missed by all but the three of us, who for the barest moment of time, shared a love that would last throughout eternity.

Our mood was broken as Peter came out of the kitchen, where he had been sampling the fare, and shouted his usual greetings to the gathered crowd.

"Get down here on the bench, Peter!" Miriamme called, "You're next to have your feet washed. I'll have no one in my house with dirty feet." With that, Miriamme insisted on washing each disciple's feet in turn, to show them the love she had for them and how our house was honored by their presence. As Peter took his turn, Jesus and I slipped out the other end of the patio into my private rooms.

I told Jesus in great detail of the murder that the High Priest and Pilate had planned. Although he knew the basic outline from my messages, I wanted to fill him in on all the subtleties he might have missed. Lastly, I told him of what was to transpire tonight, once Judas found an opportunity to leave. Jesus was quiet awhile as he absorbed what I had to say and, I am certain, pondered his moves for the night ahead. When finally he spoke, he was deadly serious, and new lines in his once smooth forehead showed the strain that he had been under. He put his hand to my arm and gave it a squeeze. "The last thing I want is for us to be found here. I will make sure Judas knows that we will be found alone at the olive press in the garden of Gethsemane. There I will await them. From there I will be able to see my Father's beloved Temple once more. I think it will help give me courage. Asher, will you pray for me?"

Hearing Jesus say these words, I was struck by a knot in my stomach, for I realized that he knew what horrible death awaited him in just a few short hours, and yet he gave himself up to it willingly. There was still time to save him: a swift horse and soldiers at the gates whom I could bribe. He could be gone in an hour, safely on his way to the protection of Galilee. But the thought passed as rapidly as it came, for he had willed himself here this night, and thus fulfilled the prophecies to see God's dream survive throughout eternity. With nothing else to say, we embraced and headed for the door. Just before going out, Jesus turned, and with compassion flowing from him like the light that he was, said, "Asher ben Ammi, I will find you again someday. Remember well this time together, keep it safe within your soul, and when it is needed, I will call you, as I did with the overflowing cup, and ask you to give the light to a thousand others, so that they too will know our Father is within their hearts."

He then turned and left.

When I could regain my composure, I came out to find that he had already taken my son and his disciples up the stairs near the front door to the room prepared on the second floor. Only Miriamme, John's wife, and I were left. I tried to tell them what was about to happen, now that the mold was cast, but I could not. So we ate a quiet meal, with my dear, sweet Miriamme intuitive enough to honor my silence and wait until I felt free enough to communicate. She spoke softly to her daughter-in-law, who was almost her own age.

Well before the end of the meal, I heard the sound of rough hinges grate as the door opened to the upstairs room. I quietly moved into the shadows of the patio and watched as Judas silently slipped his sandals on and disappeared into the dark. There was no turning back now. What was to be had begun.

The meal lasted quite a long time, or so it seemed to me, not being a part of it. But finally we heard the upstairs door open and the latch bang against the rough plaster wall, and this time it was accompanied by the sound of the muffled speech of many men and the scraping of feet on wooden stairs.

We all got up and hurried to the entry, where the stairs they now descended terminated. The covered portal opened directly onto the street outside, and its rough-sawn wooden doors served as the main entrance to our home.

It was a different group that descended the stairs than had gone up, that was evident immediately. The happy band of men that had arrived a few hours ago to celebrate the coming of the Passover holiday was now somber and introspective, each unto himself. At my insistence, the whole household gathered to wish them good-bye. Jesus went up to each person in turn and, holding their hands or giving them a hug, whispered into their ears something personal, something to remember him by. Maston, more intuitive than the rest, sensed that something was amiss and grabbed Jesus as he came to him, not letting him go for the longest time. Even with all that bore down upon him now, Jesus rushed him not, but rather held Maston in return.

When my Lord came to me, he held me close, then whispered in my ear, "Asher, my people will be criminals and lost sheep in a few hours. Please take them in and hide them if you can. And, Asher, please take my mother as your own for as long as she has need." I nodded to him in the dim light of the oil lamp along the wall, and with that, the double doors closed, and they were gone.

After Jesus and the eleven disciples left, my son John along with them, Miriamme and I started to retire as the servants cleaned up the room. As we were walking toward the stairs leading up to our quarters, Miriamme stopped as if an idea had just come into her head. "Do you mind, sweet one? Let's go up to the room where they ate."

"Why?" I asked.

"Never mind, just come along." I was deeply in love with my young, beautiful wife, and she knew I would go anywhere with her; all she had to do was ask.

We went back toward the front of the house and up the narrow stairs into the room where the girls were busy picking up dishes of leftover food. Miriamme walked to the opposite end of the low table where Jesus had been sitting and, bending over, picked up the silver goblet that was standing there. I was not present when the table had been set and was surprised to see the single silver goblet; all the rest were of common brass. As if reading my mind, Miriamme said as she returned down the length of the room, "It was a special night, and this cup was for him."

As she stopped in front of me, I looked down into the shining vessel. I noted that there was just a touch of red wine still swirling in the bottom as I thought of Jesus' words to me in the desert: "Take and drink, feel the light in you, of you, around you, and with you, in God's own peace. Then give this overflowing love you have been given to a thousand others in turn, for there is no end to His love, His peace, His bliss." Remembering his words put me at ease as I put my arm around Miriamme and we headed back down the stairs at the front of the house.

"What was that you mumbled, dear?"

"Oh, nothing, Miriamme, just something Jesus said to me in the desert." Together, arm in arm, we crossed the patio and climbed the stairs at the other end of the house to bed.

I didn't think that I had fallen asleep, but I must have, for all of a sudden I woke with a start. My mind began to work. Someone was banging on our bedroom door. It was Maston, shouting, "Come quick, master, there are Temple police at the door!"

"Tell them I will be right there," I answered while I tried to find my clothes in the dark. "Don't be frightened, Miriamme," I said, with a conviction I didn't feel myself, and rushed out the door and down the stairs into the unlit court below.

My mind was racing. What was happening? Did someone report us as harborers of Jesus? What else could it be? Wait... Caiaphas wouldn't dare do this to me with my wealth and power. I would have heard of this from my high-priced ears among the court. Could it be the trial of Jesus, then? No, it couldn't be the trial, not until after daybreak, that's the Law.

Then it hit me. Caiaphas (or more probably the crafty old Annas) had found a way to hurry the trial of Jesus so as to finish in time for Pilate to hang him by Sabbath eve. It was a desperate solution.

The answer was there before me; I just hadn't seen it. Because of the tremendous crowds present for Passover and their need to offer sacrifices, the Temple was opened at midnight and services began at the first watch; therefore it was legal to convene the Sanhedrim at this early hour. Maston had said that the police had come for me, not soldiers, which also reinforced my belief that this was exactly what had happened. For I, as a member of the high council, had to be called if Caiaphas was to follow every jot of the Law—and I knew he would. What right did they have to do this? Others would be asking that question right now as they were being awakened in the middle of the night. The answer was, of course, that they had every right. For, as the cart follows the ass, so does "right" follow power, just as surely as life itself will someday end.

I asked about John but was told that he had never returned. Maston had roused the stable, and two horses were waiting. I looked at Maston, and he said, "Sorry, master, I must go with you. I must know!" I nodded my head in agreement, and as the yard gate swung open, we rode off at a gallop.

I found out later from John that he had been with Jesus when Judas approached with some of Caiaphas' men, Temple police, and even a squad of Roman soldiers to ensure the results of the arrest. Apparently my son, not an unimportant man in his own right, demanded of the officer in charge to go with him and commanded him to state the charges. The officer, knowing that John was a member of the ruling court, allowed him to accompany them, and together they took Jesus to Annas' house. This reinforced my thought that the powerful Annas had set the planning for this miserable deed. Apparently, Jesus gave Annas nothing that would serve his needs, and thus, after being beaten by a snarling guard for insubordination, he was next sent to the Temple, which was the only place an official seal could be placed upon his fate.

When I arrived at the Chamber of Stone, Jesus was already there, his hands bound behind him, his face red and swollen from the beating he had been made to endure. In front of him in the first row was my son, who acknowledged me but didn't pause in his argument directed toward six or seven priests listening to what he had to say about this man who, in fact, had already been condemned. The whole room was filling with noisy, arguing, angry people. These were important and illustrious men here, used to being treated with deference, and they were not taking it lightly that they had been dragged here in the middle of the night.

Looking around, I saw others, too, for I had developed a shrewd political eye after this many years. I could spot those whose faces wore the satisfied and all-knowing smugness that said to me that they were of the elect who had known beforehand what the results of this night would be. Those names and faces I cataloged by habit for future use, should the knowledge be needed.

Jesus had his back to me as I entered. His presence before me was a shock for which I could not have adequately prepared. When you love someone as I loved him... I just can't explain the feelings I had. I put my hands to my mouth so as not to cry out in grief at the abject sight of him. The utter emptiness that gripped me was beyond anything I had ever experienced, even at my first wife's passing. Then, suddenly, as if I had actually uttered a cry, Jesus straightened up and slowly turned to look my way. In his peaceful eyes, already swollen from a blow, I found my courage again and my voice. I was able to return his look and let him know that I would not fail him. The words that needed to be said would be said with clarity and force, and in the end, everything he had wanted of this meeting would come to pass.

I found a place high in the back, out of my usual order, just as a hush came over the assemblage and the High Priest, adorned in all his robes, entered the chamber. Pompous ass! I thought as he took his seat. And thus, the highest court of the land was convened to "officially" decide Jesus' fate.

My son and I, as well as others in the court, argued and used every legal trick we knew to point out that Jesus was innocent of any provable charge that Caiaphas and his followers might level. Then, as prearranged, when Jesus knew his time had come to an end and this nightmare game had come to a close, he slowly lifted his head and looked straight into my eyes. Even from a distance there was no mistake. Within my head my name sounded (it imploded!) and I stood dumbly silent, stunned by the sound still reverberating within my mind. I sat strangely transfixed by his face and those incredible eyes. The arguments within me slowly died one after another—it was finished.

John, just to the right and below me, was desperately arguing now but losing the battle to the gathering silence of those still opposed to the High Priest's will. Looking back, seeking my support for some point he had just concluded, he saw my face. His mouth fell open as I stared, transfixed, at my beloved Master. He was like no other I knew upon the earth. He was the Messiah—and they knew him not.

John's eyes pleaded in vain for my help, but I held my silence as I had promised. Although the argument raged on for a short time still and John carried on the best he knew how, it was over, and the verdict was in. Finally, when Caiaphas' menacing looks had silenced all but a few, he finished the show. Slowly he stood, and respectful silence fell like a leaden curtain about the council. Then in a deep, clear voice he looked directly at Jesus and roared: "I demand, in the name of the living God, that you tell us whether you claim to be the Messiah, the Son of God!"

Jesus answered simply. "I am."

With that, the High Priest tore his vestments and shouted, "Blasphemy! What need have we for other witnesses? You have all heard him say it! What is your verdict?"

"Death! Death! Death!" was the chant that rang spontaneously throughout the Chamber as the guards grabbed Jesus under his arms and dragged him away through the council that I once thought distributed the fairest justice of any land. Caiaphas looked my way for an instant before pushing through the crowd to lead the procession across the Temple grounds to the fortress of Antonia. A smile was now openly displayed on his cunning face, thinking that he had beaten me; that he had won. "Oh, woe unto you, Caiaphas," I thought. "You think you have saved yourself and your nation, but alas, truly it is you who has lost—everything!"

I sat back down on the cold stone bench. All of a sudden, I was a very tired, weary, old man.

Chapter 19

"Come, We'll Watch From a Distance"

I have loved you even as the Father has loved me. Live within my love. When you obey me you are living in my love, just as I obey my Father and live in his love. I have told you this so that you will be filled with my joy. Yes, your cup of joy will overflow! I demand that you love each other as much as I love you. And here is how to measure it—the greatest love is shown when a person lays down his life for his friends...
John 15:9-13

The barest hint of light could be seen in the cold eastern sky, and there was a smell of moisture in the morning breeze as it drifted in from the west. John and I joined Maston in the Court of the Gentiles where Maston had been watching and waiting. Not being Jewish, Maston couldn't enter the inner court; however, he had already guessed the outcome of the trial, for he had seen the High Priest lead the parade to the gate of the Antonia and had seen Jesus with Temple guards immediately behind.

Maston said that even as we debated Jesus' fate, there had been priests out in every court quizzing people as to their feelings about him. If they professed a belief in Jesus, he noted, the priests said nothing to raise suspicion but let them on their way with a blessing. If they were against him or seemed to enjoy the questions and favors of the priest, they were gradually herded close to an angry group that was gathering near the northwestern gate that led to the fortress Antonia.

Maston pretended to be a pious Jew working his way around the Temple wall (a dangerous game that could have turned fatal had he been recognized), praying and prostrating as he went. As he came within earshot of the now righteous throng, he could hear the priests taunting them, goading them into a religious frenzy. The priests called on all their loyalties and prejudices until they felt confident that the mob would do anything they wished. Then Maston knew that even if Caiaphas lost in the court, the carefully chosen mob would ensure Jesus' fate. The High Priest was not a fool. He gained and held his position with deftness in his craft and thoroughness in his planning that even my well-paid "ears" could not penetrate. As Caiaphas led the Sanhedrim, who now followed dutifully in his tracks, and his priestly caste, the rabble also did its job by screaming for Jesus' death. When the procession reached the confines of the Temple grounds, Caiaphas would go no further, for Passover was coming that night, and he didn't want to be defiled. He sent the others on into the stone-paved court of the governor without him. Then, with an evil grin spreading across his face for having successfully delivered up a "leader" to Pilate as promised, Caiaphas turned with his two chief priests and quickly returned to the confines of his own "sacred" palace.

"What do we do now, father?" John asked limply, as if his feelings had all been drained from his body.

"Now comes the hardest task of all, son—we must watch him die.

"There could now also be much danger for his disciples, John, maybe even for us—but I doubt if Caiaphas is that bold—or dumb. Do you know where the rest of his disciples are now?"

"No, father. When they came to arrest Jesus, everyone except Peter left at a dead run down the hill through the olive trees and into the darkness of the valley. They are probably hiding somewhere in the city to be close to Jesus. They might even be hiding among this crowd, or in the city of tents just north of here.

"When they arrested Jesus," John continued, "the officer of the guards knew me personally and didn't dare tell me what I could or could not do. I could tell that he was considering arresting and holding Peter, however, for Peter seemed to care little for his life at that moment and roared his insults at Judas and the rest of them while taking a swing at one of them.

Thinking better of it, the officer of the guards turned on his heels and left, satisfied that he had his quarry. I imagine that he thought twice when he saw the look I gave him, which made him act more cautiously than he otherwise would. That officer's time will come—mark my words, he will know my wrath when this is over!"

"John," I cautioned, "have you forgotten already what our Lord taught us, why he came, why he is about to die?"

John blanched and lowered his eyes, then continued his story anew. "When we got to Annas' house the guards stopped Peter at the outer entry to the court. It took but a simple coin and my name to change his mind. When last I saw Peter, he was going over to the fire with the servants and guards to await the news. When we finished, which didn't take long, he was already gone. I have no idea where he went."

"Then go, both of you," I said to Maston and my son, "find the disciples and gather them up. They will need a place to hide. Put them in the room over the stables, behind the room where we have the grain. There are no windows, and only one door that's almost impossible to find. Even if the idiot Caiaphas is so bold as to search our home, they won't find them there. Now go, find them, they will be like frightened sheep in the city. I have other work to do. This task is just for me."

As Maston headed off for the horses and John began to search the Temple courts, I set my feet for the Fort of Antonia. Taking a deep breath, I thought, "All right, lions' den, here I come!"

The mention of Placidus' name, and also my position, sent the Roman guard off to find his captain, whose name was Caius. I knew his reputation well. I saw the guard approach him in the stone-paved court of the barracks where he had his men lined in files. The guard saluted him as he approached, then spoke of me and pointed in my direction with his spear. I saw Caius nod, bark an order to another who took charge, and head my way with a soldier's stiff gait.

I strained to look about, to see if I could find Jesus somewhere in the court. It was then that I caught sight of three men, all tied to the whipping stakes, their backs bloody from the scourge. I couldn't see their faces, as their backs were to me in the darkness of the early dawn, but none of them looked like Jesus in body or shape. Even their hair was different, for Jesus wore part of his cut and bound in the back with a thong. Of course, the guards could have removed that, but still, none of them looked like him at all.

"What do you want?" was the rude, brusque greeting I received from Caius, a soldier, not a statesman, through and through.

"I have to see Placidus. I have reason to believe he is with Pilate now."

"You can't see him now, there is a trial going on. Besides, you can see I'm too busy to be your guide. Today these men will be crucified. It's the first hour now, by your time, and I have orders to have them up by the third, or they will have my hide. Go back to your temple, see him tomorrow."

"I know very well there is a trial going on, Caius," I spit with icy precision in my words, letting him know I would not hesitate in making my position good. "The trial is for Jesus of Galilee. And, you are right; Placidus is with Pilate at the trial this very moment. Now, take me to him, Caius, or I swear by nightfall you will be the lowliest foot soldier in this garrison!"

There was a frigid silence as Caius, now crimson with rage, sized up my threat. For him to take an order from a Jew, any Jew, was more than he could abide. As he hesitated a fateful moment to decide, I felt that I needed one more weight to tip the scales in my favor. Playing my last game piece, I added with venom, "Need I ask you, Caius, how is Pilate's wife?" Many of us from the council knew from our own spies that Pilate's wife oft had a lover when Pilate was away, and Caius was her latest.

Caius exploded with all the rage of a wounded bull, but I moved not a muscle, nor did my eyes waver for an instant from their glare. Beaten, knowing that exposure would mean banishment or death, Caius turned and stormed off down the column-lined hall with me closely behind. The original guard stared after us in disbelief.

When I arrived Placidus was standing off to the side while Pilate questioned Jesus. I waved Caius off as he was about to step to Placidus' side and announce my presence in his ear, and instead I quietly walked up to my Roman friend without saying a word. Caius, glad to avoid entering the judgment hall, retreated down the gilded corridor. The heels of his military sandals echoed as he went, anger adding to their impact on the marble floor.

Placidus was so engrossed with the spectacle before him that at first he didn't notice me slip up beside him. When he did, the muscles of his massive shoulders flinched in startled surprise. My worried look said everything this man needed to know. He gave me a little resigned smile and shared a knowing in his eyes, and then once again he turned his attention back to this most amazing trial in progress. I knew that I would be "defiled" by my presence in this hall, but I no longer cared what ridiculous rules governed me. I had seen Jesus' light and knew that I could not be defiled by anything as petty as whom I saw or what I ate.

Pilate's questions were aimed at finding a rebel guilty of sedition, plotting a rebellion, a crime against the emperor punishable by death. Jesus was instead treating him to a lecture on the world of his Father God in heaven. Outside the open window the Jews who had been carefully selected by the priests were chanting, "Death! Death! Death!" just as their leaders had before in the council chambers.

Pilate's temper was naturally short, and the noise outside was making him furious. Here was not a rebel whom he could show to the people and say, "See, here is what happens when Rome is defied!" Rather, he had before him a preposterous Jew, who thought he was the Jewish Messiah, come to "save" his people with love! Ridiculous! He shot a dangerous look at the young functionary who had brought about this mess, but the young man had shifted his position nervously away from Pilate's gaze, pretending to be engrossed with what was going on outside.

Pilate had told him to bring a zealot, not a religious fanatic! I knew he couldn't care about this Jesus, pretender to a heaven-made throne. As far as he knew, all Jews were religious fanatics. Pilate couldn't tell one from another when it came to religious ranting. He wanted someone who had drawn his sword against imperial Rome, a local hero to be sacrificed as an example, a warning for all who would defy the State. There were plenty of them out there, robbing and pillaging, killing Romans whenever they could. And here before him stood not a zealot but a poor, dumb carpenter guilty of nothing—except religious blasphemy. Who cared?

Pilate wanted no part of this trial. Annoyed beyond his normal tolerance by the rabble yelling outside his room, and his own people as well, he slouched, brooding, tapping his fingers on the arm of the chair, as his face grew darker and more menacing with every moment of the drawn-out affair.

Then, with a suddenness that startled everyone in the room, he bolted from his seat and walked rapidly to the balcony above the court, motioning for the guards to drag Jesus forward as well. There he held up his arms for silence, then shouted, "You brought this man to me, accusing him of leading a revolt against the government. I have examined him thoroughly and find him innocent!"

He couldn't have spoken with more force or contempt. He fairly hissed the words, but Caiaphas' men were not taken aback for long. They were far more subtle in controlling others than Pilate. Pilate used brute force; we of the council used people's minds and emotions to serve our needs. I had participated so many times before in these ways of controlling others that I guessed immediately what was to come next in exploiting Pilate for Caiaphas' own desires—and was treated to my own just desserts.

Priests on the payroll, and those loyal to Caiaphas, were placed uniformly throughout the crowd, and as Pilate finished, I heard their individual voices clearly an instant before the throng picked up the chant. "Crucify him! Crucify him!" Once again, I saw Pilate hold up his hands to gain silence.

"I will have him scourged for you, but that is all I can do."

Now a mighty roar rose from the mob, and Pilate tried for the third time to reason with them. "Why? What crime has he committed? I find no reason to sentence him to death." But it was all over. The multitude drowned out his words and started to surge against the guards. I saw Pilate's shoulders droop as he held up his hands for the last time, appearing to wash them of the condemned man's blood. I heard him say softly as he turned to go down to the Judgment Seat on the raised platform below, "It is done Let's get rid of the fools."

My eyes betrayed my stony face as the stinging sensation once again came. Placidus kindly grabbed me by the arm, and led me away, saying, "Come, we will watch from a distance. What they are about to do to him, you do not want to see."

Placidus guided me out of the room, down some stairs, and into very opulent quarters, where he said he was staying. Once inside, he poured me wine, which I gratefully took, and there we sat in silence for the longest time. Placidus was the first to move. He quietly said again, "Come, we will watch from a distance." I rose, my old body feeling very heavy now, and went out into the streets. Placidus took me to a mercantile building where he guided me between bags piled high with what smelled like grain, then up the back stairs to the roof overlooking the street below. Beyond the street I could see the city's wall, then the ridge called the Skull past that.

We didn't have to wait long, for the noise of confusion, wailing cries, and screams of grief were growing louder in the street below, telling us that my Master and the other condemned men were coming this way. I grabbed Placidus and thanked him, then told him that I just couldn't watch.

"You'll be back, friend, you'll be back, and when you do I will still be here—until they take him down." I turned to leave just as I saw the first of the soldiers round the turn below. I pulled up the door in the rooftop floor, and as I descended the stairs I heard Placidus yell at Caius marching past in the street below, "Where's the fourth? You should have been more careful; your men are too harsh. It shouldn't have happened. See that it never happens again!"

Why did Placidus worry? What difference did it make whether the poor soul died at the whipping pole or on the cross? For a moment, I wondered whether it was Jesus who had already met his end. Then from the darkness of the room of grain, I heard the women who followed the procession wail his name. I hid my eyes and sobbed until I could cry no more. Then, empty, I headed back to our home to see if I could help any of the disciples who might be there.

I found no one at the house, neither Miriamme nor John nor his wife. The servants were gone, too. It was like a morbid tomb. Later I was to find, to my humiliation, that each of them who had been at the house had followed John up to the hill to keep watch.

Placidus was right. I couldn't stay away. I had to see the end. I felt that I was a coward. Even though I wasn't at the foot of the cross, I made myself head back to watch from the rooftop with Placidus.

Death by hanging is a long, often multi-day, excruciatingly painful way to die. I was in no hurry. I returned back through the city the long way round, an aimless path that took me by the Baths, the Hasmonean palace (where Herod Antipas was in residence), the market full of noise, and then along the Temple wall north to the fortress where I had started. I ended up there because I was not sure I could find the little storeroom if I did not take exactly the same route I had taken that morning with Placidus.

I watched the sky as I walked, for it had become dark and foreboding, and the wind had become a gale. I wrapped my cloak around me as the dust and dirt from the streets began to swirl about everywhere. A shutter to a window high above broke loose in the wind and came sailing at me, narrowly missing my head. I heard people screaming over the wailing wind and watched ahead as three stones fell from a rooftop, narrowly missing a handful of hurrying people in the street below. I looked up just in time to see a bolt of lightning rip across the ominous black sky.

Then, as the ninth hour approached, the earth began to tremble. I grabbed hold of the Temple wall as a rumbling deep within the earth began to grow. "It's Jesus, I know it, he's dead! He's dead!" My mind shrieked as I struggled to keep from falling sideways onto the ground.

I pushed away from the wall and started to run. Then I heard the sound. It was like a crack! Involuntarily, I stopped and reeled back as if the very stones of the Temple were poison to touch. And then it came, a great cry of lament from behind the Temple wall that told me something awful had just happened inside.

I turned again and headed west up the street as the shaking began to subside. People were still running every which way as I turned the first corner—and ran straight into Nicodemus and Joseph of Arimathea (who I didn't know had supported Jesus until that morning during the meeting of the Sanhedrim). They didn't see me either until we bumped headlong into each other, three old men almost knocking each other flat. "Where are you going?" I stammered as we struggled to hold each other up.

"He's dead, Asher, he's dead!" Joseph cried. "We are on our way to get permission from Pilate to let us have his body, so that we can bury him as he should be. I have a tomb not far from here that has never been used. It was going to be for my family and me, but now it will give me honor to prepare it for our Lord."

I had been running in panic, yet here were two men who had never been as close to Jesus as I, yet in this dire moment they were thinking of their Master; and I, oh God, I was thinking of me. Thus started a conflict that raged within me until my end. I found that I was either thinking of myself when I should have been thinking of his flock or flailing myself for just that cause. Not a pretty picture I paint of myself, nor one of which I am proud, but a true one just the same.

It was a miserable man who climbed the stairs to the rooftop where I had left Placidus just a few hours past, but Joseph and Nicodemus had sobered me, and my mind was once again beginning to clear. Placidus, his hands together behind his back, was staring silently at the billowing black clouds, out across the city wall to the Skull that lay beyond. I followed his gaze to see that they were just now taking Jesus from the cross and letting him to the ground. They must have been some of his followers, for he was being lowered carefully, whereas the Romans just would have let him fall.

I hadn't realized that Placidus was speaking, for I was focused on the cross, but then turning my attention his way to listen to him, I realized that he wasn't speaking to me at all but to himself and, I think, to all of history.

"Here comes Caius. Yes, Caius, you did the job for which you're paid, but this one was different, wasn't he? Not like the rest of them up there. Something strange about him. Something inside you changes, doesn't it? Yes, great, strong, hard Caius, I can even see it in you. Something is different. You can fool the others, but I know you too well.

"Stupid Jews, you don't even know what you have done. You have conquered us without lifting a sword. Damn you! Damn all of you!"

He turned to me, but I'm not sure he knew who I was, for he continued as if I were a disembodied spirit listening to his hidden thoughts. "That man up there is not a man like us. You saw him, didn't you?" I nodded my head, but I don't think he was looking for an answer. "Mark these words, his legions will conquer Rome like none of these rabble will. We'll eat these people alive someday. They can't stand against our armies, but in the end we won't be able to stand against the likes of him!" He turned and pointed at the now empty cross, silhouetted against the ominous sky. "He'll sweep through the armies into the Senate itself. Even the emperor someday will fall.

"All his people deserted him, didn't they, but they'll be back. The next time we won't be able to stop them. There's no winning this one for Pilate." Placidus laughed an eerie laugh that made my skin crawl. "I'm glad I am going back. The sooner the better."

I'm sure my face reflected a look of utter disbelief. I couldn't believe what was happening. When I left him just a few short hours ago, he was quiet, but normal. Now he was different; he had changed. He was seeing a future I could not imagine, and I thought he must have gone mad. Had Jesus done this to him? I could not imagine, but I had the greatest desire to get away from him, for truly, my instincts told me, this man could be dangerous if I but tipped him just a little off the middle of the scale.

"They took him down," Placidus said, his mouth tight. "At least somebody has some courage. What do I care. It's done. Let's go."

He started to turn, looking for the stair, but his eyes were still glassy, far from normal, and their look was far away. As I helped him down the stairs, through the room, and out onto the street, he looked up at the sky gravely and said, "It's strange. It's so quiet. I wish I'd kept back some soldiers—plenty of these people would slit my throat."

Not knowing what else to do, I started to walk him back. Then, without warning, he yanked his arm away from me and looked at me as if I were a total stranger. He shook his head, seemingly to clear it, then turned and strode down the deserted passageway alone as the thunder crashed and the rain came in a torrent.

I never saw him again.

Chapter 20

He is Not Gone

You may find him anywhere, and everywhere, for truly he lies within your heart. Go within the silence as he taught you, and find him there—he waits for you even now.

Asher ben Ammi

By daybreak, all the disciples had gathered at our home. Most had arrived under the cover of darkness the night before. As soon as I returned home from my experience with Placidus, I set about having the room over the stable readied for the men and the storeroom in front rearranged so as to show no sign of anything but staples. Finally, when I could see that John had things well under control, I let myself slip into a fitful sleep, broken every hour or so by a newcomer who needed protection and a place to rest. The next morning, I felt as if I had been drugged. I had gotten little or no sleep for two nights straight, and all of the emotion of the previous day had sapped my strength.

The next day was Passover, and it was spent at our house with all of the disciples save Judas, whom none of us had seen. In addition, Mary, Jesus' mother, now joined us too, and several others who sought protection because they followed in his name. Because it was Passover, I had no fear that Caiaphas would send anyone to search the house, and so we quietly celebrated our first holiday without Jesus, each afraid of what the night might bring. For I reasoned that if Caiaphas were to move on us, it would come soon, and what better time than by the darkness of the shadowless moon?

During the day each of us was lost in his or her own world. If the others were like me, they were reliving their lives with him, those precious moments each of us had with him wherein we found our God through him. So preoccupied was I in my own thoughts that I hadn't noticed John, son of Zebedee, when first he had come. Now I saw him in the corner of the courtyard all curled up like a ball. There was fear in him, I could tell, and my heart went out to him. He had been kind to me while I was in his homeland of Galilee, and suddenly I realized what this loss of his teacher must mean to him. I remembered that he was much afraid and never quite understood those things that were going on around him, so I sought him out to help if I could.

I sat down beside him, not saying a word. After a moment, still holding his arms around his knees, he lifted his face, tears streaming silently down his sunburned cheeks, and he spoke into the bright blue sky, anguish in his voice. "I ran, Asher, I ran! I never ran so fast or hard in my life. I didn't know where I was going. I was just running, running. I was so afraid. I've never known such panic and fear. Ohhh..." he moaned, "I left him. I deserted him. I didn't even know what happened to him. I was so afraid of the soldiers. I'm sorry, Jesus, I'm so sorry," he intoned, overcome by wracking sobs now. I could do nothing but let him cry it out.

Through his sobs he said, "At least Peter stayed with him. He's the only one of us—then even he ran! Oh, God, I'm always so afraid! Why, Asher... why?" He looked at me with pleading eyes, begging me to bring reason to the chaos that had enveloped us all.

I didn't pause to think, I only reacted with the loving pity I felt for John at this moment.

"John, look at me." I softly reached out and turned his face to me so that I could look into the depth of his eyes and have him know that I was speaking to him from the deepest part of my being. "Listen to me, John, for I tell you, he is not gone. You may find him anywhere and everywhere, for truly he lies within your heart. Go within the silence as he taught you, and find him there—he waits for you even now, John."

Gradually, I could see the change. I could see it in his eyes. Somewhere, somehow, I had touched a responsive chord, and slowly, ever so slowly, before my very eyes, I watched a boy die and a man being born.

Now, as he nervously wiped his tear-stained face, a smile worked its way across his countenance. I asked him to tell me of the supper in the upper room two nights before, if he wouldn't mind. "Of course, Asher, of course—and thank you." His eyes said everything. I dismissed his thanks with an embarrassed wave of my hand and settled down to hear the story of what happened in the room two nights prior. I realized then that I could have asked my son, but with all that had happened, it hadn't occurred to me until then.

"How did you know I was thinking of that night?" John asked. I just shrugged my shoulders. I really didn't know why I asked then, except to divert his attention and, too, I wanted to hear. "When you looked at me just now," he said, "it reminded me of how Jesus looked at me night before last. When he looked at me, I saw all my fears. Whew! You know what I mean? I don't know how, but I saw all those failings, all those things that I didn't do for him when I could have—all the things I messed up. I should have done better for him. I'm such a weak man, but I loved him."

I put my hand on his arm and invited him to look around the courtyard at all the others, each to a man brooding and glumly introspective. "See, you are not alone. I, too, yesterday went through this, for I could not bring myself to go to the cross and see him die. John, you know better than I that Jesus would be the first to forgive you and me for any weaknesses we have and ask us only to build on them, not to sit and cry. Now, continue, please, with what happened that very special night upstairs."

Watching John now was wonderful; it filled me with awe. For when he first began to speak, he was like a lamp with but little oil left and the barest flicker of life yet to burn. Then, as he began to recount the tale of that night, it was as if suddenly the lamp had been filled, and the wick was now standing tall, soaking up the fuel. Brighter and brighter he became as he now recounted the experience of this amazing dinner to me.

"He will look at you sometimes and it's like he'll look right through you. I mean, he knows what we think. I've seen him do that before lots of times, but night before last was different. When he looked at us, he stopped with each of us. He looked at us like always, but that night his eyes were ever so sad. And he was quiet. The reason I noticed was that it was a time for all of us to celebrate the coming of Passover, and everyone felt good, and we were talking and happy, but by the end of the evening everybody was quiet, too.

"Jesus was silent for a very long time," John continued. "He was holding a piece of bread, just looking quietly at it. Slowly, one by one, we all noticed, and each in turn stopped talking to stare at him, and an absolute quiet descended on the room. Then, while holding the bread, he broke off pieces and handed them all around. We were all sort of looking at each other because we didn't know what to do with it. I mean, it wasn't enough to eat, just a little piece. Then he said, slowly, pausing with each phrase, 'Eat this, this is my body, and in this you will remember me.' He looked around, and there wasn't a sound anywhere. No one even breathed. Then he kind of sighed, as if he were in some terrible pain.

"'Tomorrow, you won't find me here, you'll find me taken to the tree.' We were all wide-eyed by now, not knowing what he was talking about. He shook his head as if throwing away a thought, then said softly, 'Eat. Eat.' We did, but still no one said a word. As we ate, I watched him. He had picked up the silver goblet of wine that lay in front of him, and he was swirling it about and staring into the bottom of the cup, kind of transfixed. Then all of a sudden he held it up in the air with both hands and, in a strange and wonderful voice that seemed to come from the depths of his being and heaven itself, said, `Yahweh... Yahweh, hear me now.'

"I looked at his face, and it began to shine, I mean actually shine as if it had a light all its own. And then right before my eyes, his face changed; it became soft and peaceful and all the worry lines just vanished, and in their place was a radiance about him that I had never seen. It was almost like God was right there with us all! I felt beautiful, like the light was in me, too. 'Yahweh!' we whispered, as he had done, as we all lifted our wine, and together we drank. We drank and felt Him in us. It was like no other time I can remember. You are right, Asher. He is here, he is in me, he will always be, won't he?"

All I could manage was a small smile while saying, "Yes, John, he surely is."

As the Sabbath was ending, Miriamme came to me and said, "Husband dear, please let me talk to them, for this sadness must end. Never once did Master mourn the things he could not change, nor shrink from trials that were about to be upon him. In the worst of times, he found reason to gladden our hearts. The Father has not left him just because he is gone—nor has he departed from any of us."

Oh, how I rejoiced in her. I held her close, feeling her long, silky black hair against my rough skin, smelling the bittersweet perfume that she wore only for me, knowing that in all the world I could never have found another as sweet as she was to me. I revered and treasured her above all others for her equal veneration and sustenance. She blessed me with her light, lively, blooming youth, both day and night, in the most caring of ways. And in her caressing love, she led me in the most soft and gentle way to the highest and closest moments of ecstasy.

In her, I knew what God desired when he gave man and woman the gift of loving one another, truly sharing and trusting in each other's arms at night. In a bond of faith, we handed each other our souls to keep, to hold them dear, in a sensitive, loving trust, so that each unto the other might know the beauty of belief in someone else. Most of all, it was in the little things that she proved her love to me each day. No man could have cherished her more, and I silently swore an oath within me that if God granted me the opportunity, I would seek her out and find her again, but next time I would have a young and healthy body.

"My sweet, blessed Miriamme, what would my life have been these past few years without you? Of course, you may speak to us all." It was just what we needed.

She spoke to us of the love and joy that Jesus had brought to our lives. Then she began to admonish them all by saying, "He did not die a traitor's death by hanging on that cross. Ask Asher here," she turned and pointed toward me, "Jesus left nothing to chance, he even planned his death!

"Did he ever fail you? Did he? Even once?" Her dark-brown eyes flashed back and forth, daring any to challenge her. "No, he never did. Then why do you sit around here with faces of gloom and death? I tell you, he promised that he would be with us again, and I, for one, am going to believe it."

The disciple's mood lightened noticeably. We continued to talk of him, of course, but the lighter moments were the ones now being remembered, and even his mother joined in with stories I had never heard.

That night, as the men filed up to the room over the stable, I heard Peter's booming voice say, "It all began in the stable, why not end it here, too." Everyone laughed, and for the first time in days, they fell into a dreamless sleep. For there, on a distant mountain in the land of Judea, in the ancient city of Jerusalem, the time of the old covenant passed out of memory, and by dawn of the new day, a new life would be born.

In our bed, my Miriamme wrapped herself around me and in a sweet and dreamy voice pleaded, "Tell me more about our Master, please."

Staring up at the blackness of the ceiling I answered, "I will tell you about him by telling you what he said about you, but only if you are good."

Her interest was piqued, as I knew it would be, and placing her icy feet on my leg she said, "Tell me now, old man, or will my foot be forced to go higher?" We both laughed, for the pretended outcome of this little charade was known to us both. I got up and out of bed, lighting the lamp as I went.

"I almost forgot," I said as she watched me fumble through my private case, "he gave me this the last time I saw him in the desert and asked that I give it to you when he was gone."

From under a stack of documents came a torn piece of parchment with his writing thereon. Miriamme sat up in bed as I handed her the note and the lamp, and I climbed back into bed as she read:

> *And the soul found certain smugness and comfort in its holiness. In its aloofness blindness fell and could feel not the pain of its people.*
>
> *So God reached down in love to touch His handmaiden, and the greatest He made small.*
>
> *And from the ashes rose the phoenix of love, as understanding tempered pride. And like her Master before her, she could walk among the least of them, and cry.*

Miriamme blew out the lamp, and in the darkness I could hear her soft, aching cry. I reached out to her and wrapped myself about her, and together, in oneness, we fell sweetly asleep.

The Disciple Passes

I lived but another month or so, long enough to find that, as he had promised, Jesus tarried not long in his rock-hewn tomb. But my job was done. There were others now to carry on. My son, John, became a leader among the flock that grew now daily in our home. Mighty wonders were occurring, but my skill at politics was no longer needed as it became apparent that Caiaphas no longer found our motley group a threat once our leader was gone. And Miriamme too had found her niche. She now spent all her time counseling and tending to the homeless and the sick. It was strange; we didn't open our home to these people while he lived, yet in death we felt as if it were our responsibility to carry on in his name.

As time went on, I felt his pull stronger and stronger each day. I was just an old man now, my time having gone its way. My home had become a center of his love, and for that I was glad, but increasingly I knew this was a new world, a world in which I played no part.

The end came fast. One morning I slept late, a habit that I abhorred all my life but now had begun to acquire with my malaise.

I awoke to a morning with sunshine and bright blue sky flooding in our bedroom window. I raised myself, then sat for a while with my legs dangling over the side of the bed, finding no reason for some time to go any further.

Eventually, however, finding no counter reason to tarry any longer, I slowly rose to my feet, shuffled to the peg that held my robe, and slipped it over my head.

I put my feet in my sandals by the door and stepped over the threshold onto the landing just outside the bedrooms. I began to walk toward the stairs that led down into the inner court. Looking over the balustrade I noted my beloved Miriamme down in the courtyard below. In her arms was a basket full of fresh vegetables, fruits, and flowers from our garden.

As I stood there near the head of the stairs she looked up at me and smiled her radiant smile. Then seeing the sad, lonely look and hunched-over body that I had assumed of late, her smile became more brilliant as she looked up at me.

Thinking to get my blood running and cheer me up, she readjusted her load, gathered her basket in one arm, then reached over with her free hand and lowered the corner of her blouse. Never losing eye contact, she widened her smile as her breasts began to creep out from hiding. She knew that this little charade would excite me... and it did.

Thus, one beautiful morning as I stood at the top of the stairs, with my Miriamme beckoning me lovingly below, I felt a sudden surge of pain race up my arm and into my heart. I reached out for just a second to the woman I loved so much, who had given me more love than I had ever known, and then it was over.

Light flooded my being. The world I knew had been left behind in an instant of time, and there ahead of me was my Master, smiling, with gentle eyes, waiting for me as he had always done.

The Memory Ends

And I suppose that if all the other events in Jesus' life were written, the whole world could hardly contain the books!

John 21:25

Asher ben Ammi's story was complete. I was back. I sat there, my fingers on the computer keyboard, tears washing down my face. My wife, Trudy, came in and saw me across the room, shoulders shaking, sobbing uncontrollably. She reached out from behind me and touched me gently on the shoulder. As I turned and rose from the chair to put my arms around her, I noted out the window that our children were coming down the forest trail, home from school—and they had friends with them!

"We've got to get out of here," I said, "I can't let them see me like this." Out the door we went, down the sloping grassy hill to the dock by the edge of the lake. There I told her how physically painful those last few moments had been to me as I re-experienced the heart attack.

"Asher died," I cried, "and I felt like it was happening to me. The pain was excruciating—it sped up my arm and into my chest—then it was over. It was dark for the merest moment, and then the light came. And there was Jesus. He waited for me! He still loved me, even though I failed him in the end. I was so relieved that I hadn't disappointed him when I couldn't go to him on the cross. I thought I was a terrible man who hadn't the courage to be with him at the end." I shook my head and once again was overwhelmed by deep, wracking sobs.

We sat for some time; neither of us said a word. We stared across the placid lake with only the soft hoot of the loon occasionally breaking the quiet, and a calm began to come over me.

Trudy touched my face softly. "There's more, isn't there?"

"Yes," I said, then looked back out to the lake. It took me a few more minutes before I could relate what was next. It seemed that if I said one word, I would lose control of my emotions and start crying again. Trudy waited silently, patiently.

"There was something I saw in that last moment before the memory faded..." I paused, a bit embarrassed to relate what I had seen. "I know this sounds corny," I apologized, "but the scene was like the classical vision of Jesus in the clouds painted by some Renaissance master. Out of nowhere there was the light, a pastel light, and the clouds. He was there, Trudy, he was there waiting for me."

I cried again unashamed while Trudy waited for me to continue. "I went toward Jesus—I couldn't tell if I was walking or floating—and all of a sudden the memory was over. It was as if I had been swallowed in the light, and then I was back, and you were touching me on my shoulder."

We were sitting on the grass by our little dock, Trudy close to me, as I continued. "I have this feeling that Asher really killed himself, not with a knife, of course, but with guilt and despair. Once Jesus was gone, he no longer wanted to live. Jesus was his Master, his life.

"That's the way it came to me in those last few mental fragments of Asher's consciousness."

Trudy put her arms around me. "That's when I found you crying."

"Yes, but it's okay," I said, a smile spreading across my face. "Jesus does love me." When I said "me," I knew finally, with certainty... I was Asher, Asher ben Ammi.

I had lived during a time of great upheaval in Israel, and I had been blessed to know the man who was to become the Messiah, not only for me but also for millions more who would live during the centuries to follow. I knew him as a teacher, a man, and a friend.

For me he was the Messiah, the Anointed One of God for whom all Jews waited then—and many still do today. True enough, he came to give us freedom, but not the way many of his followers thought then, and not the way many of his followers believe today. He couldn't change the world he found himself in, ruled by Rome—the beast —anymore than we can change the world in which we find ourselves today. Instead, he came to teach us what he himself had learned, that we can be joyous, loving, giving, filled with wonder, filled from within with the miracle that is God, no matter what the world we are thrown into is like.

It has taken me a quarter of a century past the vision to learn this lesson again—hopefully for the last time. For even though I had the memories of Asher, I hadn't learned all that I had come to learn. I had to come back, reach a pinnacle of material success again, and then know total, abject failure. I had to feel the loss of a granddaughter who called me "Bapa" and the worry of losing a son as well. I had to lose all my physical possessions through bankruptcy and have the experience of being thrown out of my own home, all before I was to begin my own long climb back to experience true miracles, to learn my lessons once again.

This joining of my spirit with God, as my Master had taught me, was the one and only thing that brought me peace.

It can take a lifetime (or in my case even more) to learn, or it can occur in an instant of time. For in realizing that we are truly all sons and daughters of God—brothers and sisters one to another—the lessons of giving and love come.

Jesus was the example, the proof that anyone can find God. He touched us when he walked the earth. His parables taught all of us in vivid color, rich and poor. His laugh infected us, and his stories inspired us. His miracles of wonder were written within our very hearts. And, most importantly, as I learned as Asher, he is with us today.

We were all human, those of us who followed him then; we saw and heard the Master through the lenses of our own eyes and ears and understood him through the experiences of our own lives.

The gospel that I now bring, the "good news" of this, the Gospel, that I began to write even while I lived as Asher ben Ammi, is the example that Jesus taught in humility and love. He did have a special relationship with God, true enough, but he taught that we too could have that same relationship with God as well, and he taught us how. He taught us not to wait for "salvation" sometime in the future. He taught us that God lives within us.

I recall again the words that Asher spoke to the gentle disciple John, son of Zebedee after the Master's death. It was Asher's final gift; a testament to his Master, which now in turn, I lovingly give to you, as proof that anyone can find God here and now.

> *You may find Him anywhere, and everywhere, for truly He lives within your heart. Go within the silence and find Him there. He waits for you even now.*

To contact the author, download the first few chapters of the audio book or participate in *The Disciple's* social organization and blog go to: www.thedisciplesite.com

See also: www.crossingtheline.me for more of the author's blogs, interviews of religious and spiritual authors and thinkers and more. Comments on both sites are always welcomed.